Case Study Methodology in Business Research

Flowchart 1   p13

Flowchart 2   p40
2a   p.77
2b   p.221

(Theory Blag)

Flowchart 3   p.56
a p.218

3a   p221

(Hyp.- Building)   3b   p223

3c   p.226

To our soul mates

Case Study Methodology in Business Research

Jan Dul and Tony Hak

Routledge
Taylor & Francis Group

LONDON AND NEW YORK

First published 2008 by Butterworth-Heinemann

This edition published 2012 by Routledge
2 Park Square, Milton Park, Abingdon, Oxon OX14 4RN
711 Third Avenue, New York, NY 10017

Routledge is an imprint of the Taylor & Francis Group, an informa business

First edition 2008

British Library Cataloguing in Publication Data
A catalogue record for this book is available from the British Library

Library of Congress Control Number: 2007932103

ISBN: 978-0-7506-8196-4

Typeset by Charon Tec Ltd (A Macmillan Company), Chennai, India
www.charontec.com

Contents

Acknowledgements   xv
Foreword   xvii
List of boxes   xix
List of tables   xx
List of contributors   xxii
Preface: how to read this book   xxv

Part I: Introduction   **1**

Chapter 1   Aims and overview of this book   3
  1.1 Our definition of a case study   3
  1.2 Aims of the book   6
  1.3 Overview of the book   8
       1.3.1 Structure of the book   8
       1.3.2 Chapter 2: Case studies in business research   8
       1.3.3 Chapter 3: Principles of research   9
       1.3.4 Chapter 4: Theory-testing research (general)   9
       1.3.5 Chapters 5–7: Theory-testing case study research   10
       1.3.6 Chapters 8–9: Theory-building research   10
       1.3.7 Chapters 10–11: Practice-oriented research   10
  1.4 How to read this book   11
       1.4.1 Reading specific topics   11
       1.4.2 Suggestions for students   11
       1.4.3 Glossary and flowcharts   18
  1.5 References   18

Chapter 2   *A review of case studies in business research*   *19*
             Raf Jans and Koen Dittrich

             2.1 Published case studies in business research   20
                  2.1.1 Search strategy and sample   20
                  2.1.2 Case studies in Strategy   21
                  2.1.3 Case studies in Finance   22
                  2.1.4 Case studies in Marketing   22
                  2.1.5 Case studies in HRM   22
                  2.1.6 Case studies in Operations   22
                  2.1.7 Types of case study research   23
             2.2 Review of methodological discussions on case study research   24
                  2.2.1 Objectives of case study research   24
                  2.2.2 Guidelines for case study research   25
                  2.2.3 Evaluations of case study research   26
             2.3 Conclusion   27
             2.4 References   27

Chapter 3   *Principles of research*   *30*

             3.1 Theory-oriented and practice-oriented research   30
                  3.1.1 General research objectives of theory-oriented and
                         practice-oriented research   30
                  3.1.2 Orientation: how to choose between theory-oriented or
                         practice-oriented research   33
             3.2 Principles of theory-oriented research   34
                  3.2.1 Theory   34
                  3.2.2 Theory-oriented research: contribution to theory
                         development   38
                  3.2.3 Replication   40
                  3.2.4 Representativeness, external validity, and generalizability 45
                  3.2.5 Exploration of theory-oriented research   48
                         3.2.5.1 Exploration of theory   48
                         3.2.5.2 Exploration of practice for finding a proposition 49
                         3.2.5.3 Exploration of practice for confirming the
                                  relevance of a proposition   51
                  3.2.6 Contributions to theory development   51
             3.3 Principles of practice-oriented research   52
                  3.3.1 Practice   52
                  3.3.2 Practice-oriented research: contribution to a
                         practitioner's knowledge   53
                  3.3.3 Exploration for practice-oriented research   55
                         3.3.3.1 Exploration of practice   57

3.3.3.2 Exploration of theory for finding a hypothesis 58
3.3.3.3 Exploration of theory for confirming relevance of
a hypothesis 58
3.3.4 Contributions to a practitioner's knowledge 59
3.4 References 59

Part II: Theory-testing research **61**

Chapter 4 *Theory-testing research (general)* 63

4.1 Research objectives in theory-testing research 64
4.2 Specifying propositions in theory-testing research 65
4.2.1 Propositions that express a sufficient condition 67
4.2.2 Propositions that express a necessary condition 68
4.2.3 Propositions that express a deterministic relation 69
4.2.4 Propositions that express a probabilistic relation 70
4.3 Business relevance of propositions 71
4.4 Research strategies in theory-testing research 76
4.4.1 Strategy for testing a proposition that expresses a
sufficient condition 78
4.4.2 Strategy for testing a proposition that expresses a
necessary condition 80
4.4.3 Strategy for testing a proposition that expresses a
deterministic relation 81
4.4.4 Strategy for testing a proposition that expresses a
probabilistic relation 82
4.4.5 Testing more complex conceptual models 84
4.5 Outcome and implications 87
4.6 Summary 88
4.7 References 89

Chapter 5 *Testing sufficient and necessary conditions with a case study* 90

5.1 How to test a sufficient or a necessary condition with a
case study 91
5.1.1 Introduction 91
5.1.2 Candidate cases 92
5.1.3 Case selection 92
5.1.4 Hypothesis 93
5.1.5 Measurement 94
5.1.6 Data presentation 94
5.1.7 Data analysis 94

5.1.8 Implications for the theory   95
5.1.9 Replication strategy   96
5.2 Case Study 1: Theory-testing research: testing a necessary condition.
Testing a theory of collaboration characteristics of successful
innovation projects   98
Koen Dittrich
5.2.1   Introduction   98
5.2.2   Theory   99
        5.2.2.1 Object of study   99
        5.2.2.2 Concepts   99
        5.2.2.3 Propositions   100
        5.2.2.4 Domain   101
        5.2.2.5 Conceptual model   101
5.2.3   Research objective   102
5.2.4   Research strategy   102
5.2.5   Candidate cases   103
5.2.6   Case selection   103
5.2.7   Hypotheses   104
5.2.8   Measurement   105
5.2.9   Data presentation   105
        5.2.9.1 Radical innovation projects   105
        5.2.9.2 Incremental innovation projects   108
5.2.10 Data analysis   110
5.2.11 Implications for the theory   111
5.2.12 Replication strategy   112
5.3 Methodological reflection on Case Study 1   112
5.3.1   Theory   112
5.3.2   Research objective   113
5.3.3   Research strategy   113
5.3.4   Candidate cases   115
5.3.5   Case selection   115
5.3.6   Hypothesis   116
5.3.7   Measurement   116
5.3.8   Data presentation   117
5.3.9   Data analysis   117
5.3.10 Implications for the theory   117
5.3.11 Replication strategy   118
5.4 Case Study 2: Theory-testing research: testing a necessary condition.
Testing a theory of ideal typical organizational configurations for
successful product innovations   119
Ferdinand Jaspers and Jan Van den Ende
5.4.1   Introduction   119

	5.4.2	Theory	119
		5.4.2.1 Object of study	119
		5.4.2.2 Concepts	120
		5.4.2.3 Proposition	122
		5.4.2.4 Domain	122
		5.4.2.5 Conceptual model	123
	5.4.3	Research objective	123
	5.4.4	Research strategy	123
	5.4.5	Candidate cases	124
	5.4.6	Case selection	124
	5.4.7	Hypothesis	124
	5.4.8	Measurement	125
	5.4.9	Data presentation	127
	5.4.10	Data analysis	127
	5.4.11	Implications for the theory	129
	5.4.12	Replication strategy	130
5.5	Methodological reflection on Case Study 2	130
	5.5.1	Theory	130
	5.5.2	Research objective	131
	5.5.3	Research strategy	131
	5.5.4	Candidate cases	131
	5.5.5	Case selection	132
	5.5.6	Hypothesis	132
	5.5.7	Measurement	132
	5.5.8	Data presentation	133
	5.5.9	Data analysis	133
	5.5.10	Implications for the theory	134
	5.5.11	Replication strategy	135
5.6	References	136

Chapter 6	*Testing a deterministic relation with a case study*	*138*
	6.1 How to test a deterministic relation with a case study	138
	6.1.1 Introduction	138
	6.1.2 Candidate cases	139
	6.1.3 Case selection	139
	6.1.4 Hypothesis	140
	6.1.5 Measurement	141
	6.1.6 Data presentation	141
	6.1.7 Data analysis	141
	6.1.8 Implications for the theory	142
	6.1.9 Replication strategy	142

6.2 Case Study 3: Theory-testing research: testing a deterministic relation. The
     influences of urban time access windows on retailers' distribution costs   142
     Hans Quak
     6.2.1   Introduction   142
     6.2.2   Theory   143
           6.2.2.1 Object of study   143
           6.2.2.2 Concepts   143
           6.2.2.3 Proposition   144
           6.2.2.4 Domain   144
           6.2.2.5 Conceptual model   144
     6.2.3   Research objective   145
     6.2.4   Research strategy   145
     6.2.5   Candidate cases   146
     6.2.6   Case selection   146
     6.2.7   Hypotheses   147
     6.2.8   Measurement   148
     6.2.9   Data presentation   149
     6.2.10 Data analysis   149
     6.2.11 Implications for the theory   151
6.3 Methodological reflection on Case Study 3   151
     6.3.1   Theory   151
     6.3.2   Research objective   152
     6.3.3   Research strategy   152
     6.3.4   Candidate cases   152
     6.3.5   Case selection   153
     6.3.6   Hypotheses   153
     6.3.7   Measurement   153
     6.3.8   Data presentation   153
     6.3.9   Data analysis   154
     6.3.10 Implications for the theory   154
     6.3.11 Replication strategy   154
6.4 References   154

Chapter 7 *Testing a probabilistic relation with a case study*   *156*

7.1 How to test a probabilistic relation with a case study   156
     7.1.1   Introduction   156
     7.1.2   Candidate cases   157
     7.1.3   Case selection   157
     7.1.4   Hypothesis   158
     7.1.5   Measurement   158
     7.1.6   Data presentation   158
     7.1.7   Data analysis   158

7.1.8   Implications for the theory   159
7.1.9   Replication strategy   159
7.2 Case Study 4: Theory-testing research: testing a probabilistic relation.
     The influence of a retailer's distribution strategy on a retailer's
     sensitivity to urban time access windows   159
     Hans Quak
     7.2.1   Introduction   159
     7.2.2   Theory   160
             7.2.2.1 Object of study   160
             7.2.2.2 Concepts   160
             7.2.2.3 Propositions   160
             7.2.2.4 Domain   161
             7.2.2.5 Conceptual model   162
     7.2.3   Research objective   162
     7.2.4   Research strategy   162
     7.2.5   Candidate cases   162
     7.2.6   Case selection   162
     7.2.7   Hypotheses   163
     7.2.8   Measurement   163
     7.2.9   Data presentation   165
     7.2.10 Data analysis   166
     7.2.11 Implications for the theory   168
     7.2.12 Replication strategy   169
7.3 Methodological reflection on Case Study 4   169
     7.3.1   Theory   169
     7.3.2   Research objective   170
     7.3.3   Research strategy   170
     7.3.4   Candidate cases   170
     7.3.5   Case selection   170
     7.3.6   Hypotheses   171
     7.3.7   Measurement   171
     7.3.8   Data presentation   171
     7.3.9   Data analysis   171
     7.3.10 Implications for the theory   172
     7.3.11 Replication strategy   172
7.4 References   172

Part III: Theory-building research   **173**

Chapter 8   *Theory-building research (general)*   *175*

8.1 Research objectives in theory-building research   176
     8.1.1   Specifying the relation between known concepts   177

        8.1.2 Discovering a not yet known concept   178
        8.1.3 Discovering concepts and their relation   179
        8.1.4 Discovering concepts   180
    8.2 Principles of theory-building research   180
    8.3 Research strategies in theory-building research   181
    8.4 Outcome and implications   183
    8.5 Summary   183

Chapter 9   *The theory-building case study*   *184*

    9.1 How to design and conduct a theory-building case study   184
        9.1.1 Introduction   184
        9.1.2 Candidate cases   185
        9.1.3 Case selection   185
        9.1.4 Extracting relevant evidence   187
        9.1.5 Coding   188
        9.1.6 Data presentation   188
        9.1.7 Data analysis   189
            9.1.7.1 Sufficient condition   189
            9.1.7.2 Necessary condition   190
            9.1.7.3 Deterministic relation   190
            9.1.7.4 Probabilistic relation   191
        9.1.8 An example of data analysis   191
            9.1.8.1 Sufficient condition   191
            9.1.8.2 Necessary condition   193
            9.1.8.3 Deterministic relation   194
            9.1.8.4 Probabilistic relation   194
        9.1.9 Outcome   195
    9.2 Case Study 5: Theory-building research. Building propositions
         about the kind of company representatives involved in
         communication with providers of business services   197
         Wendy Van der Valk and Finn Wynstra
        9.2.1 Introduction   197
        9.2.2 Candidate cases   199
        9.2.3 Case selection   200
        9.2.4 Extracting relevant evidence   200
        9.2.5 Coding   202
        9.2.6 Data presentation   204
        9.2.7 Data analysis   204
        9.2.8 Outcome   206
    9.3 Methodological reflection on Case Study 5   207
        9.3.1 Justification of a theory-building case study   207
        9.3.2 Candidate cases   208

9.3.3 Case selection 209
9.3.4 Extracting relevant evidence 209
9.3.5 Coding 210
9.3.6 Data presentation 210
9.3.7 Data analysis 210
9.3.8 Outcome 212
9.4 References 213

Part IV: Practice-oriented research **215**

Chapter 10 Practice-oriented research (general) 217
10.1 Hypothesis-testing research 218
10.1.1 Research objective in hypothesis-testing research 219
10.1.2 Research strategy in hypothesis-testing research 220
10.2 Hypothesis-building research 222
10.2.1 Research objective in hypothesis-building research 222
10.2.2 Research strategy in hypothesis-building research 224
10.3 Descriptive research 224
10.3.1 Research objective of descriptive practice-oriented research 225
10.3.2 Research strategy of practice-oriented descriptive research 226
10.4 Summary 227

Chapter 11 The practice-oriented case study 229
11.1 How to design and conduct a practice-oriented case study 229
11.1.1 Introduction 229
11.1.2 Case selection 230
11.1.3 Implications of the research results 230
11.2 Case Study 6: Hypothesis-testing practice-oriented research. Assessing whether a company has sufficient flexibility to develop successfully a new product 233
Murthy Halemane and Felix Janszen
11.2.1 Introduction 233
11.2.2 Hypothesis 234
11.2.3 Measurement 235
11.2.4 Data analysis 236
11.2.5 Results and implications 237
11.3 Methodological reflection on Case Study 6 237
11.3.1 Practice 237
11.3.2 Research objective 237

	11.3.3 Research strategy	238
	11.3.4 Candidate cases	238
	11.3.5 Case selection	238
	11.3.6 Measurement	239
	11.3.7 Data presentation	239
	11.3.8 Data analysis	239
	11.3.9 Implications for practice	239

11.4 Case Study 7: Descriptive practice-oriented research.
Building a model of best practice of company standardization   240
Henk J. De Vries and Florens Slob

	11.4.1 Introduction	240
	11.4.2 Absence of guidelines or criteria	241
	11.4.3 Measurement	244
	11.4.4 Data presentation	245
	11.4.5 Concept definition	245
	11.4.6 Implications	248

11.5 Methodological reflection on Case Study 7   249

	11.5.1 Practice	249
	11.5.2 Research objective	249
	11.5.3 Research strategy	250
	11.5.4 Candidate cases	250
	11.5.5 Case selection	250
	11.5.6 Measurement	250
	11.5.7 Data presentation	251
	11.5.8 Data analysis	251
	11.5.9 Implications for practice	251

11.6 References   252

Appendices   253
1: Measurement   253
2: Business journals that publish case studies   265
3: Flowcharts   267
4: Writing a case study research report   276
5: Glossary   278

Index   293

Acknowledgements

Case studies deserve a prominent role in business research. The case study research strategy can be used for analysing and solving practical business problems, as well as for building and testing business theories. However, in order to acquire that prominent role, case studies must be designed and conducted with scientific rigour. We wrote this book with the ambition of giving a methodological framework that supports such high quality case study research.

We think that our approach to case study research is useful in all (social) sciences, but we have explicitly written this book with an audience of students and novice case study researchers in business and management in mind. For several years now, we have taught research methods, including case study methodology, to undergraduate, graduate, and doctoral students in business administration, using various textbooks. This book is based on that experience and uses examples from this discipline. The limitation to research in business and management also enabled us to make good use of examples of case study research in our research school.

We realize that our thinking on case study methodology in business research was shaped not only by our own experience as researcher and teacher, but also by the uncountable interactions that we had with researchers, methodologists, teachers, and students who liked (or disliked) the use of case studies. We thank them for stimulating discussions. Although we cannot name them all here, we would like to mention a few persons who influenced the content of the book.

First of all we acknowledge the contributions of our colleagues and co-authors from RSM Erasmus University: Koen Dittrich, Jan Van den Ende, Murthy Halemane, Raf Jans, Felix Janszen, Ferdinand Jaspers, Hans Quak, Florens Slob (alumnus), Wendy Van der Valk, Henk De Vries, and Finn Wynstra. They provided the data and draft versions for the example chapters in this book (5.2, 5.4, 6.2, 7.2, 9.2, 11.2, and 11.4) and accepted the considerable cuts and changes that we proposed in their texts because of our aim to fit the presentation of these studies to our methodological framework. The full richness of the original studies can be read in other research publications referred to in the respective chapters.

We are grateful to Bert Balk, Harrie Jansen, Ruud Smit, Peter Swanborn, Piet Verschuren, and Fred Wester for their valuable comments based on their extensive methodological knowledge and experience.

We also express thanks to several researchers for their comments on draft versions of our book: Floortje Blindenbach, Paul van Fenema, Helleke Hendriks, Dianne Heijink, Wim Hulsink, Jos van Iwaarden, Katariina Kemppainen, and Allen S. Lee.

Our Master students Mirjam van Dijk, Michiel Elshof, Fieke Göritzlehner, Eveline Hogenes, Hubert van de Vecht, and Martijn Put provided us with helpful feedback after applying our case study methodology in their Master's thesis research.

We learned from comments from Bachelor students that our book might be somewhat concise. In an attempt to serve both students and experienced researchers, we decided that virtually each sentence of our book must be precise and informative. This choice might require some additional effort from students, as well as guidance from seniors. We thank our Bachelor students Patricia van Beek, Shakti Kapoerchan, and Merel Piekaar for giving us specific feedback on the book.

Finally we are grateful to our soul mates who were a necessary (though not sufficient) condition for finalizing our book.

Dear reader, we hope that our book will contribute to the quality of your research. We would welcome any comment, for which we thank you in advance.

Jan Dul and Tony Hak
September 2007

Foreword

The role of case studies in research is a paradox. On the one hand, case studies are widely used by many communities in business research; for example case study research has consistently been one of the most powerful methods in operations management, particularly in the building of new theory. It is clearly accepted that case study research in management can be rigorous, as is evidenced by case-based papers in both top European and US journals. On the other hand there is strong resistance to case study research in some communities and its use has been rather narrow, often restricted just to exploratory research. In addition there is confusion in the minds of many as to what exactly is case study research: is it about practice or theory, and is it about theory-building or testing?

The contribution of exploratory case study research to theory-building is well documented. Despite challenges (it is time consuming, it needs skilled interviewers, and care is needed in drawing generalizable conclusions from a limited set of cases and in ensuring rigorous research) the results of case study research can have very high impact. Unconstrained by the rigid limits of questionnaires and models, it can lead to new and creative insights, building of new theory, and have high validity with practitioners – the ultimate user of research. Through triangulation with multiple means of data collection, the validity can be increased further. Many of the breakthrough concepts and theories in my field – Operations Management – from lean production to manufacturing strategy have been developed through exploratory case study research. Finally, case study research enriches not only theory, but also the researchers themselves. Through conducting research in the field and being exposed to real problems, the creative insights of people at all levels of organizations, and the varied contexts of cases, the individual researcher will personally benefit from the process of conducting the research. Increasingly, new ideas are being developed, not by distant academics, but by those working in close contact with multiple case studies – management consultants! Exploratory case study research is not only good at investigating how and why questions, but it is also particularly suitable for developing new theory and ideas.

Although there has been a number of important articles and books on case study research in business, their focus has been primarily on theory-building through exploratory case study research. In this book, Jan Dul and Tony Hak have set out to provide a structured and broader view of the use of case study research. They make clear the differences between the varying uses of case studies including the difference between practice-oriented and theory-oriented research. In particular, in addition to theory-building, they pay attention to two areas: first, theory-testing and, second, replication, with its consequent impact on generalizability. They have produced a valuable addition to the armoury of the business researcher. It is important that case study research is conducted well, so that the results are both rigorous and relevant. Case study research is not an excuse for "industrial tourism" – visiting lots of organizations without any preconceived ideas as to what is being researched. For the achievement of the potential of case study research it is important that it is done with rigour. This book sets out structures and guidelines that will assist researchers from a wide range of disciplines to develop rigorous use of case studies in research.

Chris Voss
Professor of Operations and Technology Management
London Business School

List of boxes

1   The difference between practice-oriented and theory-oriented research   31

2   What is a theory, and when is it "true"?   37

3   Scientific realism   41

4   Replication of survey results   44

5   Multiple case study   45

6   Domain, instance, case, population, sample, and replication   46

7   The term hypothesis in practice-oriented research   57

8   Is business reality deterministic or probabilistic? A note on "pragmatic determinism"   72

9   How the survey can become a case study   83

10   More complex conceptual models   85

11   An example of a theory-testing single case study   97

12   Michael Porter's case selection   186

13   Building a theory on successfully helping city government   196

14   Other propositions that can be derived from Table 9.9   212

15   A practice-oriented "flash case study"   231

List of tables

1.1 Main difference between the case study and the experiment 5
1.2 Main differences between the case study and the survey 6
1.3 Suggestions for reading specific topics 11
1.4 Suggestions for students to design and conduct a research project 12
1.5 A stepwise approach for research: activities, results, quality criteria, and references to relevant chapters in this book 14
2.1 Number of publications with case study research in all scholarly journals in Proquest and in ISI journals in the period 2000–2005 21
2.2 Three types of case studies in five fields of business research (2000–2005) 23
4.1 Correspondence between theoretical terms and theory-oriented research terms 66
4.2 Preferred research strategies for testing different types of propositions 77
5.1 Radical innovation projects 108
5.2 Incremental innovation projects 110
5.3 Six types of innovation that change a product's components and interfaces 120
5.4 Typology of ideal organizational configurations for product innovation success 122
5.5 Data for 15 successful product innovation projects 128
5.6 Number of selected cases by product innovation type 132
6.1 Main case characteristics 147
6.2 Scenarios of time access window pressure 148
7.1 Vehicle types sorted on capacity 164
7.2 Distribution strategy dimensions per case 166

9.1   Data matrix regarding "success" factors of innovation
       projects   192

9.2   Data matrix regarding successful innovation projects   193

9.3   Data matrix regarding unsuccessful innovation projects   193

9.4   Data matrix regarding team size   194

9.5   Data matrix regarding management commitment   195

9.6A   Selected cases, descriptions, and informants KPN   201

9.6B   Selected cases, descriptions, and informants UWV   201

9.7A   Representatives involved in interaction with the service
       provider   203

9.7B   Level of perceived risk   203

9.8   Type of buying company representatives involved   205

9.9   Type of buying company representatives involved   211

10.1   Preferred research strategies for testing different types of
       hypotheses   220

A.2.1 Scholarly business journals that have published five or more
       case studies from 2002–2005   265

List of contributors

Koen Dittrich (Chapters 2 and 5.2)
Koen Dittrich received an MSc degree in Economics from the University of Maastricht, the Netherlands, an MA degree in Science and Technology Studies from the University of Maastricht and the University of Oslo, Norway, and a PhD degree in Technology, Policy and Management of Delft University of Technology, Delft, the Netherlands. He is Assistant Professor in Management of Innovation at RSM Erasmus University. His research interests include the organization and management of innovation processes, R&D networks and collaboration for innovation (http://www.rsm.nl/kdittrich).

Jan Dul
Jan Dul obtained an MSc degree in Mechanical Engineering from Twente University of Technology, the Netherlands, and a PhD degree in Biomedical Engineering from Vanderbilt University, USA. He is Professor of Technology and Human Factors at RSM Erasmus University. His research interests include human centred design of products and processes, in particular human factors in operations systems, and employee creativity for innovation (http://www.rsm.nl/jdul).

Jan Van den Ende (Chapter 5.4)
Jan Van den Ende obtained a PhD degree from Delft University of Technology, the Netherlands. He is Associate Professor of Management of Technology and Innovation at RSM Erasmus University. His research focuses on the organization and management of product and service development processes. He leads a research programme on systemic innovation in ICT. Van den Ende has (co-)authored books and numerous articles in, amongst others, *Research Policy, Journal of Management*

Studies, IEEE Transactions on Engineering Management, Business History, R&D Management, and *Group and Organization Management* (http://www.rsm.nl/jende).

Tony Hak

Tony Hak received an MSc degree in Medical Sociology from Erasmus University Medical Centre, Rotterdam, the Netherlands, and a PhD degree in Social Sciences from the University of Amsterdam, the Netherlands. He is Associate Professor of Research Methodology at RSM Erasmus University. His research interests include the response process in business surveys, questionnaire pre-testing, and qualitative methods (http://www.rsm.nl/thak).

Murthy Halemane (Chapter 11.2)

Murthy Halemane has a doctorate in engineering from the University of Technology in Delft, the Netherlands. He is currently Assistant Professor of Management of Technology and Innovation at RSM Erasmus University. Capability analysis of firms and synergy development of their technologies with business strategies are his research themes. His current research extends these themes to business process outsourcing (http://www.rsm.nl/mhalemane).

Raf Jans (Chapter 2)

Raf Jans holds a PhD degree in Applied Economics with a specialization in Operations Research from the Katholieke Universiteit Leuven in Belgium. He is an Assistant Professor of Operations Management at RSM Erasmus University. His research interests are in decision and risk analysis, optimization modelling and their application to industrial problems, mainly in the area of operations management. His current research focuses on production planning problems (http://www.rsm.nl/rjans).

Felix Janszen (Chapter 11.2)

Felix Janszen has a PhD degree in Biochemistry from Erasmus University. He is Professor of Management of Technology at RSM Erasmus University. His research areas are technology management, innovation, complexity theory, and computer modelling (http://www.rsm.nl/fjanszen).

Ferdinand Jaspers (Chapter 5.4)

Ferdinand Jaspers received an MSc degree in Business Administration from RSM Erasmus University. He is a PhD student at RSM Erasmus University. His research interests include typological theories and strategy and innovation in complex product settings (http://www.rsm.nl/fjaspers).

Hans Quak (Chapters 6.2 and 7.2)
Hans Quak obtained an MSc degree in Business Administration from RSM Erasmus University. Currently, he is a PhD student at RSM Erasmus University. His research interests include urban goods movements, city logistics, retail distribution, and sustainability (http://www.rsm.nl/hquak).

Florens Slob (Chapter 11.4)
Florens Slob received an MSc degree in Business Administration from RSM Erasmus University. His Master thesis project dealt with company standardization. Currently he is project manager at Van Gansewinkel Groep BV, specialists in waste management services, Eindhoven, the Netherlands.

Wendy Van der Valk (Chapter 9.2)
Wendy Van der Valk obtained an MSc degree in Industrial Engineering and Management Science from Eindhoven University of Technology, the Netherlands. She is a PhD candidate at RSM Erasmus University. Her research deals with buyer–supplier interaction in purchasing and developing business services (http://www.rsm.nl/wvalk).

Henk J. De Vries (Chapter 11.4)
Henk J. De Vries obtained an MSc degree in Geodesy at Delft University of Technology, the Netherlands, and a PhD degree in Business Administration at Erasmus University. He is an Associate Professor of Standardization at RSM Erasmus University. His research and teaching concern standardization from a business point of view. His books include *Standardization – A Business Approach to the Role of National Standardization Organizations* (Kluwer Academic Publishers, 1999) (http://www.rsm.nl/hdevries).

Finn Wynstra (Chapter 9.2)
Finn Wynstra received a Licentiate-degree from Uppsala University, Sweden, and a PhD degree from Eindhoven University of Technology in the Netherlands. He is a Professor of Purchasing and Supply Management at RSM Erasmus University. His research focuses on the integration of supply and innovation processes, combining qualitative research methods with (experiment-based) survey studies. He is the co-author of two books; *Buying Business Services* (Wiley, 2002) and *Developing Sourcing Capabilities* (Wiley, 2005) (http://www.rsm.nl/fwynstra).

Preface: How to read this book

One way of reading and using this book is linear. This is recommended particularly if the book is used as a textbook. The reader could start with Chapter 3 and then follow the development of the narrative through Chapters 4, etc. If this book is used as a companion guide for students in the process of designing and conducting their own research project, we strongly recommend using the flowcharts which specify each separate stage of the project (see 1.4.2 "Suggestions for students" and Appendix 3). The contents of the boxes and the flow-charts are discussed and explained in the corresponding chapters of the book.

Some readers might be interested in reading about specific topics only. Tables 1.3 and 1.5 map the contents of this book in such a way that these readers will be able to locate the text parts that are relevant to them.

Our approach to research in general and the case study in particular is characterized by a consistent conceptual structure which is only partly visible in the linear structure of the text. This conceptual structure is made explicit in the Glossary (see Appendix 5) which contains definitions of all important terms. **Bold print** in the text refers to this glossary. Because some of our definitions differ considerably from definitions in the literature, we recommend the reader who encounters a term in **bold**, to *always* read the relevant entry in the glossary, and to follow the references to other terms in the glossary.

Part I

Introduction

CHAPTER 1

Aims and overview of this book

1.1 Our definition of a case study

It is an understatement that there is confusion among students, teachers, researchers, and methodologists about the definition and the main characteristics of **case study research**. Case study research is presented by some as a strictly exploratory research strategy in which nothing can be proven, most often by referring to the alleged impossibility to "generalize". Others, such as Yin (1984, 1994, 2003), have claimed that the problem of "generalization" can be solved and that, therefore, theories can also be tested in (preferably) "multiple case studies". A major difficulty for students and novice case study researchers is that proponents of these different perspectives give different meanings to similar methodological terms without clearly defining these meanings, making it almost impossible to grasp the nature of the debate and to infer solutions to problems in designing their own research. Ragin (1992) has argued that the work of any given case study researcher often is characterized by some hybrid of various approaches, which are usually difficult to disentangle.

Most definitions of case study research, as found in the literature, are statements about the most frequently used measurement techniques (such as using "multiple sources of evidence", or "qualitative methods") and research objectives (such as "exploration"). Such definitions are attempts to capture in one statement the most important practical characteristics of a diverse array of studies that present themselves as case studies. Yin's (2003: 13–14) definition is an example of such an all-inclusive descriptive definition: "A case study is an empirical inquiry that investigates a contemporary phenomenon within its real-life context, especially when the boundaries between object of study and context are not clearly evident. It copes with the technically distinctive situation in which there will be many more variables of interest than data points, and as one result relies on multiple sources of evidence, with data needing to converge in a triangulating fashion, and as another result benefits from the prior development of theoretical propositions to guide data collection and analysis".

But one methodological characteristic by which a case study is distinct from other research strategies such as the survey is not captured in Yin's work, or most other definitions found in the literature, namely the fact that a **case study** basically is an inquiry of only *one single* **instance** (the case), or sometimes a small number of instances, of the object of study. Yin's and others' definitions only highlight another distinctive characteristic of the case study, namely that in a case study the object of study or its environment are not manipulated ("**real life context**"). Our definition wants to capture both, and the two really distinctive features of the case study in comparison to the survey and the experiment create our definition of the case study:

A case study is a study in which (a) one case (single case study) or a small number of cases (comparative case study) in their real life context are selected, and (b) scores obtained from these cases are analysed in a qualitative manner.

With "study" we mean a research project in which a practice-oriented or theory-oriented research objective is formulated and achieved. With a **case** we mean an instance of an object of study. (We will explain our concept of "object of study" in Chapter 3.) With "real life context" we mean the object of study as it occurs (or has occurred) in reality, without manipulation. With "analysis in a qualitative manner" we mean an analysis based on visual inspection of the scores of the case (in contrast to a statistical analysis).

We distinguish two main types of case study: the **single case study**, a case study in which data from one instance is enough to achieve the research objective, and the **comparative case study**, a case study that requires data from two or more instances to achieve the research objective.

Table 1.1

Main difference between the case study and the experiment

Case study	Experiment
Real life context	Manipulated

The difference between the **experiment** and the case study is that the experiment *manipulates* instances, whereas the case study does not. An experiment is a study in which one or more variable characteristics of an object of study are manipulated in one or multiple ("experimental") instances of an object of study and in which scores obtained in the experimental instance or instances are analysed.

The **survey** also studies instances in their real life context. A survey is a study in which (a) a single population in the real life context is selected, and (b) scores obtained from this population are analysed in a quantitative (statistical) manner.

Our definition of the case study reflects our idea that the survey and the case study are different in two aspects; (a) the number of instances from which data are collected for the analysis, and, consequently, (b) the method of **data analysis**. The instances and data can be available from earlier studies (allowing for a secondary analysis) or it may be necessary to select new instances and collect new data. The case study draws conclusions on the basis of a "**qualitative**" **analysis** ("**visual inspection**") of scores from one single instance (single case study) or from a small number of instances (comparative case study), whereas the survey draws conclusions on the basis of a **quantitative (statistical) analysis** of data from a population with a large number of instances. These main differences between the case study and the survey are summarized in Table 1.2.

Our definition of the case study does *not* include statements on **data collection** or **measurement** techniques. In our view research strategies do not differ, in principle, in terms of methods of measurement. For all three research strategies discussed here, the data analysed can be quantitative or qualitative! Measurement methods that are usually associated with case studies, such as the "qualitative" interview and using "multiple sources of evidence", could also be used in the other research strategies. Similarly, measurement methods that are usually associated with other research strategies, such as standardized questionnaires in surveys and quantitative measurements in experiments, could also be used in case studies. Principles of measurement and the quality criteria that apply to it, such as reliability and validity,

Table 1.2

Main differences between the case study and the survey

Case study	Survey
Small N	Large N
Qualitative data analysis ("visual inspection")	Quantitative data analysis (statistical)

apply to any measurement in any research strategy (see Appendix 1: "Measurement"). Although in a case study quantitative data can be used to generate the scores to be analysed, the interpretation of scores of the (small number of) cases in order to generate the outcome of the study is done qualitatively (by visual inspection) and not statistically.

We do *not* limit case studies to the study of *contemporary* events, as suggested in, among others, Yin's definition of the case study. Our definition of the case study is applicable also to the study of instances (cases) of objects of study that existed or occurred in the past. Therefore, the study of instances of an object of study as occurring "in its real-life context" (as formulated in our definition) includes both the study of contemporary instances and of past instances.

In this book, thus, we discuss the case study as a **research strategy** defined by the number of instances (N = 1 or N = small) that is studied as well as the "qualitative" or non-statistical method of analysis of all kinds of (quantitative and qualitative) data.

1.2 Aims of the book

Our book has four main aims. One aim is to present to students and novice case study researchers a broad spectrum of types of case study research (including practice-oriented case studies, theory-building case studies and theory-testing case studies) in one consistent methodological framework. We define methodological notions (such as "theory", "theory-building", "theory-testing", "concept", "variable", "proposition", "hypothesis", "generalizability", "replication") and use our definition of these technical terms in a consistent way (see the glossary in Appendix 5). We describe in detail how to design and conduct different types of case study research. In that sense this book is a *textbook* from which readers can learn how to conduct a case study (see section 1.4.2 "Suggestions for students" on how to use this book as a textbook).

A second aim of this book is to contribute to the methodological debate about the appropriateness of the case study as a research strategy for **theory-testing**. Business researchers usually make a choice between the survey and the case study as the main strategy in their research, particularly if an experiment is not feasible. We emphasize and clearly illustrate (in Chapters 4 and 5) that the case study is the preferred research strategy for testing deterministic propositions case by case and that the survey is the preferred research strategy for testing probabilistic propositions in a population, if the experiment is not feasible. This implies that choosing either the case study or the survey as the research strategy in a theory-testing study depends on the type of proposition, and not on, for example, the method of measurement or what is common in the field. We believe that the main reason for confusion regarding the role of case study research in theory-testing research is that, most often, propositions are not precisely specified.

Our third main aim of the book is to emphasize the role of replication in *all* theory-testing research, irrespective of which research strategy is chosen for a specific test. The relevance of emphasizing this fundamental principle of theory development in this book is that a common criticism of case study research concerns the alleged "lack of generalizability" of the results of a case study. We think it is important to emphasize that *every test result needs replication*: a one-shot survey of a population, a one-shot experiment, and a one-shot case study. Our "how to" guide for how to design and conduct the theory-testing case study, therefore, includes a final step in which not only the significance of the test result for the theory is discussed, but also the replication strategy that is required for further theory development.

Finally, our fourth aim is to give more weight to the importance of theory-testing relative to theory-building. We claim that it is relatively easy to build relevant propositions but much more difficult to find out whether they are supported and, if so, for which domain. It certainly takes much more effort and time to test propositions (particularly because theory development requires many replications) than to build them. This is a general statement about theory development, and as such is not related to the case study only. However, we think it is important to make this point because case study research is often promoted as particularly suited for generating new propositions in "exploratory" studies. We think it is important to emphasize, contrary to such promotion, that designing and *conducting a case study with a theory-building ("exploratory") aim is often not useful* because (a) it is usually more important for the development of a theory that already formulated propositions are tested (and that such tests are replicated), and (b) there are usually much more effective and efficient ways of building propositions (see Chapter 3).

A large part of this book (Chapters 4–7) discusses theory-testing case studies, although such studies are rare in current research practice. This mismatch between our emphasis in this book on the theory-testing case study and the rare occurrence of such studies in current research practice does not reflect our misunderstanding of current research practice, but rather our deliberate attempt to correct what we see as an under-representation and under-utilization of the case study as an appropriate research strategy for theory-testing.

1.3 Overview of the book

1.3.1 Structure of the book

This book is divided into four parts. Part I (Chapters 1, 2, and 3) is an introduction to research in general and the role of case study research in particular. In Part II we discuss principles of theory-testing research in general (Chapter 4) and of the theory-testing case study in particular (Chapters 5, 6, and 7), illustrated with examples. Part III discusses theory-building research in general (Chapter 8) and the theory-building case study in particular (Chapter 9). Part IV deals with practice-oriented research in general (Chapter 10) and the practice-oriented case study in particular (Chapter 11). Below is an overview of the content of each chapter.

1.3.2 Chapter 2: Case studies in business research

In Chapter 2 ("A review of case studies in business research") Raf Jans and Koen Dittrich present a literature review of recently published case studies in business research. A distinction is made between practice-oriented case studies and theory-oriented case studies. The review shows that most studies are practice-oriented and describe the design, implementation, and/or evaluation of some interventions, or illustrate the usefulness of a theory or approach to a specific company or situation. Although such studies might make use of theories, their aim is not to contribute to the development of those theories but rather to use them in practice. Within the group of theory-oriented case studies, most studies are formulated as exploratory: building theory by exploring instances of the object of study. The review also shows that case studies are only very rarely aimed at theory-testing.

Review articles on case study research show that many case studies suffer from a lack of scientific rigour.

1.3.3 Chapter 3: Principles of research

In Chapter 3 we discuss general principles of research. We make a distinction between practice-oriented research and theory-oriented research, and discuss general features of research objectives for each of these two types. We define "practice" and we formulate the aim of practice-oriented research: to contribute to the knowledge (through research) of practitioners in order to support them in acting effectively. When we focus on theory-oriented research, we define theory as a system of statements (propositions) about relations between concepts that describe aspects of the object of study in a domain of instances of that object of study. We distinguish three types of activity that contribute to theory development: exploration (gathering information from a variety of sources), theory-building research (developing propositions through research), and theory-testing research (testing propositions through research). We claim that replication is essential for making a theory robust and for assessing its "generalizability". We argue that generalizability is not a characteristic of the results of a study, but a characteristic of the theory, which needs to be achieved through replications.

1.3.4 Chapter 4: Theory-testing research (general)

Chapter 4 further focuses on theory-testing research in general. A theory can only be tested properly if its propositions are specified in detail. We formulate four types of propositions: A is a *sufficient condition* for B ("if there is A there will be B"), A is a *necessary condition* for B ("B exists only if A is present"), a *deterministic relation* between A and B ("if A is higher, then B is higher"), and a *probabilistic relation* between A and B ("if A is higher then it is likely that B is higher"). We argue that the choice of a research strategy (i.e. making a choice between an experiment, a survey, and a case study) depends on the type of proposition. For each type of proposition, a specific strategy is preferred, second best, or third best. Despite the widespread belief that case study research is not an appropriate research strategy for theory-testing, we argue that the case study is actually the preferred research strategy for the testing of specific types of proposition, if an experiment (i.e. manipulation of aspects of the object of study) is not possible (which is often true in business research).

1.3.5 Chapters 5–7: Theory-testing case study research

In Chapters 5–7, we discuss in detail the different types of theory-testing case studies: first we describe how to design and conduct a case study for testing a sufficient or necessary condition (Chapter 5), then for testing a deterministic relation (Chapter 6), and finally for testing a probabilistic relation (Chapter 7). In each chapter, we first discuss "how to do" such a case study. Next we provide one or two examples of such a case study. These examples are intentionally not selected because they are "exemplary". On the contrary, the examples are actual case studies and as such provide a realistic picture of what is involved in conducting such a theory-testing case study. After each example of a case study we add a "methodological reflection" in which we discuss the contingencies with which the study in the example had to deal, as well as the resulting methodological limitations. This emphasizes our conviction that designing and conducting a research project is not the execution of a protocol but rather a process in which a researcher makes trade-offs all the time.

1.3.6 Chapters 8–9: Theory-building research

In Chapter 8 we discuss theory-building research in general, and in Chapter 9 the theory-building case study (aimed at the "discovery" and formulation of new propositions). As in Chapters 5–7, we first discuss "how to do" such a case study, followed by an example and a methodological reflection.

1.3.7 Chapters 10–11: Practice-oriented research

We conclude this book with two chapters on practice-oriented research. After a discussion (in Chapter 10) on practice-oriented research in general, we discuss practice-oriented case study research in Chapter 11. As in Chapters 5–7, we first discuss "how to do" such a case study, followed by an example and a methodological reflection.

1.4 How to read this book

This book can be read from the beginning to the end. However, it is also possible to read the book in another sequence, or to select for reading some specific topics of interest. Below we give suggestions to readers who are interested in specific topics, and readers (such as students) who want to use the book as a textbook for designing and conducting a research project.

1.4.1 Reading specific topics

Table 1.3 refers to specific topics that can be read separately from other parts of the book.

Table 1.3
Suggestions for reading specific topics

Topic	Chapter
Principles of research in general (not only case study research)	3, 4, 8, 10
Overview of the authors' main ideas on case study research	1, 4
Literature review of case studies in business research	2
Case studies for theory-testing	5, 6, 7
Case studies for theory-building	9
Case studies for practice-oriented research	11
"How to" design and conduct case study research	5.1, 6.1, 7.1, 9.1, 11.1
Examples of case study research	5.2, 5.4, 6.2, 7.2, 9.2, 11.2, 11.4
Methodological reflections on the examples of case study research	5.3, 5.5, 6.3, 7.3, 9.3, 11.3, 11.5

1.4.2 Suggestions for students

This book provides guidance for designing and conducting a case study. In Flowchart 1 (all flowcharts are presented additionally in Appendix 3) we present a stepwise approach for the process of designing and conducting research in general, from the formulation of the first ideas about a research topic to the final reporting of its results. In this stepwise approach, three phases can be distinguished:

- preparation phase – steps 1, 2, 3;
- research phase – steps 4, 5, 6, 7;
- implications and report phase: steps 8, 9.

Table 1.4

Suggestions for students to design and conduct a research project

Phase	Step	Chapter
Preparation	1. Define research topic	–
	2. Define the general research objective and the general type of research	3
	3. Define the specific research objective and the specific type of research	4, 8, 10, Appendix 3
Research	4. Choose the research strategy	5, 6, 7, 9, 11
	5. Select instances	
	6. Conduct measurement	Appendix 1
	7. Conduct data analysis	5, 6, 7, 9, 11
Implications and report	8. Discuss results	5, 6, 7, 9, 11
	9. Report the research	

In the *preparation phase* of the research, Flowchart 1 and the corresponding Table 1.4 can be studied to get a general picture of the steps that are needed for designing and conducting a research project. In Table 1.5, we indicate the required activities for each step of Flowchart 1, the expected results, and the applicable quality criteria, and where the reader can find support in the book. In the next step of the preparation, general Chapter 3 "Principles of research", could be studied followed by an inspection of all the flowcharts shown in Appendix 3. After that Chapters 4 "Theory-testing research (general)", Chapter 8 "Theory-building research (general)", and Chapter 10 "Practice-oriented research (general)" could be studied.

In the *research phase*, most research activities depend on the research strategy. Since our book focuses on the case study, we provide only advice for the case study strategy. If an experiment or survey was selected, the researcher must use references other than this book. If the decision was made to do a case study, one of the Chapters 5, 6, 7, 9, or 11 could be studied depending on the specific type of case study that is conducted. Information on measurement can be found in Appendix 1: "Measurement". This appendix applies to any type of research strategy.

In the *implications and report phase*, the outcome of the research is discussed and reported. Here the example chapters (always in combination with the methodological reflections!) could be read for discussing the implications of the research for theory and practice, for getting ideas on the outline of the research report, and for possible other topics to be discussed (see Appendix 4: "Writing a case study research report").

Flowchart 1

A stepwise approach to research

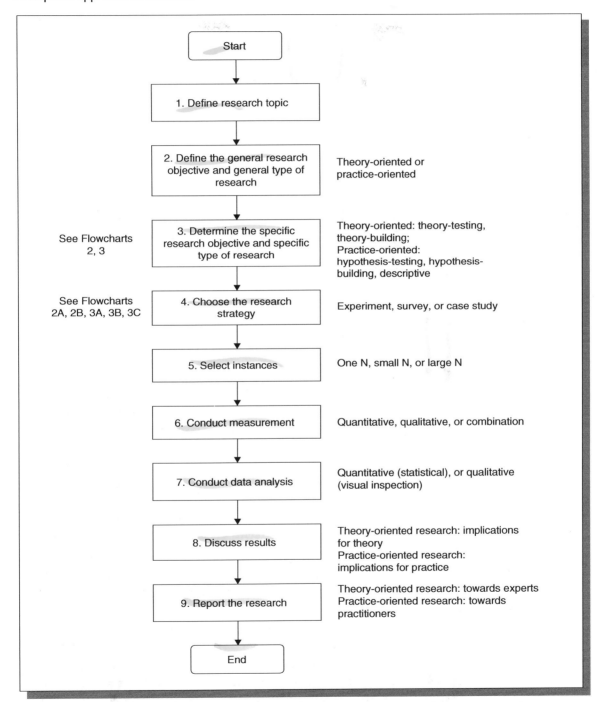

Table 1.5

A stepwise approach for research: activities, results, quality criteria, and references to relevant chapters in this book

Step	Activity	Result	Quality criterion	Chapter in this book (for all research strategies)	Chapter in this book (for case studies only)
1. Research topic	Generate ideas for research topics	Selection of the research topic	Specific, well-defined topic	–	–
2. General research objective	Orientation of practice and theory about the research topic	Choice of the general research objective	Clear choice between practice-oriented and theory-oriented research objective	3.1 Theory-oriented and practice-orientd research	–
3. Specific research objective	Exploration: for theory-oriented research using the empirical cycle; for practice-oriented research using the intervention cycle	Specification of the research objective by specifying the propositions (for theory-oriented research) or hypotheses or variables (for practice-oriented research)	Research objective is specific. For theory-oriented research: initial theory-testing, replication, or theory-building, including specification of propositions; for practice-oriented research: hypothesis-testing, hypothesis-building, or descriptive, including specification of the hypotheses or variables	3.2 Principles of theory-oriented research; 3.3 Principles of practice-oriented research; 4.2 Specifying propositions (theory-testing); 4.3 Business relevance of propositions; 8.2 Principles of theory-building research; 10.1 Hypothesis-building research (practice-oriented research); 10.2 Hypothesis-testing research (practice-oriented research); 10.3 Descriptive research (practice-oriented research)	5.1 How to test a sufficient or a necessary condition with a case study; 6.1 How to test a deterministic relation with a case study; 7.1 How to test a probabilistic relation with a case study; 9.1 How to design and conduct a theory-building case study; 11.1 How to design and conduct a practice-oriented case study; 5.3, 5.5, 6.3, 7.3, 9.3, 11.3, 11.5 Methodological reflections on example case studies
4. Research strategy	Evaluation of possible research strategies (experiment, survey, case study)	Determination of the research strategy	Fit between research strategy and specific research objective	4.4 Research strategies in theory-testing research; 8.3 Research strategies in theory-building research; 10.1 Hypothesis-testing research (practice-oriented research);	5.1 How to test a sufficient or a necessary condition with a case study; 6.1 How to test a deterministic relation with a case study; 7.1 How to test a

			10.2 Hypothesis-building research (practice-oriented research); 10.3 Descriptive research (practice-oriented research)	probabilistic relation with a case study; 9.1 How to design and conduct a theory-building case study; 11.1 How to design and conduct a practice-oriented case study; 5.2, 5.4, 6.2, 7.2, 9.2, 11.2, 11.4 Example case studies; 5.3, 5.5, 6.3, 7.3, 9.3, 11.3, 11.5 Methodological reflections on example case studies
5. Selection of instances	Evaluation of possible instances of the object of study	Selection of the instances	Fit between research objective and selection of instances	4.4 Research strategies in theory-testing research; 8.3 Research strategies in theory-building research; 10.1 Hypothesis-testing research (practice-oriented research); 10.2 Hypothesis-building research (practice-oriented research); 10.3 Descriptive research (practice-oriented research)	5.1 How to test a sufficient or a necessary condition with a case study; 6.1 How to test a deterministic relation with a case study; 7.1 How to test a probabilistic relation with a case study; 9.1 How to design and conduct a theory-building case study; 11.1 How to design and conduct a practice-oriented case study; 5.2, 5.4, 6.2, 7.2, 9.2, 11.2, 11.4 Example case studies; 5.3, 5.5, 6.3, 7.3, 9.3, 11.3, 11.5 Methodological reflections on example case studies

(Continued)

Table 1.5
(Continued)

Step	Activity	Result	Quality criterion	Chapter in this book (for all research strategies)	Chapter in this book (for case studies only)
6. Measurement	Evaluation of possible data sources, methods for accessing data sources (e.g. interview, measurement instrument, observation), procedures	Determination of measurement methods	Measurement validity and reliability	Appendix 1 Measurement	Appendix 1 Measurement; 5.2, 5.4, 6.2, 7.2, 9.2, 11.2, 11.4 Example case studies; 5.3, 5.5, 6.3, 7.3, 9.3, 11.3, 11.5 Methodological reflections on example case studies
7. Data analysis	(Statistical) analysis; visual inspection ("pattern matching")	Formulation of or rejection/confirmation of proposition (for theory-oriented research). Formulation of concepts or rejection/confirmation of hypothesis (for practice-oriented research)	Internal validity	4.4 Research strategies in theory-testing research; 8.3 Research strategies in theory-building research; 10.1 Hypothesis-testing research (practice-oriented research); 10.2 Hypothesis-building research (practice-oriented research); 10.3 Descriptive research (practice-oriented research)	5.1 How to test a sufficient or a necessary condition with a case study; 6.1 How to test a deterministic relation with a case study; 7.1 How to test a probabilistic relation with a case study; 9.1 How to design and conduct a theory-building case study; 11.1 How to design and conduct a practice-oriented case study; 5.2, 5.4, 6.2, 7.2, 9.2, 11.2, 11.4 Example case studies; 5.3, 5.5, 6.3, 7.3, 9.3, 11.3, 11.5 Methodological reflections on example case studies

			Critical reflection		
8. Results	Reflection and discussion of results with experts and practitioners	Discussion on: limitations of the study due to methodological and practical choices; contribution of the study to the research objective – consequences of the results for the theory, or consequences of the results for practice (for practice-oriented research); suggestions for replications (in theory-oriented research); speculations regarding the consequences of the results for practice (for theory-oriented research) or speculations regarding the consequences of the results for theory (for practice-oriented research)	Critical reflection	4.5 Outcome and Implications; 8.4 Outcome and Implications; 10.1 Hypothesis-testing research (practice-oriented research); 10.2 Hypothesis-building research(practice-oriented research); 10.3 Descriptive research (practice-oriented research)	5.2, 5.4, 6.2, 7.2, 9.2, 11.2, 11.4 Example case studies; 5.3, 5.5, 6.3, 7.3, 9.3, 11.3, 11.5 Methodological reflections on example case studies
9. Report	Writing and rewriting	Report that includes at least the sections: Introduction, Methods, Results, Discussion	Logical coherence between paragraphs and sentences	–	5.2, 5.4, 6.2, 7.2, 9.2, 11.2, 11.4 Report of example case studies; Appendix 4: Writing a case study research report

Although the research process is depicted here as a sequence of consecutive steps, in practice it is an iterative process that often requires stepping back to previous phases of the research process. Also many "trade-off" decisions must be made, for example between depth of the research and progress of the project. Then it is important to justify decisions and to estimate its consequences for the outcome of the research.

1.4.3 Glossary and flowcharts

One of the aims of this book is to define technical terms precisely and to use them in a consistent way. We refer to the glossary in Appendix 5 for an overview of these terms. In order to keep track of the steps that are needed for designing and conducting different types of research we present flowcharts at several places in the book. For an overview, these flowcharts are also presented in Appendix 3.

1.5 References

Ragin, C.C. 1992, Introduction: cases of "what is a case?", pp. 1–17 in: Ragin, C.C. and Becker, H.S. (eds) (1992), *What is a case?* Cambridge: Cambridge University Press.

Yin, R.K. 1984, *Case study research: design and methods.* Thousand Oaks (CA): Sage.

Yin, R.K. 1994, *Case study research: design and methods* (2nd, revised edn). Thousand Oaks (CA): Sage.

Yin, R.K. 2003, *Case study research: design and methods* (3rd, revised edn). Thousand Oaks (CA): Sage.

CHAPTER 2

A review of case studies in business research

Raf Jans and Koen Dittrich

The aim of this chapter is to provide a background to this book's approach to case study research. We want

- ▧ to find out how common the case study is in business research and in which scientific journals case studies are published and to describe the types of case studies that were published in a variety of business research areas in the period 2000–2005; and
- ▧ to review how the aims, strengths, weaknesses, and requirements of case study research have been discussed in those scientific journals.

In this chapter we review studies that are presented as case studies by their authors and the journals in which they were published. We have accepted the definition of "case study" as used in these publications (which differ considerably), and have not used our own definition of the case study. This implies that publications of research that could be considered case study research but presents itself as something else (such as "ethnography") are not included, and that an unknown number of publications of research that is not case study research according to our definition is included. We have limited our analysis of case study methodology in business research to five main fields; (1) Strategy, (2) Finance and Accounting (Finance), (3) Marketing, (4) Organizational Behaviour and Human Resource Management (HRM), and (5) Operations and Supply Chain Management (Operations). In our selection and classification of business fields, we did not aim to be exhaustive. Rather, these areas were chosen to provide a general picture of some main research streams within business research.

We found that case study research is mostly used for illustration and exploration. A minority of published case studies in business research is theory-oriented, and theory-testing case studies are very rare. Review articles on case study research show that many case studies suffer from a lack of scientific rigour.

2.1 Published case studies in business research

2.1.1 Search strategy and sample

First we identified *all publications* in scholarly journals in Strategy, Finance, Marketing, HRM and Operations in the Proquest bibliographical database for the period 2000–2005. We used the following search strings:

- Strateg*;
- Financ*, Accounting or Accountancy;
- Marketing;
- Human resourc* or Organizational Behavior;
- Operations Management, Supply Chain or Logistics.

In the search strings above, the asterix (*) represents wildcard characters. Our search was done on subject terms, which are representative for a specific field in business research. As such, we did not only look for the subjects within the list of specialized journals (e.g. only looking for marketing topics in marketing journals), but we considered papers related to a specific subject in all business journals. Note that the chosen subjects do not cover the whole field of business and management.

Second, within this first set, we identified papers reporting *case study research* by selecting those publications that had the term "case study", "case studies", or "case research" in the title or abstract. Next, within this set of publications, we only considered papers published in journals that are part of the *bibliographical databases of the Institute for Scientific Information* (ISI), assuming that this subset would contain publications of relatively high quality. We were unable to select publications on case study research directly from the ISI databases, since the search term "case study" resulted in all publications with only the word

Table 2.1

Number of publications with case study research in all scholarly journals in Proquest and in ISI journals in the period 2000–2005

Subject	Total number of publications in scholarly journals in Proquest database	Number of case study publications in scholarly journals in Proquest database	Number of case study publications in ISI journals
Strategy	10,166	930 (9.1%)	206 (22.2%)
Finance	13,912	436 (3.1%)	47 (10.8%)
Marketing	4,334	255 (5.9%)	39 (15.3%)
HRM	9,492	778 (8.1%)	153 (19.6%)
Operations	7,457	720 (9.7%)	244 (33.9%)

"case" (not combined with "study"), which mostly were not case studies. We omitted those publications from the list that were not actually publications dealing with an empirical case study, although they mentioned such terms in the title or the abstract. For example, we identified 18 publications on case studies in *Harvard Business Review*, but ten of these appeared to be fictional. We analysed the abstracts of all publications on this final list of case study publications.

Table 2.1 documents our results in the different phases of this search. The percentages of case study publications in the last two columns are relative to the total number in the respective previous column. The table shows that 8–10 per cent of the publications in Strategy, HRM, and Operations report case study research. In Marketing and in Finance the *relative* contribution of case study research is lower (3–6 per cent). Also, in *absolute* numbers, most case study research is published in Strategy, HRM, and Operations. In Finance and Marketing, relatively few publications on case study research have been published, and a relatively small proportion of these publications have been published in ISI journals. Appendix 2 of this book presents a list of the journals that published five or more papers on case study research between 2000 and 2005.

2.1.2 Case studies in Strategy

In Strategy we found 206 publications on case studies in ISI journals. The journals with most case study publications were *International Journal of Operations & Production Management*, *International Journal of Technology Management*, and *Long Range Planning*. Although the *International Journal of Operations & Production Management* is not a Strategy research journal, it also publishes many articles on case study research on the interface of Strategy and Operations.

2.1.3 Case studies in Finance

We found 47 publications in ISI journals on case studies in finance and accountancy. Only the journal *Accounting, Organizations & Society* published more than five articles. The majority of the publications in ISI journals appeared in categories other than the ISI category "Finance and Accounting". This may indicate that case study research is not well accepted in this field.

2.1.4 Case studies in Marketing

We found 39 ISI publications on case studies in Marketing. The only journal with more than five case study research publications was *Industrial Marketing Management*, with seven papers. About half of the publications were published in journals outside the field of marketing research. None of the top marketing research journals (e.g. *International Journal of Research in Marketing, Journal of Consumer Research, Journal of Marketing, Journal of Marketing Research*, and *Marketing Science*) have published on case study research. In Marketing, also, case study research seems to be not well accepted.

2.1.5 Case studies in HRM

We found 153 ISI publications on case studies in HRM. These papers were mainly published in HRM journals such as *Human Relations, Human Resource Management*, and *Journal of Business Ethics*, but, again, the *International Journal of Operations & Production Management* was an important outlet for publications on case study research.

2.1.6 Case studies in Operations

We found 244 ISI publications on case studies in Operations. These publications were concentrated in the typical operations management and operations research journals, with the *International Journal of*

Operations & Production Management and *International Journal of Production Research* as the most common outlets.

The review shows that the *International Journal of Operations & Production Management* is the one most important channel by which case study research is published. Not only are studies in Operations published in this journal, but also articles on the interface of Operations with Strategy and HRM. Almost 10 per cent (62) of all ISI listed publications on case study research in 2000–2005 (689) have been published in this journal.

2.1.7 Types of case study research

We were not only interested in the number of publications on case study research but also in what types of case study research were reported in these publications. In particular we were interested in how the published studies are divided over the categories theory-testing, theory-building, and practice-oriented research. In order to classify these publications, we relied on the authors' statements in the abstracts of the publications. We did not analyse all publications in their entirety.

Most case studies that are meant as a contribution to theory (either building or testing theory) state this explicitly in their title and/or abstract. Therefore, we categorized studies with explicitly stated theory-oriented aims (either theory-testing or theory-building) first. Most of the remaining case studies describe the design, implementation, and/or evaluation of some intervention, or illustrate the usefulness of a theory or approach to a specific company or situation. Although such studies might make use of theories or theoretical notions, their aim is not to contribute to the development of those theories. We use the label "practice-oriented" for this category of case studies.

The results of our categorization are presented in Table 2.2. The large majority of published case studies are practice-oriented, namely

Table 2.2

Three types of case studies in five fields of business research (2000–2005)

	Strategy	Finance	Marketing	HRM	Operations	Total
Practice-oriented	153	24	19	104	154	454
Theory-building	48	21	19	41	83	212
Theory-testing	5	2	1	8	7	23
Total	206	47	39	153	244	689

454 out of 689. Of the 235 remaining theory-oriented case study publications only 23 are presented as theory-testing studies. This is only 3 per cent of the total number of published case studies in ISI journals.

2.2 Review of methodological discussions on case study research

A number of journals in business research have published articles in which the methodology of case study research is discussed and, sometimes, promoted as a valuable research strategy (see below). These articles:

- argue that case study research is useful for some topics or questions or research objectives (*objectives*);
- claim that case study research can meet general quality criteria (such as validity and reliability) and illustrate this by giving lists of advice and criteria (*guidelines*); or,
- use such guidelines in evaluations of published research (*evaluation*).

We will comment on these three themes (objectives, guidelines, and evaluation), rather than discuss these articles in detail, because the following chapters of this book will explicitly or implicitly deal with the arguments of these articles.

2.2.1 Objectives of case study research

Case study research has been advocated as a valid research strategy in marketing (Bonoma, 1985), operations management (McCutcheon and Meredith, 1993), management information systems (Benbasat *et al.*, 1987), and strategy (Mintzberg, 1979; Eisenhardt, 1989; Larsson 1993). Most of these authors consider case study research as a useful research strategy (a) when the topic is broad and highly complex, (b) when there is not a lot of theory available, and (c) when "context" is very important. It is claimed that all these three conditions hold for many topics in business research. Based on such arguments, most authors advocate the use of case study research for studies with exploratory aims. Several authors provide a list of topics or questions for which they deem case study research particularly useful. Suggested topics in marketing include, marketing strategy development and implementation, business reengineering and customer service, and the formation of organizational ethical orientations as they pertain to marketing

(Valentin, 1996; Perry, 1998; Johnston *et al.*, 1999). In Operations, the management of environmental policies in operations, the dynamics of technology implementation, and differences between manufacturing and service operations management provide, according to these authors, interesting opportunities for case study research (McCutcheon and Meredith, 1993; Ellram, 1996; Meredith, 2002; Stuart *et al.*, 2002).

Some authors elaborate on the use of case study research for testing purposes. Bonoma (1985), for instance, proposes a four-step process for conducting case study research that is oriented to theory-testing. Johnston *et al.* (1999), Wilson and Woodside (1999), and Hillebrand *et al.* (2001) also advocate case study research as a strategy that is useful for theory-testing.

2.2.2 Guidelines for case study research

Several articles such as McCutcheon and Meredith (1993), Ellram (1996), Perry (1998), Hill *et al.* (1999), Stuart *et al.* (2002), and Voss *et al.* (2002), provide broad guidelines for applying case study research. Perry (1998) provides a blueprint for case study research in marketing at the Master's and PhD level. The section on implementing case study research methodology discusses how to formulate questions and set up an interview protocol, how to select cases (for replication), how many cases to select (based on the information richness), and how to analyse the cases (within case and cross-case analysis). McCutcheon and Meredith (1993) give a basic introduction to the methodology of case study research in which they focus on case study research for exploration, although they also acknowledge that it can be used for explanation. Based on their experience as reviewers of papers using case study research in academic operations management journals, Stuart *et al.* (2002) describe a number of weaknesses that they believe are common in case study research papers. Based on this analysis, they provide suggestions for designing and conducting the research itself but also for writing the research paper. They discuss how to anticipate the common criticisms of reviewers in order to increase the chances of acceptance of the paper. Voss *et al.* (2002) provide guidelines for the design, execution, and analysis of case study research. The paper discusses both theoretical issues and practical recommendations. Halinen and Törnroos (2005) provide general guidelines for doing case study research on business networks in a similar vein. They provide a list of 11 consecutive steps with specific issues related to each of them, from problem formulation to the publication of the case study results. Other authors focus on one specific methodological aspect, such as on the use of existing cases in Lewis (1998). Barnes (2001) discusses the advantages and disadvantages of several measurement methods that can be used within case study research (ethnography, interviews, strategy charting, questionnaires, and documentation). Welch (2000) focuses specifically on the use of archival records. Larsson (1993) advocates using case surveysto bridge the gap between surveys analysing too few variables and the in-depth, multi-aspect single case study.

2.2.3 Evaluations of case study research

Several authors claim that case study research can achieve the same scientific rigour as other research methodologies when correctly applied (Lee, 1989; Meredith, 1998; Hudson, 2003; Peck, 2003). This of course begs the questions of how rigorously case studies are done in business research.

Dubé and Paré (2003) list 53 quality criteria that they applied to published case study papers in management information systems (MIS). They only considered papers that used case study research for theory-building or theory-testing purposes. In total, 183 such papers were found in seven major information system journals in the period 1990–1999. Dubé and Paré discovered that only 42 per cent of the publications stated a clear research question and only 8 per cent clearly stated their unit of analysis. In 85 per cent of the single case studies and 68 per cent of the multiple case studies, no case selection criterion was discussed. A total of 42 per cent did not discuss how data were collected and of the other 58 per cent, only 5 per cent described a case study protocol. Methods of data analysis were not sufficiently discussed in 77 per cent of the publications and a clear chain of evidence was provided in only 19 per cent of the cases. Dubé and Paré concluded that a large portion of these publications lack rigour and that there is plenty of room for improvement.

These results are consistent with the observation by Stuart *et al.* (2002) as well as by Hilmola *et al.* (2005) that most case study articles in the operations management and supply chain management literature do not sufficiently discuss methodological issues. Hilmola *et al.* further found that only 12 out of the 55 studied publications made adequate references to the literature on case study research methodology. Based on their experience as reviewers for case studies in operations management journals, Stuart *et al.* (2002) state that many case study research papers indeed lack a discussion of fundamental aspects, such as a statement about the research aim, descriptions of the protocol, case selection criteria, measurement, and analysis. Also Meredith (2002) noted that case study methodology is often not well understood and not applied rigorously.

2.3 Conclusion

Whereas other researchers have investigated the use of case study research in a specific field, we provide an analysis of the broad field of business in the recent period 2000–2005. This allows us to compare the different business subfields. First of all, we observe that there are substantially more publications in ISI journals using case research on the subjects of Strategy, HRM, and Operations Management compared to only a few in Finance and Marketing. This conclusion is true for both absolute numbers and relative percentages compared to the total number of publications in the field. Furthermore, the case-based publications on Finance and Marketing topics do not appear in the core Finance and Marketing journals. This indicates that case study research is not a well-accepted method in Finance and Marketing research. The Operations Management case study publications, on the other hand, appear mainly in core operations management and operations research journals. Also in areas of HRM and Strategy, case study research is published in the respective core journals. We observe that publications related to these fields appear as well in Operations Management and Marketing journals.

When we compare the review of the methodological papers with our findings from the first part of this chapter, we observe some gaps. First, while many authors advocate the use of case study research for either exploratory purposes or theory-testing, we found previously that cases are mostly used for illustration and exploration. A minority of published case studies in business research is theory-oriented, and theory-testing case studies are very rare. Second, review articles on case study research show that many case studies suffer from a lack of scientific rigour.

It is against this background that this book was written in order to emphasize and clearly illustrate the usefulness of case study research for theory-testing, and how scientific rigour can be obtained.

2.4 References

Barnes, D. 2001, Research methods for the empirical investigation of the process of formation of operations strategy. *International Journal of Operations & Production Management*, 21(8): 1076–1095.

Benbasat, I., Goldstein, D.K., and Mead, M. 1987, The case research strategy in studies of information systems. *MIS Quarterly*, 11(3): 369–386.

Bonoma, T.V. 1985, Case research in marketing: opportunities, problems, and a process. *Journal of Marketing Research*, 22: 199–208.

Dubé, L. and Paré, G. 2003, Rigor in information systems positivist case research: current practices, trends, and recommendations. *MIS Quarterly*, 27(4): 597–635.

Eisenhardt, K.M. (1989), Building theories from case study research. *Academy of Management Review*, 14(4): 532–555.

Ellram, L.M. 1996, The use of the case study method in logistics research. *Journal of Business Logistics*, 17(2): 93–138.

Halinen, A. and Törnroos, J.-Å. 2005, Using case methods in the study of contemporary business networks. *Journal of Business Research*, 58(9): 1285–1297.

Hill, T., Nicholson, A., and Westbrook, R. 1999, Closing the gap: a polemic on plant-based research in operations management. *International Journal of Operations & Production Management*, 19(2): 139–156.

Hillebrand, B., Kok, R.A.W., and Biemans, W.G. 2001, Theory-testing using case studies: a comment on Johnston, Leach, and Liu. *Industrial Marketing Management*, 30: 651–657.

Hilmola, O.P., Hejazi, A., and Ojala, L. 2005, Supply chain management research using case studies: a literature analysis. *International Journal of Integrated Supply Management*, 1(3): 294–311.

Hudson, R. 2003, Fuzzy concepts and sloppy thinking: reflections on recent developments in critical regional studies. *Regional Studies* 37(6/7): 741–746.

Johnston, W.J., Leach, M.P., and Liu, A.H. 1999, Theory-testing using case studies in business-to-business research. *Industrial Marketing Management*, 28: 201–213.

Larsson, R. 1993, Case survey methodology: quantitative analysis of patterns across case studies. *Academy of Management Journal* 36 (6): 1515–1546.

Lee, A.S. 1989, A scientific methodology for MIS case studies. *MIS Quarterly*, 13(1): 33–50.

Lewis, M.W. 1998, Iterative triangulation: a theory development process using existing case studies. *Journal of Operations Management*, 16: 455–469.

McCutcheon, D.M. and Meredith, J.R. 1993, Conducting case study research in operations management. *Journal of Operations Management*, 11: 239–256.

Meredith, J. 1998, Building operations management theory through case and field research. *Journal of Operations Management*, 16: 441–454.

Meredith, J. 2002, Introduction to the special issue: case study and field research. *Journal of Operations Management*, 20: 415–417.

Mintzberg, H. 1979, An emerging strategy of "direct" research. *Administrative Science Quarterly*, 24: 582–589.

Peck, J. 2003, Fuzzy old world: a response to Markusen. *Regional Studies* 37(6/7): 729–740.

Perry, C. 1998, Processes of a case study methodology for postgraduate research in marketing. *European Journal of Marketing*, 32(9/10): 785–802.

Stuart, I., McCutcheon, D., Handfield, R., McLachlin, R., and Samson, D. 2002, Effective case research in operations management: a process perspective. *Journal of Operations Management*, 20: 419–433.

Valentin, E.K. 1996, Managerial marketing education and case research. *Marketing Education Review*, 6(1): 55–62.

Voss, C., Tsikriktsis, N., and Frohlich, M. 2002, Case research in operations management. *International Journal of Operations & Production Management*, 22(2): 195–219.

Welch, C. 2000, The archaeology of business networks: the use of archival records in case study research. *Journal of Strategic Marketing*, 8: 197–208.

Wilson, E.J. and Woodside, A.G. 1999, Degrees-of-freedom analysis of case data in business marketing research. *Industrial Marketing Management*, 28: 215–229.

CHAPTER **3**

pp 30 - 59

Principles of research

1 3

Empirical research is building and testing statements about an object of study by analysing evidence drawn from observation. In this chapter we discuss a number of fundamental issues regarding research. After a research topic has been identified (step 1 in Flowchart 1; selecting a research topic is not discussed in this book), the next decision that a researcher must make is to determine the general **research objective**: will the **study** be theory-oriented or practice-oriented (step 2 in Flowchart 1)? We make a distinction between these two types of objective because which is chosen determines:

1. the way in which the exploration (step 3) must be conducted;
2. the selection of instances for study (step 5);
3. the implications of the study's outcome (step 8).

In this chapter we first discuss the main differences between theory-oriented and practice-oriented research. Then we discuss each of these two types of research in more detail.

3.1 Theory-oriented and practice-oriented research

3.1.1 General research objectives of theory-oriented and practice-oriented research

We define **theory-oriented research** as research that is aimed at contributing to the development of theory. The academic community is the primary user of research findings. We define **practice-oriented research** as research that is aimed at contributing to the knowledge of specific practitioners responsible for a specific practice. A **practice** is the real life situation for which a practitioner has either a formal or an informal responsibility, and in which he acts or must act. Members of the business community are the primary users of these research outcomes. Although, as Van de Ven (1989; quoting Lewin) famously stated, "Nothing is quite so practical as a good theory", theory-oriented research and practice-oriented research are (at least partially) different activities that must be evaluated according to partially different types of criteria (see Box 1).

Box 1 The difference between practice-oriented and theory-oriented research

Practice-oriented research	Theory-oriented research
Practice-oriented research is research where the objective is to contribute to the knowledge of one or more specified practitioners.	Theory-oriented research is research where the objective is to contribute to theory development. Ultimately, the theory may be useful for practice in general.

The difference between practice-oriented and theory-oriented research can be illustrated with the difference between management practice and management theory. Managers evaluate the success of an intervention in terms of the change that is observable in the specific organization. For this evaluation, it is not relevant whether there is a theory that explains the observed success. The specific organization benefits from the intervention and celebrates this success, whether this success is theoretically explained or not. In this context, practice-oriented research is the systematic, methodologically correct, collection and evaluation of observable facts in the organization by which it is proven that "success" occurred as the result of an intervention. The criterion for success of practice-oriented research is thus whether an empirically correct conclusion about a practical object of study is reached (such as the conclusion that a specific outcome has been achieved).

Theory-oriented research regarding the same intervention in the same organization would have another objective and, therefore, another criterion for success. Its aim would not be to conclude anything about this practice (this intervention in this organization) but rather to conclude something about a theoretical statement or proposition. The empirical finding that the intervention benefits the organization in this setting (if proven in a methodologically correct way) would not be evaluated as informative about what to do next in this organization, but only (or primarily) as a contribution to the robustness and generalizability of a specific theoretical explanation (or proposition). That theory, if proven correct in a series of independent tests, might eventually have a practical value (e.g. if it can predict in which organizations the intervention will be successful and why) but the success of this particular theory-oriented research project would not be evaluated in terms of its contribution to the specific organization.

has a specific outcome been reached

The difference between practice-oriented and theory-oriented research is particularly relevant if a theory consists of probabilistic propositions, e.g. a proposition that an intervention with a specific feature has a higher chance of being successful than one without that feature. Such a proposition is still true if some interventions with that feature are not successful. In theory-oriented research we collect and analyse data about multiple interventions (with and without the feature) in order to establish the correctness of the proposition. In practice-oriented research we are only interested in knowing whether or not the feature makes a positive difference in the concrete circumstances of the practice to which the study is oriented. Whether or not the feature makes a difference in other practices (and in what direction) is not relevant.

We emphasize the distinction between these two types of research objectives (practice- and theory-oriented) because not making this distinction explicitly at the beginning of a study (in the design phase) and in its evaluation at the end of the project, usually results in severe misunderstandings about what was achieved in the study. The clearest examples of such misunderstandings are occasions in which practice-oriented research is criticized for lacking "generalizability" (which usually is not a relevant criterion in such cases) and occasions in which practical conclusions are inferred from a first test of an interesting theoretical proposition (which cannot be considered robust and generalizable before it is tested in a series of replication studies).

For theory-oriented research, the general objective of the study can be formulated as follows:

> *The general objective of this study is to contribute to the development of theory regarding topic T* {specify the research topic}.

For practice-oriented research, the general objective of the research can be formulated as follows:

> *The general objective of this study is to contribute to the knowledge of practitioner P* {specify the practitioner by mentioning a name and by referring to the real life context in which this practitioner acts or must act}.

These general research objective formulations do not specify which knowledge must be generated in order to make the intended contribution. We will discuss in 3.2 and 3.3 how the research objective can be further specified by specifying propositions (in theory-oriented research) and hypotheses (in practice-oriented research).

3.1.2 Orientation: how to choose between theory-oriented or practice-oriented research

How can one, at the beginning of a research project, make the "right" decision regarding one's general research objective? Often there is hardly a choice. For example, if the research is commissioned by an organization with the aim of getting recommendations regarding solving a practical problem, then the research is practice-oriented and should be designed as such. On the other hand, if the goal is to advance theoretical knowledge (e.g. at universities), then only theory-oriented research might be acceptable. In such cases the research is theory-oriented and should be designed as such. Sometimes researchers or students might be free to choose the one or the other research objective. In this situation, one should reflect about what one wants to achieve with the research project (e.g. a thesis project).

We recommend that everyone who is at the beginning of a research project but, in particular, those researchers who do not have a clear research objective from the start, conduct an **orientation** of both the "practice" in which the topic of interest occurs, and the "theory" that is published in the scientific literature on that topic, before making the decision to conduct a practice-oriented or a theory-oriented study.

Regarding "theory", the orientation could entail activities such as:

- searching the core scientific literature, e.g. by using bibliographic databases to identify scientific publications regarding the research topic;
- identifying suggestions for further research, usually formulated in the discussion section of papers;
- identifying interesting propositions, which were supported in an initial test and need further replication for enhancing their robustness and generalizability;
- discussions with **experts** in this theoretical field to check whether the core literature was found as well as whether the "diagnosis" of current knowledge gaps is correct.

Regarding "practice", this orientation could entail activities such as:

- searching literature on the topic, both in the general media (such as newspapers and television) and in specialized media (such as the managerial, professional, and trade literature);
- identifying "problems" (i.e. issues that practitioners describe as "yet to be solved" or "difficult"), "explanations" (i.e. ideas about causes of problems that are formulated by practitioners),

and "solutions" (i.e. ideas about what can be done about problems); and

■ discussions with practitioners who deal with the chosen topic in practice to identify what knowledge they need in order to act. Would there be interest in research aiming at providing these practitioners with knowledge they need?

It is helpful to think about different possible outcomes of a theory-oriented or practice-oriented study, and to judge how valuable specific outcomes would be. A useful tool is to write at least two different (fictional) press releases about the study results (before even having started to design the research), one of them reporting the expected ("positive") results and the other reporting very different ("negative") results. Would any of these results make any difference (to theory or to practice)? Is it desirable to get results that contribute to the development of a theory that, in the event, after many more tests, might be "generalizable" to many more situations (theory-oriented research), or is it more desirable to contribute to the knowledge of practitioners who will (ideally) be able to act upon your results (practice-oriented research)?

3.2 Principles of theory-oriented research

Theory-oriented research aims at contributing to the development of a theory. Although a theory might be used as a basis for advice in practice, what matters only in theory-oriented research is whether the study's results contribute to one or more steps in the theory development process, as will be discussed in 3.2.2. Before that we first discuss the characteristics of theory (3.2.1).

3.2.1 Theory

A **theory** is a set of *propositions* about an *object of study*. Each proposition in the theory consists of concepts and specifications of *relations between concepts*. Such relations are assumed to be true for the object of study defined in the theory and they can, therefore, be seen as predictions of what will happen in instances of the object of study under certain circumstances. The set of instances to which the predictions apply is called the *domain* (i.e. the field to which the predictions can be "generalized"). Therefore, a theory has four characteristics that need to be defined precisely: the object of study, the concepts, the propositions (relations between concepts), and the domain.

The **object of study** is the *stable* characteristic in the theory. The object of study can be very different things, such as activities, processes, events, persons, groups, organizations. If, for example, a theory is developed about "critical success factors of innovation projects", then *innovation projects* is the object of study. This object of study is the characteristic of the theory that is "stable" – other characteristics are not stable: the values of the concepts vary (hence "variables" when operationalized in a specific study), and the expected relations between concepts, and the domain to which they apply, can change over time because of new insights.

The **concepts** of the theory are the *variable characteristics of the object of study*. The aspect described by a concept can be absent or present, more or less existing, etc. For instance, if the research topic is "critical success factors of innovation projects" the *factors* that presumably contribute to success are variable characteristics. In each instance of the object of study, these factors can be present or absent or present to a certain extent. Also, *success* is a variable characteristic of the object of study that can be present or absent or present to a certain extent in an instance of the object of study (i.e. in one specific innovation project).

Concepts need to be *defined* precisely to allow for the measurement of their value in instances of the object of study. When we measure the value of a concept in such instances, we call it a **variable**. For instance, if we deal with a theory of critical success factors of innovation projects, the concept "success" needs to be defined such that it is clear what counts as "success" and what does not. Also, the different "factors" need to be defined so that we can measure the extent to which each factor is present.

Most often, defining concepts involves making assumptions about their meaning. For example, when defining the "success" of innovation projects, it must be decided whether this is an aspect that "belongs" to the innovation project itself, or that it is an evaluation attributed to it by stakeholders (and, thus, "belonging" to them). Such a decision determines how "success" could be measured in actual instances, e.g. as a return on investment (which could be calculated from financial data) or as a personal or institutional judgement. Appendix 1 "Measurement" contains a more detailed discussion on measurement.

The **propositions** of a theory formulate *causal relations* between the variable characteristics (concepts) of the object of study. A **causal relation** is a relation between two variable characteristics A and B of an object of study in which a value of A (or its change) permits or results in a value of B (or in its change). A proposition does not only state that there is a causal relation between two concepts but also what type of causal relation is meant. For instance, a success factor could be "necessary" for success, or it could be "sufficient" for success, or the relation could be probabilistic, meaning that a higher level or extent of that factor results in a higher chance of success, etc. (see Chapter 4: "Theory-testing research").

The **domain** of a theory is a specification of the universe of the instances of the object of study for which the propositions of the theory are believed to be true. The boundaries of the domain should be specified clearly. For instance, if a researcher develops a theory of critical success factors of innovation projects, it must be clearly stated whether it is claimed that the theory is (or, eventually, will be proven to be) true for all innovation projects, or only for innovation projects of specific types, or in specific economic sectors, or in specific regions or countries, or in specific time periods, etc. Hence the domain might be very generic (e.g. all innovation projects in all economic sectors in the whole world) or quite specific (e.g. limited to innovation projects in a specific economic sector, in a specific geographical area, or of a specific type).

The propositions of a theory can be visualized by means of a **conceptual model**, i.e. a visual representation of how the concepts of the theory are related to each other. Usually such a model has inputs (**independent concepts**) on the left hand side and outputs (**dependent concepts**") on the right hand side, linked to each other by unidirectional pathways, which are represented by arrows that point to the dependent concepts. The arrows are indications of the direction of the relations between the concepts. The nature of these arrows needs to be defined more precisely in the wording of the proposition. Figure 3.1 illustrates this. It represents the basic idea of a conceptual model by depicting its most simple building block: a relation between two concepts. In this figure we (only) illustrate that concept A ("the independent concept") has an effect on concept B (the "dependent concept").

In this book we consider the independent concept A as the **cause** of the dependent concept B, which is the **effect**; so we presume that there is information or an expectation about the direction between A and B, indicated by the direction of the arrow in the conceptual model. The arrow represents the assumption that causes precede the effect, which

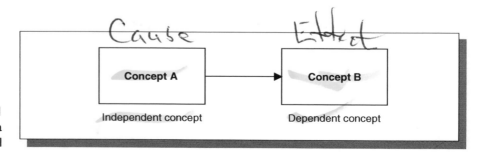

Figure 3.1
Simplest form of a
conceptual model

"depends" on these causes, hence the term "dependent concept". Causes are assumed to be "independent" from their effects, hence the term "independent concept".

Note that the object of study (e.g. "innovation project") is *not* depicted in a conceptual model because the model represents only the variable characteristics (concepts) that are linked in the theory, and not the invariable object of study that the theory is about. Nor is the domain depicted in a conceptual model.

More complicated models might depict relations of the concepts A and B with other concepts C, D, E, etc. For instance, in a conceptual model of the "critical success factors of innovation projects", the model would depict a number of different factors (A, B, C, D, E, etc.) on the left hand side, "success" on the right hand side, and an arrow originating from each factor pointing to "success".

Examples of more complex conceptual models are discussed in Box 10 "More complex conceptual models" in Chapter 4.

Box 2 What is a theory, and when is it "true"?

In this book we have a broad view of what counts as a "theory", but a strict view on when a theory is considered to be "true". First corresponding to what most people associate with the word "theory", a theory can be a set of propositions that together are known as a theory with a specific name, such as "Porter's theory" or "transaction cost theory", and with which a list of publications can be associated. Secondly, a theory could also be a new combination of (parts of) extant theory and empirical knowledge published in the scientific literature that is constructed by the researcher in the preparation of a study. Thirdly, a theory could be a well-formulated new theoretical notion, without any reference to theoretical notions published in the literature, constructed by an individual researcher after exploration of existing knowledge and ideas from the literature as well as experts. In our view, a theory is a theory if it can be expressed explicitly in terms of these four characteristics:

- object of study;
- concepts;
- relations between concepts (propositions);
- the domain to which the propositions apply.

A theory cannot be "proven" to be correct, but the degree of confidence that it is correct for a specified domain (or its generalizability) can be enhanced by repeated tests of its propositions in different parts of its domain until eventually a situation occurs in which researchers do not consider further testing useful. A single ("one-shot") study cannot be conclusive.

3.2.2 Theory-oriented research: contribution to theory development

The goal of theory-oriented research is to contribute to the development of theory. As discussed above, a theory is a system of propositions (relations between concepts) regarding an object of study in a specified domain. "**Theory development**" consists of two main activities: (a) the formulation of propositions and (b) testing whether they can be supported. If the research objective is theory-oriented, it does not matter whether the propositions have any practical implication and, generally speaking, it is even not commendable to assume that any proposition has practical relevance before it is tested thoroughly in a series of replicated tests.

We distinguish three types of activity contributing to theory development:

1. *Exploration*: Exploration for theory development is collecting and evaluating relevant information about theory and practice in order to assess how exactly research could best contribute to the development of theory.
2. *Theory-building research*: Theory-building research is research with the objective of formulating new propositions based on the evidence drawn from observation of instances of the object of study.
3. *Theory-testing research*: Theory-testing research is research with the objective of testing propositions.

Figure 3.2 is a representation of these three types of activity that contribute to theory development. Together they constitute the **empirical cycle**.

We use the term **exploration** for creatively combining information from different practical and theoretical sources in order to (re)formulate propositions. This information might come from any source that is in contact with the object of study (insights from experts, practitioners, stakeholders, existing research, the researcher's experiences, and imagination, etc.). Exploration is not research.

With **theory-building research** we mean research that is explicitly designed to gather empirical evidence for the formulation of propositions.

Theory-testing research is aimed at the testing of formulated propositions. After the test has been conducted the results of theory-testing research can be used for (re)formulating propositions, particularly if a proposition is not supported by the test.

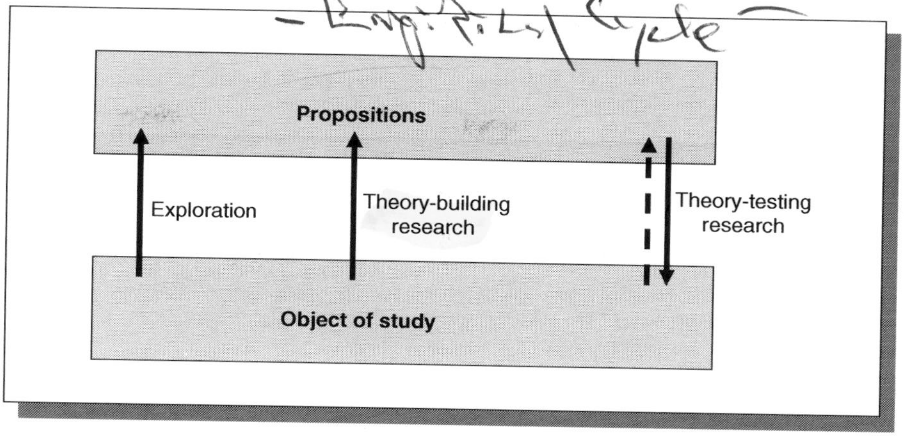

Figure 3.2
The empirical cycle for developing theory by formulating and testing propositions about an object of study

We propose that any theory-oriented research starts with an exploration of theory and practice to find out whether or not a proposition regarding the research topic of interest is available, and, if so, if it has yet been tested in one or more tests. This exploration helps to decide whether theory-building research, initial theory-testing research, or replication theory-testing research is needed.

Flowchart 2 presents a flow diagram with the order of activities that are needed for deciding about the type of theory-oriented research that should be conducted: theory-building, initial theory-testing, or replication. Theory-oriented research starts with exploration of theory in order to find propositions on the research topic. If one or more relevant propositions are available, practice is explored in order to find support for the relevance of the proposition or to select one or more propositions for testing from a larger number of candidate propositions. If no such propositions are found in theory, then the practical exploration may yield ideas for relevant propositions. Based on the exploration of theory and practice, the researcher will be able to formulate a proposition for testing. If exploration has not been successful in this regard, theory-building research is needed to formulate propositions. If a proposition has been identified for testing, theory-testing research is asked for. This type of research can be *initial theory-testing* if the proposition has never been tested before or *replication* if the proposition was tested before. A series of replications is needed in order to enhance a proposition's generalizability. If the proposition is not supported in a number of tests, the researcher may want to conduct an exploration again in order to identify other propositions for testing.

Flowchart 2
Deciding on the type of theory-oriented research

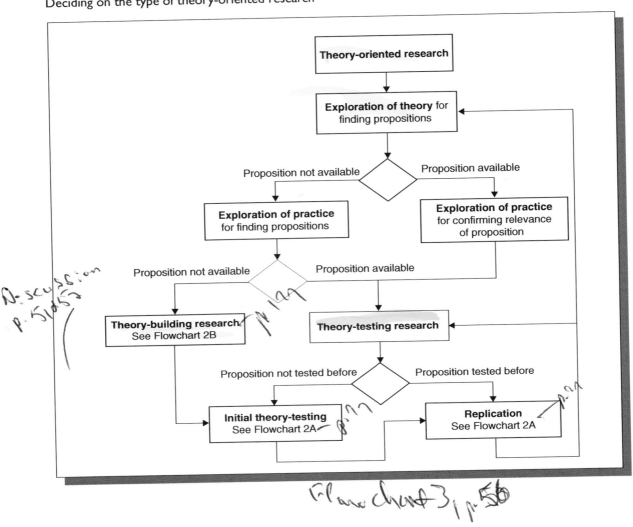

Discussion p. 51-52

Flowchart 3, p. 56

3.2.3 Replication

We emphasize the importance of **replication**, which is a much-underestimated contribution to theory development. The scientific literature is replete with reports of outcomes of initial theory-testing research: single studies in which a hypothesis is formulated, tested, and confirmed ("one-shot studies"). The study might be a single experiment in which it is demonstrated that an experimental stimulus has an effect, or a single case study in which evidence confirms the hypothesis, or a single survey of a population in which the likelihood of the correctness of the hypothesis is proven to be "significant".

Box 3 Scientific realism

We define the survey as a study in which (a) a single population in the real life context
is selected and (b) scores obtained from this population are analysed in a quantitative
manner.

We define the case study as a study in which (a) one case (single case study) or a small
number of cases (comparative case study) in their real life context are selected and
(b) scores obtained from these cases are analysed in a qualitative manner.

A conclusion based on one or a small number of observations cannot be generated
by statistical means and can be characterized as "qualitative". This distinction between
quantitative (or statistical) and qualitative methods of analysis does not imply a difference in epistemological grounding of these methods. Epistemologically, both approaches
are the same in all relevant respects: "they attempt to develop logically consistent
theories, they derive observable implications from these theories, they test these implications against empirical observations or measurements, and they use the results of
these tests to make inferences on how to modify the theories tested" (George and
Bennett 2005: 6). Basic assumptions underlying this epistemology are (a) that there are
phenomena that exist independent of our theory and that they have attributes that
exist independent of our scientific observations, (b) that we can make these attributes
observable through (scientific) instruments even in those cases in which the relevant
phenomena are not observable in the everyday sense of the word, and (c) that, subject
to a recognition that scientific methods are fallible and that most scientific knowledge
is approximate, we are justified in accepting findings of scientists as true descriptions of
phenomena and, therefore, as facts that matter in practice. We adhere to this common
sense conception of science, known as *scientific realism*, in this book. We see no reason to
ground this position in philosophical arguments or to defend it against alternative
ones, such as constructivism and other positions that argue against the possibility of
approximately true knowledge of aspects of a really existing world.

Although one-shot tests of propositions can be valuable contributions to theory development, results should always be treated with caution because of two reasons. First, erroneous conclusions might be
drawn regarding the instances studied. Second, one instance or one
group of instances is not representative of the domain to which the
proposition is assumed to be applicable.

With respect to the first problem, even though the study would have
been set up according to scientific standards, the study might have
been flawed and the reported conclusion regarding the hypothesis
(rejection or confirmation) might be erroneous. The usual checks on
the veracity of published empirical work – mainly through peer review

and critical commentary – are not sufficient protection against these problems. Replicating the study in the same situation (the same instance for case study research, or the same population of instances for survey research) can address this problem. If the results of such replication studies are in agreement with the original findings, there is more confidence in the correctness of these findings. The bottom line is that we cannot be sure of the correctness of any published test result of one-shot studies that have not been replicated. Unfortunately, many theories in business research have not been put to such a test.

With respect to the second problem, even though the study was adequately conducted and the reported conclusion regarding the hypothesis was correct, the test result might be different if the hypothesis were tested in another experimental situation (for the experiment), another instance (for the case study), or another population (for the survey). If in a one-shot study the *hypothesis* is *confirmed,* it is tempting to assume that the test has shown that the proposition is supported in general (for the entire domain covered by the theory) and, from it, to formulate practical advice for managers. In particular, survey outcomes might be thought to be generalizable to the whole domain claimed by the theory, often because no distinction is made between the population from which a (probability) sample is drawn and the larger theoretical domain from which the sample is not drawn (see Box 6 "Domain, instance, case, population, sample, and replication").

Principles of statistical sampling do not apply to the choice of a population for a survey (either for a first test or for replication). If we take seriously the claim of a theory that it applies to a domain of instances (such as other instances and populations, in other time periods, in other organizations, in other geographical areas, in other experimental contexts, etc., than the one in which the single test was conducted), we must test it in many other situations that belong to this domain. In other words, we need a series of replications. Research outcomes that have not been replicated, even those that are highly statistically significant, are "only speculative in nature and virtually meaningless and useless" regarding the wider domain (Hubbard *et al.,* 1998: 244). A serious problem in business research literature is that "negative" outcomes (rejections of hypotheses in single studies) tend not to be published. The resulting selection bias in published results exacerbates the risk of drawing conclusions about the correctness of a theory based on a one-shot confirmation. Similarly, if the hypothesis is *rejected* in the one situation that it is studied, it is usually concluded that something is wrong with the proposition. However, it might be that the single instance did not belong to the domain for which the theory is correct. The only way to assess whether this is true is through replication.

We emphasize the need of a series of replications before it can be claimed that a theory is generalizable to the specified domain. Given the fact that the knowledge base in business studies mainly consists of propositions that have been tested only once and have not been put to replication tests, an effective and appropriate way to contribute to a specific theory is by replicating published one-shot studies in the same and in other instances or sets of instances (populations). The common emphasis of journals on "originality" as a criterion for good and publishable research may hamper the much-needed increase of the number of replication studies.

With every new replication another study is added to the previous ones, creating a situation in which a theory has not been tested in a single test but rather in *serial* tests. If one research project consists of a series of replications one could call that project a serial study. If such replications make use of the same research strategy (experiment, case study, or survey), which, however, is not a prerequisite, then we could call the project a *serial experiment*, a *serial survey*, or a *serial case study*. The number of replications within one study (reported in a single research article) depends only on time and money constraints. We do not consider this a methodological choice.

Publications on experimental research often present the results of a series of experiments that replicate one another. The situation is very different in survey research. Most reports on survey research present the results of a single survey (with a single population of instances) in which a series of hypotheses is tested of which some are confirmed and some are rejected in that study. Replication of survey results is rather rare. The situation for case study research is more diverse. Theory-testing case studies of which the explicit aim is to test a proposition are rare, and so is replication of test results. Many writers on case study research, such as Yin (2003) who explicitly supports the idea of replication, recommend the "*multiple* case study" as the preferred research design. However, case studies in business research that are presented as multiple case studies are most often a series of case studies in which theories are built or applied, and not a series of replications of tests of propositions. We think that these differences in replication habits between experiments, surveys, and case studies have practical origins. Experiments are considered "smaller" (less costly in terms of time and money) than surveys and case studies, and replications in experimental research can be conducted relatively efficiently once the infrastructure and preparations for an experimental setting have been established. These are practical reasons, not methodological ones.

> ### Box 4 Replication of survey results
>
> Yin (2003: 47–48) clearly explains the difference between replication logic (which he applies to results of the case study and of experiments) and sampling logic (which he applies to procedures within a survey). Although this is not mentioned by Yin, replication logic also applies to survey results (see for example Hubbard *et al.*, 1998 and Davidsson, 2004). Davidsson (2004: 181–184) demonstrates the necessity of replication of survey results with the example of three studies of small owner–managers' expected consequences of growth, using the same measurement instruments for the same variables. Relations that were "significant" on the 5 per cent risk level in one study were absent in the other studies. Davidsson's comment is that "we would be in serious error" if conclusions about the propositions were drawn based on only one of these studies (p.183).

We coined the term **serial** study for a study in which a series of replications is conducted. We prefer the term "serial" instead of "multiple" (as in "multiple case study") because it makes explicit that every single replication can best be seen as a next test in a series of replications. In this perspective, every replication study begins with an evaluation of the results of all preceding tests of the proposition and a study is designed such that it maximally contributes to the current theoretical debate about the **robustness** of the proposition and the domain to which it applies. A temporal order is assumed. This approach implies that for every next replication a new test situation is chosen or designed on theoretical grounds: in an experiment this might be another version of the experimental stimulus or another category of experimental subjects; in a survey this might be another sample of a same population or a sample of a new population; in a case study this might be another, carefully selected case. Replication thus involves most often also the *selection* of a new case (in a case study) or a new population (in a survey). The new case or new population is selected from the universe of cases or populations to which the theory is supposed to be applicable. In actual practice, however, many multiple experiments and most multiple case studies do not use this replication logic. These studies are often designed as **parallel** (not serial).

Multiple experiments are usually pre-planned parallel replications of the same experiment with different samples of subjects. In multiple case studies usually a number of cases are selected beforehand and the test is conducted in parallel (i.e. **parallel replication**).

> ## Box 5   Multiple case study
>
> In our book we do not use the term **multiple case study** for the case study with more than one case. Instead, we distinguish: the comparative case study, the parallel single case study, and the serial single case study.
>
> A **comparative case study** is a study in which (a) a small number of cases in their real life context are selected and (b) scores obtained from these cases are analysed in a qualitative manner.
>
> A **parallel single case study** is case study research with a replication strategy in which a number of single cases are selected at the same time and the same proposition is tested in each of them without taking into account the outcome of any of the separate tests.
>
> A **serial single case study** is case study research with a replication strategy in which each test takes into account the outcome of previous tests.

3.2.4 Representativeness, external validity, and generalizability

One of the reasons that we emphasize the terms "serial" and "parallel" *study* is that we want to stress the difference between the selection of cases and populations (for testing) from a domain on the one hand, and sampling from a population on the other hand. The alleged lack of "generalizability" of the case study has its origin in confusion about these two issues as well as in confusion about what it is that is generalized (the study, its outcome, or a proposition). We will here define the three concepts that are most used in discussions about this issue: representativeness, external validity, and generalizability:

Representativeness is a characteristic of a group of instances in relation to a larger group (which is usually a domain or a population) of which it is a subset. The representativeness of the smaller group for the larger group is the degree of similarity between the distribution of the values of the variables in the two groups, as well as the degree of similarity between the causal relations in this group and in the larger group. We distinguish two main types, domain representativeness and population representativeness.

Domain representativeness is the degree of similarity between the distribution of the values of the variables in an instance of an object of study (or a group of instances or a population) and their distribution

Box 6 Domain, instance, case, population, sample, and replication

In this book, we define the domain of the theory (represented by the rectangle in the picture below) as the universe of all possible **instances** (represented by the symbol x) of the object of study to which the theory applies. The domain is a characteristic of the theory. It does *not* refer to the set of instances that is selected for a study.

For a test in a survey, a subset of instances must be selected from the domain. We call such a subset a **population** (represented by an ellipse in the picture below, in which three populations are depicted). Usually a smaller subset of instances is selected from the population for the study. We call such a subset from the population, selected for a study, a **sample**. A sample from a population must be representative for the population, which can be achieved by using **probability sampling** techniques. Populations are never "representative" for an entire domain. The significance of a test result for the theory in a survey must always be assessed by means of replications in other, equally unrepresentative, populations from the domain. A **candidate population** is not just any group of instances selected from the domain, but is defined by one or more criteria. This allows a researcher to claim that a proposition has been tested in a named population (such as, "the population of European airline companies") rather than in a group of instances selected for the study.

For a test in a single or a comparative case study, instances of the object of study must be selected from the domain. We call such instances cases. Cases are never "representative" for a domain. The significance of a test result for the theory in a case study must always be assessed by means of replications in other, equally unrepresentative, instances from the domain.

A group of cases is rarely a sample as defined for a population, with the exception of a **group of instances** selected for a quasi survey (see Chapter 7: "Testing a probabilistic relation with a case study").

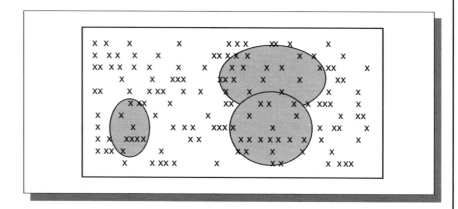

in the theoretical domain, as well as the degree of similarity between the causal relations in these instances and in the domain. The actual extent of domain representativeness of a group of instances cannot be determined because the distribution of values of the variable characteristics of all instances in a theoretical domain cannot be known.

Population representativeness is the degree of similarity between the distribution of the values of the variables in a sample and their distribution in the population from which the sample is drawn as well as the degree of similarity between the causal relations in the sample and in the population. The actual degree of population representativeness can be determined (in principle) because it is possible in principle (though usually unfeasible) to determine the distribution of values of the variable characteristics of all instances in the population. The degree of population representativeness of a **probability sample** can be estimated if the distribution of the values of the variables in the instances of the sample is known.

External validity is a characteristic of a study outcome. External validity is the extent to which the outcome of a study in one instance or in a group of instances applies (or can be generalized) to instances other than those in the study. Two important forms of external validity are ecological validity and statistical generalizability. **Ecological validity** is the extent to which the outcome of a laboratory experiment applies to instances of the object of study in its real life context. **Statistical generalizability** is the likelihood that research results obtained in a sample of a population are also true for the population.

Generalizability is a characteristic of a proposition and therefore of a theory. It is the degree of confidence that a proposition is correct and applies to the entire theoretical domain. Generalizability is enhanced if the proposition is supported in a series of replications. Generalizability decreases if the proposition is not supported in a number of such tests.

The *alleged lack of "generalizability" of the case study* is a misunderstanding. First, generalizability is not a characteristic of a study but of a proposition. Second, external validity (which is a characteristic of a study's outcome) is not an issue in most forms of case study research because usually there is no population to which results are "generalized" (with exception of the quasi survey; see Chapters 4 and 7). Third, cases (in case study research) are equally unrepresentative of a theoretical domain as populations (in survey research).

There is, however, a *general "lack of generalizability" of propositions* in the sense that most propositions are tested only once in one-shot studies. This problem, however, applies in principle to all types of propositions, irrespective of the research strategy by which they are tested. With more replication studies, the generalizability of propositions could be enhanced. Generalization, thus, is an aim rather than a claim. It is something a research community aims to be able to do after a series of replications rather than claiming to be able to do on the basis of an assumed degree of representativeness of the instances in which a test was conducted.

3.2.5 Exploration for theory-oriented research

Before a theory can be tested or built by research, an exploration must be performed.

As can be seen in Flowchart 2 we distinguish between an exploration of theory (which comes first) and a (consecutive) exploration of practice. If propositions have been found in the exploration of theory, the goal of the exploration of practice is to find support for the relevance of the propositions and to find reasons for prioritizing one or more of them for testing. If no propositions have been found in the exploration of theory, the goal of the exploration of practice is to find propositions. We will discuss each of these three types of exploration separately. Hence, there are three types of exploration for theory-oriented research that will be discussed below:

- exploration of theory;
- exploration of practice for finding a proposition; and
- exploration of practice for confirming the relevance of a proposition.

3.2.5.1 Exploration of theory

The aim of **exploration of theory** in theory-oriented research is, first, to *find candidate propositions for testing* and, second, to *select one or more of these propositions for being tested in the study*. Initial exploration will consist of conducting a literature review in order to identify potentially relevant texts (such as books, review articles, research articles, and theoretical articles) and of reading a selection of these sources. These sources must be evaluated and contradictory statements must be interpreted. A literature review will describe what is considered to be "known" about the object of study and what is not yet known. A critical literature review weighs the evidence for what is considered to be "known". For instance, assumptions and not yet tested propositions cannot be accepted as "knowledge" and, more importantly, the number and quality of replications of each "proven" proposition must be critically assessed. The literature review will conclude with a list of

- ▓ propositions that need further replication,
- ▓ propositions that have never been tested, and
- ▓ aspects of the object of study about which no proposition has been found.

Usually a literature review does not describe the most recent insights in the field because publications lag several years behind actual developments known only to experts who attend conferences and exchange information among them. Such experts usually also know important sources that will not be found in a literature search and they will also have explanations for the presence or absence of certain ideas. In other words, it is necessary not only to conduct "desk research" but also to communicate with insiders. Experts on the theory are usually quite eager to convey their insights to students and to interested colleagues.

If this exploration of theory (consisting of a literature review as well as communicating with experts) has been successful (which it usually is), this phase of the research process can be concluded with

- ▓ a description of the current body of knowledge,
- ▓ a list of propositions that have some support but need further testing (replication),
- ▓ a list of propositions that have been proposed but not yet tested,
- ▓ a description of aspects of the object of study about which no proposition has yet been formulated, and
- ▓ reasoning about what needs to be done next.

The last result is, obviously, the most important. It specifies either a proposition that should be further tested (and why this one) or a proposition that should be tested for the first time (and why this one) or an aspect of the object of study about which a new proposition should be built (and why).

3.2.5.2 Exploration of practice for finding a proposition

If the conclusion of the exploration of theory is that a new proposition should be built, it is usually concluded that theory-building *research* should be conducted. In our view, however, an **exploration of practice** should be conducted first before a decision is made to conduct theory-building research. The aim of this exploration of practice is the same as the aim of the exploration of theory, i.e. to *find candidate propositions for testing* and, second, to *select one or more of these propositions for being tested in the study.* One difference is that the exploration of practice is aimed at identifying other types of theory than "academic theories" published in the scientific literature, namely **"theories-in-use"**. A theory-in-use is a practitioner's knowledge of "what works" in practice, expressed in terms of an object of study, variables, hypotheses, and a practice domain.

The assumption underlying most theory-building (or "exploratory") research is that "nothing is known yet" about the relevant aspects of the object of study. This might be true for the theory (as explored in the first phase of exploration of theory) but is usually not true for practitioners. In an exploration of practice, it is usually discovered that a whole set of more or less explicit theories about relevant aspects of the object of study exists. Practitioners formulate them all the time, and could be the basis for ideas for propositions of a theory. How could such "theories-in-use" as formulated and exchanged by practitioners be discovered? Some of the relevant strategies are the following:

- gathering information from general media such as newspapers, television, and the internet;
- reading professional literature, such as the managerial, professional, and trade literature regarding (or related to) the object of study;
- communicating with practitioners with experience regarding the object of study;
- visiting places where the object of study occurs and observing it;
- participating in situations in which the object of study occurs.

Regarding the actual discovery of propositions in what is read, observed, or heard in this exploration of practice, it is important to recognize that the relevant sources are not "theoretical" in the academic sense and, therefore, will rarely present their insights as "propositions" or "hypotheses". However, if, for instance, managers of innovation projects are asked why some of these projects were successful and others not, the answers might be formulated as: "We did not have sufficient resources {of such and such a type}, so it could not be successful" or "Commitment of top management helped a lot". Each of such statements can be formulated as a (usually more abstract) proposition, such as: "Having sufficient resources is a necessary condition for success of projects in this firm", and "More management commitment will result in more success of projects in this firm".

If this exploration of practice is successful, this phase of the research process can be concluded with a list of candidate propositions. Next, it should be decided which of these propositions is worth testing. It is useful to contact again an expert in the theory to discuss the results of this exploration and to decide which of the resulting propositions should be tested in order to make the study a relevant contribution to development of the theory.

In terms of Flowchart 2, we can now move to theory-testing research, which will be discussed in Chapter 4. If this exploration of practice is *not* successful, we can then move to theory-building research, which will be discussed in Chapter 8.

3.2.5.3 Exploration of practice for confirming the relevance of a proposition

If the exploration of theory has resulted in the identification of a proposition for testing, we still also advise conducting some form of exploration of practice. The aim of this exploration is to *acquire real life experience regarding the object of study.* This real life experience can be acquired in the same way as when we are aiming at discovering "theories-in-use", as discussed in 3.2.5.2.

The result of such an exploration of practice is knowledge regarding the actual variation of aspects of the object of study. For instance, if the object of study is innovation projects, an exploration of practice will yield an insight into the number of such projects in different economic sectors, an idea about how successful they usually are, some knowledge about ways these projects are organized, etc. Such insights are also very helpful in later stages of the research process, such as in identifying, selecting, and accessing instances for measurement as well as for developing ideas about how measurement could be organized.

3.2.6 Contributions to theory development

A contribution to the development of a theory is, thus, any activity that can be located in Flowchart 2. The different types of *exploration* do not entail "research". Nevertheless we consider exploration as an import- ant activity in theory development in which the researcher must creatively combine ideas from others and his/her own ideas.

Theory-oriented *research* is either theory-building or theory-testing. The fact that there is no output at the end of the flowchart but rather

a replication loop is significant. This means that, although a single project that contributes to theory development will have an end (see Flowchart 1), there is usually no end to the further development of a theory (see Flowchart 2). Theory-oriented research is hardly ever "finished". This also means that every contribution in any place in Flowchart 2 is relevant. Contributing to the development of a theory entails always adding a small brick to a large building.

Many theory-oriented research proposals mention as their objective to "fill a gap" in our theoretical knowledge. Usually this means that the authors have found that a relevant proposition has not yet been formulated. "Filling the gap", then, means formulating a new proposition: theory-*building* research. Flowchart 2 helps to identify other types of "gap" in a theory. It is, for instance, also a "gap" if a proposition is not, or not yet, sufficiently tested. Thus, theory-*testing* research can also be seen as "filling a gap" in our theoretical knowledge, and perhaps an even more important one.

3.3 Principles of practice-oriented research

The objective of practice-oriented research is to contribute to the knowledge of a practitioner (not practitioners in general). A **practitioner** is a person or group of persons with either a formal or an informal responsibility for a real life situation in which he/she acts or must act. A practitioner can be a person (a manager, an entrepreneur, a policy maker, a staff member, etc.) or a group of persons (a team, a company, a business sector, a nation, etc.). A practitioner needs knowledge to solve or clarify a "problem" in an identified practice. Before we discuss (in 3.3.2) the different types of contribution to a practice that practice-oriented research can make, we first discuss the concept of a practice (3.3.1).

3.3.1 Practice

We define a **practice** as the real life situation for which a practitioner has either a formal or an informal responsibility and in which he/she acts or must act. A practice cannot be defined "objectively" but is defined through and by the perspective of the practitioner (a person or an organization) and by how he conceives his duties and responsibilities. The idea of practice-oriented research is based on the assumption that practitioners can make use of knowledge about their practice when they act or make decisions, and that they have knowledge needs (i.e. knowledge that they do not yet have but need in order to act or decide more effectively or efficiently). Practice-oriented research is designed and conducted in order to produce the knowledge that is needed by practitioners. However, if they ask researchers to design and conduct a study, practitioners normally have not yet formulated their specific knowledge needs. Similar to theory-oriented research, in which the most relevant proposition to be put to test (and in what precise formulation) should be ascertained through a thorough exploration (of the theory), in practice-oriented research a thorough exploration (of practice) is necessary in order to ascertain the most relevant knowledge need in this practice (and in what precise formulation).

When we use the term "theory" (as in "theory-oriented research" and in "exploration of theory"), we do not refer to a specific theory but rather to the field of theories. One of the aims of exploration of theory is to identify in that field one or more specific theories that are relevant to the research topic. We have used the *empirical cycle* to define different ways (theory-building, initial theory-testing, and replication) by which a research project can contribute to the development of a specific theory. Theory-oriented research, thus, begins with the general aim to contribute to a (yet unknown and thus to be specified) theory regarding the chosen research topic, but after a successful exploration the more specific aim of contributing to a specific theory can be formulated.

Similarly, if we use the term "practice" as in "practice-oriented research" and in "exploration of practice", we do not refer to an already specified problem to be solved, but rather to the yet unstructured set of problems with which the practitioner is dealing. One of the aims of exploration of practice is to identify in that set one or more specific knowledge needs that need to be addressed. We will use the *intervention cycle* to prioritize a practitioner's challenges and the corresponding knowledge needs. Practice-oriented research, thus, begins with the general aim to provide the practitioner with some knowledge that he might need in order to act, but, after a successful exploration, a more specific knowledge need can be formulated.

3.3.2 Practice-oriented research: contribution to a practitioner's knowledge

Practice-oriented research is (only) useful if it delivers the knowledge that a practitioner can actually use in his actual situation and, therefore, it is of paramount importance that his knowledge need is precisely

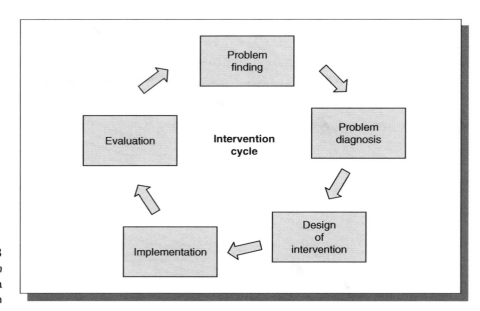

Figure 3.3
The *intervention cycle* for solving a practical problem

specified. This can only be achieved if the practitioner's circumstances as well as his options for action (both "objectively" and "subjectively", i.e. seen from the practitioner's viewpoint) are precisely known. It is, therefore, necessary to explore and map the practice in which knowledge needs have emerged, to formulate these needs as precisely as possible, and to prioritize them, before one of these is chosen as the one that should be addressed in the research project. We advise using the "intervention cycle" as a tool for this process of mapping and prioritizing knowledge needs.

The **intervention cycle** (see Figure 3.3) depicts problem solving as an iterative process consisting of five distinct phases:

1. *problem finding*: identification and definition of a problem;
2. *problem diagnosis*: finding out why a problem exists (causes);
3. *design of intervention*: designing an intervention (based on a diagnosis) that should (help to) solve the problem;
4. *implementation*: implementing the intervention that has been designed;
5. *evaluation*: ascertaining whether the aims of the intervention have been achieved and whether (or to what degree) the problem has been solved.

The five phases of the intervention cycle define the stages through which a "problem" progresses. The basic underlying assumption is that the logical and temporal order that is depicted in this cycle must not be violated. One phase needs to be completed sufficiently before the problem can move to the next phase. Based on this assumption, we believe that practitioners' knowledge needs can be prioritized by "locating" where they are in terms of phases of this cycle.

As shown in Flowchart 3, there are three forms of practice-oriented research:

- descriptive practice-oriented research;
- hypothesis-building practice-oriented research;
- hypothesis-testing practice-oriented research.

We recommend beginning any practice-oriented research project with a thorough exploration of the practice to which the research is oriented in order to determine whether hypotheses can be found that should be tested. If no hypothesis can be found in this way, it must be decided whether or not a hypothesis (and hypothesis-testing) is needed in order to generate the knowledge that the practitioner needs. If it is decided that it is not necessary to find and test a hypothesis, *descriptive practice-oriented research* should be designed and conducted. If, however, it is decided that the practitioner definitely needs knowledge about a relationship between aspects of the practice, *hypothesis-building practice-oriented research* should be designed and conducted. If a hypothesis is available, and assuming that the result of the test of this hypothesis will provide knowledge on which the practitioner can act in the current circumstances, *hypothesis-testing practice-oriented research* should be designed and conducted.

3.3.3 Exploration for practice-oriented research

The aims of exploration for practice-oriented research are:

- to specify the problem as precisely as possible;
- to identify its current phase in terms of the intervention cycle;
- to identify knowledge needs; and
- to prioritize these needs according to their urgency in relation to the phase in the intervention cycle to which the problem has progressed.

The main result, thus, of the exploration of practice is a specification of the main **practitioner's knowledge need**, i.e. the knowledge that the practitioner currently needs most in order to act effectively in the

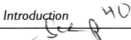

Flowchart 3
Deciding on the type of practice-oriented research

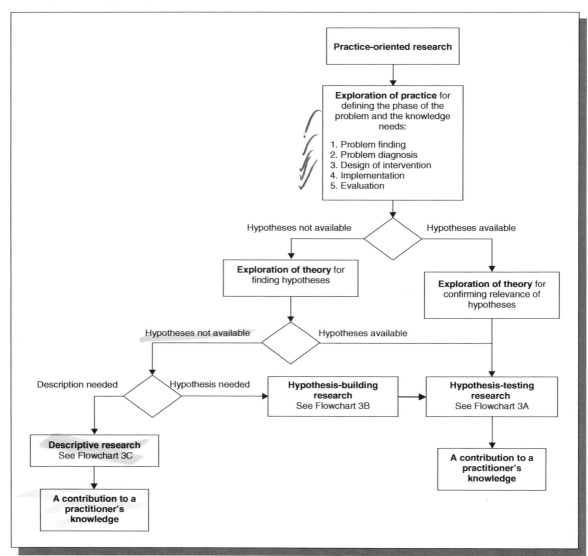

current circumstances. As can be seen in Flowchart 3 we distinguish, first, between an exploration of practice (which comes first) and a consecutive exploration of theory and, second, between two types of exploration of theory, depending on the knowledge need that is formulated as the result of the exploration of practice. We will discuss each of these three types separately.

Box 7 The term hypothesis in practice-oriented research

In the context of practice-oriented research we use the word hypothesis instead of proposition because practice-oriented research does not aim at contributing to theory or any other generalization. Assumed relations apply only to the local context of the research. Generalization to a theoretical domain is not relevant for the problem at hand and, thus, not an aim of the research. If the aim of the research was to "generalize" the outcomes to similar practices, then practice-oriented research is not the right research strategy. For such an aim, theory-oriented research must be designed and conducted, and the present practice might or might not be useful as an instance, depending on the specific proposition.

3.3.3.1 Exploration of practice

The aims of this exploration are (a) to specify the problem as precisely as possible, (b) to identify its current phase in terms of the intervention cycle, (c) to identify knowledge needs, and (d) to prioritize these needs according to their urgency in relation to the phase in the intervention cycle to which the problem has progressed. The main activities by which these aims can be achieved are:

- communicating with people, initially the "problem owner" (the manager or the team that must act and, therefore, also "owns" the knowledge need), but also to all other parties that are involved in the practice to which the research is oriented; and
- visiting places where the problem occurs and, if possible, participating in activities related to the problem in order to get a "feel" for relevant aspects of the problem and of the context in which it occurs.

These activities will not only be helpful in deciding the problem's current phase in the intervention cycle but also in understanding better what kind of knowledge is needed.

Often, the knowledge need is formulated in the form of a hypothesis or as a question in which a hypothesis is implied. A practitioner, for instance, could need to know whether a cause X is the main cause of the practitioner's problem, implying a hypothesis "X is the (main) cause of this problem". The exploration of practice usually provides the researcher with a number of such hypotheses, which could be parts of larger "theories-in-use", similar to how exploration of practice in theory-oriented research will provide for a set of such theories. As in theory-oriented research, these "theories-in-use" can be formulated as hypotheses.

3.3.3.2 Exploration of theory for finding a hypothesis

If no hypothesis has been formulated as part of the exploration of practice, theory might be explored that is related to the problem at hand. This exploration of theory would be aimed at finding hypotheses or, more correctly, of finding propositions on which hypotheses regarding relevant aspects of the current problem can be based. This exploration will, as with any exploration of theory, consist of conducting a literature review in order to identify and read potentially relevant texts (such as books, overview articles, research articles, and theoretical articles). It is useful also to talk to experts in relevant theories in order to find out whether new developments in those theories have occurred or are emerging, which might be relevant to the problem at hand.

If this exploration has been successful and has resulted in the formulation of one or more hypotheses regarding the practice problem at hand, hypothesis-testing practice-oriented research should be designed and conducted.

If no hypothesis has been identified, it needs to be decided whether the practitioner needs knowledge about relations between aspects of the practice in order to be able to act effectively or whether it is sufficient to get descriptive knowledge. If knowledge about relations is needed, hypothesis-building research needs to be designed and conducted.

3.3.3.3 Exploration of theory for confirming relevance of a hypothesis

If a hypothesis is formulated in practice-oriented research, support for that hypothesis should be sought in an exploration of theory. There might already be much theoretical knowledge that might be relevant to the practice to which the research is oriented. The hypothesis might already have been discarded in theory after a series of tests in which the corresponding proposition had been rejected. It might also be the case that new, additional propositions are emerging in the theory and that it is useful (for the solution of the problem at hand) to test the corresponding hypotheses in this practice. This exploration will, again, consist of conducting a literature review and communicating with experts.

If this exploration has been successful and has resulted in the formulation of one or more additional hypotheses (or in the belief that the current hypothesis is worth testing) hypothesis-testing research should be designed and conducted.

3.3.4 Contributions to a practitioner's knowledge

A contribution to a practitioner's knowledge is, thus, any activity that can be located in Flowchart 3. Some of them, such as exploration of practice and exploration of theory, do not entail "research". Practice-oriented *research* is descriptive, hypothesis-building, or hypothesis-testing. The fact that there is a clear output at two ends of the flow-chart, labelled "Contributions to a practitioner's knowledge", means that practice-oriented research is finished if the specific knowledge need of the practitioner is satisfied.

In Chapter 10 "Practice-oriented research (general)" we give more information on these three types of research.

3.4 References

Davidsson, P. 2004, *Researching entrepreneurship.* New York: Springer.

George, A.L. and Bennett, A. 2005, *Case studies and theory development in the social sciences.* Cambridge (MA): MIT Press.

Hubbard, R., Vetter, D.E. and Little, E.L. 1998, Replication in strategic management: scientific testing for validity, generalizability, and usefulness. *Strategic Management Journal,* 19(3): 243–254.

Van de Ven, A.H. 1989, Nothing is quite so practical as a good theory. *Academy of Management Review,* 14(4): 486–489.

Yin, R.K. 2003, *Case study research: design and methods* (3rd, revised edn). Thousand Oaks (CA): Sage.

Part II

Theory-testing research

pp 63~89

Theory-testing research (general)

Theory-testing research is one of the types of theory-oriented research. The objective of theory-oriented research is to contribute to the development of theory. The general format of the research objective of theory-oriented research was formulated as follows (see 3.1.1 "General research objectives of theory-oriented and practice-oriented research").

The general objective of this study is to contribute to the development of theory regarding topic T {specify the research topic}.

This very general format of a theory-oriented research objective must be further specified as one of two different types, (a) theory-testing research, and (b) theory-building research. We described in section 3.2.5 "Exploration for theory-oriented research" how this specification could be achieved through an exploration of theory followed by an exploration of practice (see Flowchart 2). In this Part II we discuss theory-testing research and in Part III theory-building research.

The objective of theory-testing research is to test propositions. Theory-testing research consists of:

1. choosing the research strategy for the test, depending on the specific proposition – experiment, survey, or case study;
2. selecting instances of the object of study, depending on the chosen research strategy – one instance for a single case study, a group of instances for a comparative case study, a population for a survey;
3. formulating a **hypothesis** about these instances, derived from the proposition of the theory;

4. conducting measurement, depending on the concepts – qualitative, quantitative, or both;
5. conducting data analysis – comparing the observed pattern of scores with the predicted pattern.

In theory-testing research two types of research can be distinguished: (a) initial theory-testing, and (b) replication.

4.1 Research objectives in theory-testing research

After the exploration of theory and practice and (sometimes) after conducting theory-building research, propositions have been identified for testing. If the proposition has not been tested before, *initial testing* is needed to confirm that there is at least one situation in which the proposition is true. In order to check whether theory-testing is appropriate the following questions could be raised.

■ Do relevant persons (usually experts, but sometimes practitioners) agree on what exactly is the topic about which theory should be further developed?
■ Is it established beyond reasonable doubt that as yet no propositions on this topic have been tested?
■ Which criteria are used to select one or more propositions for testing from the list of candidate propositions that resulted from the exploration? Is it possible to justify the choice of propositions-to-be-tested?

If the answers to such questions are conclusive, initial theory-testing research needs to be designed and conducted. Then the specific research objective can be formulated as follows.

The objective of this study is to contribute to the development of theory T {specify the object of study} by testing the following new propositions P:

■ {specify proposition P1}
■ {specify proposition P2}
■ {... etc.}.

If the proposition has been tested before a replication is usually needed. There are two reasons for a replication:

■ to increase the robustness of the theory;
■ to make the theory more generalizable.

In order to check whether replication theory-testing research is appropriate the following questions could be raised:

- Do relevant persons (usually experts, but sometimes practitioners) agree on what exactly is the topic about which theory should be further developed?
- Which core propositions of the theory have not been sufficiently tested in replication studies?
- What exactly is the aim of the replication? Is it a test to see whether outcomes of earlier tests can be reproduced (increase robustness of the theory)? Is it a further investigation of the generalizability of the proposition by exploring the boundaries of the domain to which the proposition can be extended or must be restricted?

If the answers to such questions are conclusive, replication theory-testing research needs to be designed and conducted. Then the specific research objective can be formulated as follows:

The objective of this study is to contribute to the development of theory T {specify the object of study} by re-testing the following existing propositions P:

- {specify proposition P1}
- {specify proposition P2}
- {… etc.};

in order to {specify the aim of the replication}.

4.2 Specifying propositions in theory-testing research

In our general discussion of theory in Chapter 3, we use the word **proposition** to designate a statement about the relation between **concepts**. A proposition, therefore, belongs to the realm of the theory. We use the term **hypothesis** in the context of a study. A hypothesis is a statement about a relation between **variables**, representing concepts, in the instances studied. A hypothesis, thus, belongs to the realm of the empirical situation in which the proposition (represented by this hypothesis) is tested.

Many propositions in business research have the form "A results in B" or "A contributes to B" or "A affects B", etc. in which A is, for

Table 4.1
Correspondence between theoretical terms and theory-oriented research terms

Theory	Theory-oriented research
Propositions	Hypotheses
Concepts	Variables

instance, something that a manager can or cannot do (or can do to a larger or lesser degree) and B is the desired result of that action. If the topic of the research is "critical success factors of innovation projects" then a proposition regarding innovation projects could be that "factor A results in success B" where A may be *top management commitment* and B is *successful financial performance.*

There is a **probabilistic** and a **deterministic** way of expressing "A results in B". These two ways are fundamentally different and represent two different theories about the effect of A on B. In a theory-testing research project, the assumed relationship between A and B needs to be specified precisely in the proposition before we can determine which research strategy fits best.

In this book we make a distinction between three types of deterministic proposition and one type of probabilistic proposition. Within the category of deterministic propositions we distinguish:

- propositions that express that concept A is a **sufficient condition** for concept B;
- propositions that express that concept A is a **necessary condition** for concept B;
- propositions that express a **deterministic relation** between concept A and concept B.

Within the category of probabilistic propositions we have the following type of propositions:

- propositions that express a **probabilistic relation** between concept A and concept B.

In business research, the proposition "A results in B" is usually implicitly considered as a probabilistic relation: if there is more A, then it is likely that there is more B. A corresponding hypothesis would predict that for higher levels of the value of A the *average* level of the value of B would be higher.

In terms of the example above, the hypothesis would predict that in a group of innovation projects selected for the study, the average success of

B will be higher in the projects in which the factor A (e.g. *top management commitment*) is high than in projects in which the factor A is low. The practical implication of the theory (if supported after many replications) would be that managers could increase the *chance* of success by making sure that the success factor (e.g. *top management commitment*) is in place. Such a theory would be a theory on "factors that increase *chance of success*".

If the word "critical" means that success is very unlikely to occur if the factor is absent or, in other words, that success is not possible without the assumed "success factor", then the word "critical" designates an almost complete determinism (see Box 8 in 4.3, below). In terms of the example above, the hypothesis would then predict that in innovation projects in which the factor A (e.g. *top management commitment*) is higher, the success will be higher in comparison to projects in which the factor A is lower. The practical implication of the theory (if proven to be correct) would be that managers could increase the success by making sure that the success factor (e.g. *top management commitment*) is in place. Then, such a theory would be a theory on "factors that increase *success*".

4.2.1 Propositions that express a sufficient condition

Propositions that express that concept A is a **sufficient condition** for concept B can be formulated as follows:

> **If there is A, then there will be B.**

Alternative ways to express that A is sufficient for B are:

- "If A then B";
- "If there is A there must be B";
- "A is enough for B".

In our example this would mean: "If there is top management commitment, then the innovation project will be successful".

In propositions that express a deterministic (sufficient or necessary) *condition,* the condition A and the effect B can each have only two values: the condition A can be present or absent, and the effect B can be present or absent. Then there are four possible combinations of the presence or absence of A and B, as shown in Figure 4.1. If A is a sufficient condition for B for all instances of the domain, then an instance of the object of study can only be in three of the four cells. There can be no instances of the object of study in the cell "A present/B absent".

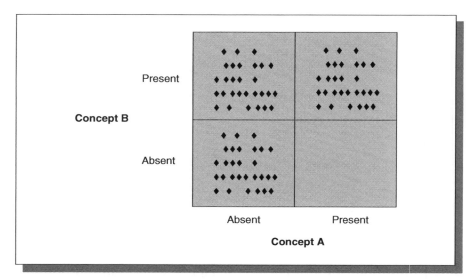

Figure 4.1
Scatter plot of
instances indicating
a sufficient
condition

4.2.2 Propositions that express a necessary condition

Propositions that express that concept A is a **necessary condition** for concept B can be formulated as:

B exists only if A is present.

Alternative ways to express that A is necessary for B are:

- "B does not exist without A";
- "If there is B then there is A";
- "A is needed for B";
- "There must be A to have B";
- "Without A there cannot be B";
- "If there is no A there cannot be B".

In our example this would mean: "In a successful innovation project there is management commitment" or "Management commitment is required for success".

Again, there are four possible combinations of A and B. If A is a necessary condition for B for all instances of the domain, then an instance can only occur in three of the four cells. There can be no instances of the object of study in the cell "A absent/B present".

A proposition can also express that A is both sufficient for B and necessary for B. Then both corresponding cells are empty. Such a

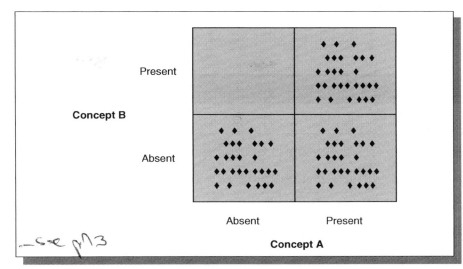

Figure 4.2
Scatter plot of
instances indicating
a necessary
condition

proposition will not be discussed further in this book, as the proposition can be treated as a combination of two single propositions.

If a very small number of instances is located in the, presumably, empty cell in comparison to the vast majority that is located in the other ones, we argue that this situation can be considered as a pragmatic deterministic sufficient or necessary condition (see Box 8 in 4.3, below).

4.2.3 Propositions that express a deterministic relation

Propositions that express a **deterministic relation** between concept A and concept B can be formulated as:

If A is higher, then B is higher.

This type of relation is depicted in Figure 4.3 as a continuous increasing relation between A and B: B increases with A. In our example this would mean: "if there is more top management commitment, then the innovation project will be more successful". The deterministic relation between A and B could also be a continuous decreasing relation, depending on the proposition. A deterministic relation between A and B is not always a continuous increasing or decreasing relation. It can also be a relation that is partly increasing and partly decreasing. For a deterministic relation it only matters that there is one specific value of B for one specific value of A.

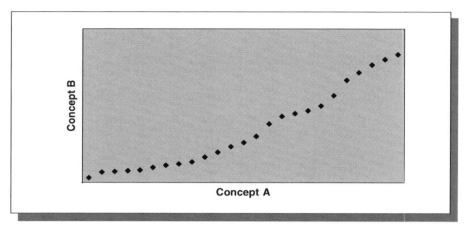

Figure 4.3
Scatter plot of
instances indicating
a continuous
increasing
deterministic
relation between
concept A and
concept B

Concept A in a deterministic relation can be forced (or "recoded") into a *condition* by specifying a cut-off point that dichotomizes this concept. For values below the cut-off point, condition A is considered to be absent; for values above the cut-off point condition A is considered to be present. In a similar way, the effect concept B can be forced into a dichotomous concept.

4.2.4 Propositions that express a probabilistic relation

Propositions that express a **probabilistic relation** between concept A and concept B can be formulated as:

If A is higher, then it is likely that B is higher.

A probabilistic relation is a relation in which both A and B on average increase or decrease at the same time. It is assumed that A causes B. A probabilistic relation can be visualized as a scatter plot of instances of the object of study of interest, as shown in Figure 4.4, which, on the average, illustrates an increase in concept B due to an increase in concept A.

Note that there can be pairs of instances in which A increases and B decreases, which would not be possible in a deterministic relation. In our example this could be formulated as: "If there is more top management commitment, then it is likely that the innovation project is more successful". Probabilistic relations between A and B can be (on

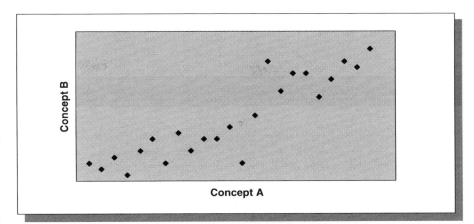

Figure 4.4
Scatter plot of
instances indicating
a probabilistic
relation between
concept A and
concept B

average) increasing, or decreasing, continuously, or not continuously,
depending on the proposition. Also note that we do not mean that variation as shown in Figure 4.4 is due to "measurement error". Figure 4.4
depicts the variation of the actual values of the *concepts* of the object of
study. These actual values are interpreted as a representation of an
underlying, "realistic", probabilistic relation.

4.3 Business relevance of propositions

We have presented two different types of propositions: deterministic
propositions and probabilistic propositions. We consider deterministic propositions as "stronger" than probabilistic ones because
they explain more (and sometimes all) variation in a dependent concept and, therefore, can often predict effects in individual instances.
Deterministic propositions make the theory more powerful. Furthermore, deterministic propositions (if supported in many replications)
are very useful for practitioners. An insight that tells you how to act (or
not to act) in order to create a "critical" condition for success (or for
the absence of failure) is often more useful in managerial practice
than an insight that tells you how to increase the *likelihood* of success.
This is not to say that absolute certainty about an effect can be achieved,
but an "almost certainty" (see Box 8) is a powerful ground for decision
making.

The distinction between deterministic conditions and probabilistic
relations reflects two different types of knowledge that managers
might need for their decision making. Typically, managerial problems

Box 8 Is business reality deterministic or probabilistic? A note on "pragmatic determinism"

In Chapter 4.3 we claim that many causal relations in real life situations in business and management can be formulated as deterministic necessary conditions. This claim is usually received with scepticism. Most business researchers assume that deterministic conditions and relations do not exist in the actual practice of management and business. It is assumed that every causal relation that is of interest to business research is multi-causal or multi-factorial and, thus, must be expressed in probabilistic statements. Our response to such criticisms consists of three parts:

1. academic theories in business and management in fact express deterministic conditions and relations;
2. even if reality is probabilistic, this does not undermine the usefulness of deterministic theories;
3. managerial theories-in-use are deterministic.

Many theories are deterministic

Goertz (2003) reviewed the political science literature in search for theories that do not present themselves as deterministic but actually are. He found no less than 150 necessary condition hypotheses covering large areas of political science, sociology, and economic history (2003: 76–94). On the basis of this finding he formulated Goertz's First Law: "For any research area one can find important necessary hypotheses" (2003: 66). We are confident that we would find an equally impressive list of necessary condition hypotheses in a review of management theories. A prominent example is Porter's theory of the conditions of competitive advantage of nations (see Box 12; 9.1). Other examples are the theories-in-use tested by Sarker and Lee (see Box 11; 5.1) and the examples of case studies in Chapter 5 of this book (5.2 and 5.4).

In this book we use the concept of "necessary condition" as formulated in classic mathematical and philosophical logic. The necessary character of A for B is expressed in this formulation by "if": "B only if A". The sufficient character of A for B is expressed by "B if A" (meaning "always B if A"). In this logic such expressions are always either true or false. This leads to the common view in theory that a necessary condition is dichotomous: true or false (Figure A).

But conditions and effects can also be continuous. Various authors have shown that it is possible to express necessary conditions for continuous variables using multi-value logic. Goertz and Starr (2003) present these authors and their ideas. They show how it is possible to express a continuous expression of a necessary condition, as illustrated in Figure B (adapted from Goertz and Starr, 2003: 10). In the upper left part of the graph there are no instances. The basic idea of a necessary condition as depicted in Figure B is that a specific value of A is necessary for a specific value of B, which is expressed in the graph by the necessity that every instance is situated below a sloping line between the

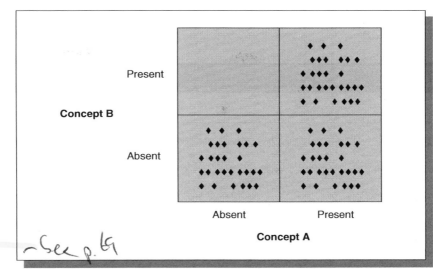

Figure A
Concept A is a
"dichotomous"
necessary condition
for concept B

⌐See p. 69

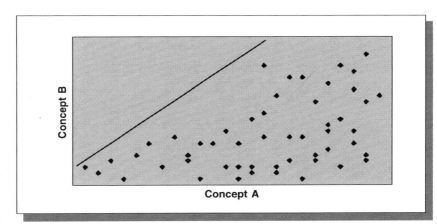

Figure B
Concept A is a
"continuous"
necessary condition
for B

area with and without instances. This idea was formulated by Ragin (2000) and by Goertz (2003).

Reality is probabilistic

The standard view of a theory with a proposition that expresses a necessary condition is the absence of even one exception of the necessary condition in the entire domain. Finding one single instance would fatally undermine the correctness of the presumed

(Continued)

necessary condition. This situation is depicted in Figure C for the dichotomous necessary condition and in Figure D for the continuous necessary condition.

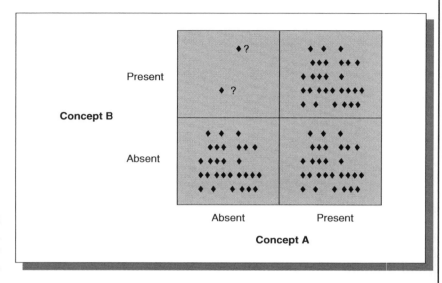

Figure C
Concept A is a "nearly" necessary condition for B

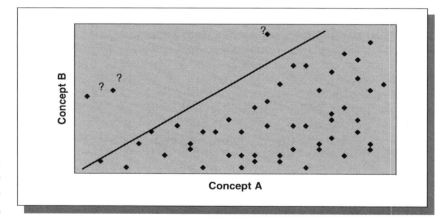

Figure D
Concept A is a "nearly continuous" necessary condition for concept B

Figures C and D depict situations in which a large majority of instances "behave" according to the formulated necessary condition statement, but there are a small number of exceptions. But what would be a better formulation of the reality depicted in these figures? Not a probabilistic one. Despite the exceptions, a continuous necessary

(Continued)

condition statement is a more fitting formulation of this reality than a formulation of a regression through the points in Figure D. In practice and in empirical research, exceptions to deterministic relations can always be found but the fact that reality probably is probabilistic does not undermine the usefulness of deterministic theories.

Ragin and other authors have formulated the idea of "almost always necessary conditions", i.e. probabilistic statements that express a very high chance (e.g. up to 0.99) that there is a deterministic relation. These authors have developed mathematical expressions for such "probabilistic necessary conditions". Ragin has also developed a statistical tool by which data as presented in Figure D are analysed in such a way that the proportion of cases on the "wrong" side of a sloping line are calculated and the "significance" of this proportion is tested against a benchmark.

Managerial theories-in-use are deterministic

Managerial relevance is not dependent on the few exceptions. Even if managers would know that the probabilistic necessary condition hypothesis is true, they would act as if the condition was completely deterministic and make sure that the necessary condition is in place.

We use the term **pragmatic determinism** for the view that it is sometimes preferable to act as if a complete determinism exists, although it is acknowledged that there might be some exceptions to the assumed determinism.

have the form "How can the company or our management team, etc., achieve the success of a project, an investment, etc.?"

For critical decision making (e.g. when a decision must be made about whether or not a huge investment should be made, or when a go/no-go decision must be made about a merger) a practitioner would prefer deterministic knowledge of the factors that would "guarantee" success (in other words, of "sufficient" conditions for success) or of conditions that are minimally required (in other words, of "necessary" conditions) for success. Probabilistic knowledge, such as "If a certain condition is present, then success is more likely" may entail too much risk for such critical decision making and, therefore, may not be enough for decision making. Obviously, this does not imply that, in this type of situation, having no knowledge at all would be better than having some probabilistic knowledge, quite the contrary. But it does imply that having knowledge about a deterministic condition would be even better.

For less critical management decisions (e.g. on ways of maximizing the average financial result of projects) probabilistic knowledge could be sufficient. If the manager knows which factors increase the *likelihood* of success of projects, he will be able to increase the average project performance or the relative number of successful projects. Hence, depending on criticality of the management decision, deterministic knowledge may be required, or probabilistic knowledge may be enough.

Although most research articles published in business research journals deal explicitly or implicitly with probabilistic propositions, such articles often conclude with a discussion of "managerial implications" in deterministic formats (such as "This study has shown that managers must do A in order to be successful"). We believe that much of such "deterministic" advice does reflect the fact that many managerial problems actually require (or, at least, would be helped with) knowledge of necessary conditions for success (see Box 8). Many research problems could, therefore, from the outset better be explicitly formulated in terms of necessary conditions than of probabilistic relations.

The question arises whether or not true determinism does exist, or that there is always an exception to the general rule, which makes reality probabilistic. Our position in this debate is that if the researcher wants to contribute to Van de Ven's (1989) idea that "Nothing is quite so practical as a good theory" he could best have a "pragmatic deterministic" view. Pragmatic determinism is the view that it is sometimes preferable to act as if a complete determinism exists, although it is acknowledged that there might be some exceptions to the assumed determinism in reality (see Box 8).

4.4 Research strategies in theory-testing research

Different research strategies (e.g. experiment, survey, case study) can be used in theory-testing research. The experiment *manipulates* the independent concept and measures the effect on the dependent concept. The survey establishes the statistical relation between the independent and the dependent concepts in a *population of instances* of the object of study. The case study determines the relation between the independent and the dependent concepts in *one instance* or a *small group of instances* of the object of study as it occurs in its real life context. Some strategies are more appropriate for testing specific types of proposition than for others. Some propositions allow for testing in single instances or a small number of instances. Other propositions require testing in a large number of instances.

Table 4.2 shows the preferred research strategies for the different types of propositions. The research strategies for testing each of the types of propositions are shown in Flowchart 2A and will be discussed below.

Table 4.2
Preferred research strategies for testing different types of propositions

Proposition	Experiment	Case study	Survey
Sufficient condition	Preferred	Second-best (single case study)	Third-best
Necessary condition	Preferred	Second-best (single case study)	Third-best
Deterministic relation	Preferred	Second-best (longitudinal single case study or comparative case study)	Third-best
Probabilistic relation	Preferred	Third-best (comparative case study)	Second-best

see p.46

Flowchart 2A
Theory-testing research (initial theory-testing or replication)

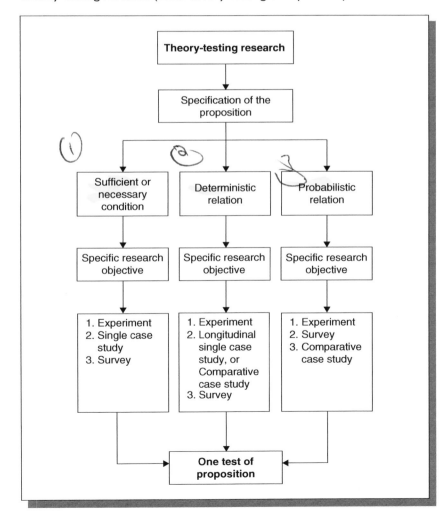

4.4.1 Strategy for testing a proposition that expresses a sufficient condition

A proposition that expresses a deterministic sufficient condition implies that for *each* single instance in the domain the proposition is true according to the theory. This means that the proposition can be tested in a single instance.

The preferred strategy for *confirming* a sufficient condition is the experiment. In an experimental test, condition A is introduced to an instance that initially does not have condition A, nor the effect B. If B occurs in the instance that has received "treatment" A, the hypothesis is confirmed and the proposition is supported. If B does not occur (and, thus, the hypothesis is rejected in this study), doubt will arise about the correctness of the proposition. An experiment, thus, is particularly preferred for confirming a sufficient condition. After the test in the single instance, another test could be conducted in another instance without A and B (replication).

If conducting an experiment is difficult or impossible, which it is on many occasions in business research, the single case study is a good alternative research strategy. With the case study a sufficient condition might be *rejected*. One instance of the object of study (a case) in which *condition A is present* is selected, and it is observed whether B is present or not. If not, then the hypothesis is rejected. Referring to Figure 4.1, the hypothesis is rejected if the case is located in the lower-right cell because, according to the hypothesis, that cell must stay empty. An alternative test is that one instance of the object of study (a case) in which *effect B is absent* is selected, and it is observed whether condition A is present. If A is present, then the hypothesis is rejected because, according to the hypothesis, that cell must stay empty. After the test with the single case, another case could be tested (replication).

Note that the single case study cannot be used as a strategy for confirming a hypothesis, because the co-occurrence of A and B (or the co-concurrence of non-A and non-B) in an instance does not prove that A is a sufficient cause for B. The presence of B can be the result of another factor than A. The occurrence of A without B, or the absence of B with the presence of A, however, implies a rejection of the hypothesis. Although strictly speaking a sufficient condition cannot be confirmed in a single case study, a failure to find rejections of the hypotheses in many different attempts (replications) provides confidence that the proposition might be generalizable to the theoretical domain, particularly if "least likely" instances are selected for the test. Such "least likely" instances are instances in which, for other reasons than the presence of A, it is very unlikely that B is present, or for other reasons than the absence of B it is very unlikely that A is absent.

The survey could be used to test a sufficient condition as well. Remember that we define a survey as a study in which (a) a single population in the real life context is selected, and (b) scores obtained from this population are analysed in a quantitative manner. For a test in a survey, a population can be selected in which the dependent concept B is known to be present or the independent sufficient condition A is known to be absent. If the values of the concepts are unknown, any population could be selected from the domain. It is tested in this population whether the frequency of occurrences of instances with the values A present/B absent is zero (as expected if the proposition is true in the population) or is very small (according to a "pragmatic determinist" criterion, as discussed in Box 8). The hypothesis is rejected if the proportion of instances with the values A present/B absent is larger than zero or larger than the proportion specified.

Such a survey might seem an efficient way of testing a sufficient condition, because it is an efficient way of computing the proportion of the instances in which the proposition is not correct. We have classified the survey as the third-best strategy for testing a sufficient condition for the following two reasons.

1. When the survey strategy as discussed here is used for testing a sufficient condition it is one test in the set of all instances of (a sample from) the selected population. This strategy for testing the sufficient condition is comparable with a case study with many (parallel) replications at the same time, in which for each instance it is determined whether it is (or is not) an instance with the values A present/B absent. In section 3.2.2 "Replication" we showed that parallel replication may not be efficient. If a rejection of the hypothesis is found in a number of instances, this might be a reason to stop further testing of the proposition. But, in the survey strategy, scores of all instances (of the population or of the sample) must be known because the test is by definition conducted in the entire (sample of the) population. The parallel single case study, thus, is much more cost effective in terms of measurement costs.

2. The survey tests the proposition in only one population, which is selected from all possible populations in the domain. Other surveys are needed to replicate the test in other parts of the domain, which again implies measurement costs. If the

same number of instances would be observed in a serial single case study, these could be selected much more purposively from all parts of the domain. The serial single case study, thus, is considerably more flexible and efficient.

4.4.2 Strategy for testing a proposition that expresses a necessary condition

A proposition that expresses a deterministic necessary condition implies that for *each* single instance in the domain the proposition is true according to the theory. Again, this means that the proposition can be tested in a single instance.

A proposition with a necessary condition can be confirmed with an experiment in a situation where A and B are both present and by taking away the condition A and observing whether the effect B disappears.

If conducting an experiment is not feasible, the best strategy for testing a necessary condition is the single case study. One instance of the object of study (a case) in which *effect B is present* is selected, and it is observed whether condition A is present or not. If not, then the hypothesis is rejected. Referring to Figure 4.2, the hypothesis is rejected if the case is located in the upper left cell, because according to the hypothesis that cell must stay empty. An alternative test is that one instance of the object of study (a case) in which *condition A is absent* is selected, and it is observed whether effect B is present or not. If B is present, then the hypothesis is rejected. Referring to Figure 4.2, the hypothesis is rejected if the case is located in the upper left cell because according to the hypothesis that cell must stay empty.

Again, as with testing for a sufficient condition, it is not possible to confirm the correctness of the proposition for all instances of the domain without repeating the test in all of them, but finding one instance in which the proposition is rejected is sufficient for concluding that the proposition is not correct (for at least one instance from the domain to which it was assumed to apply). As with testing for a sufficient condition, a failure to find rejections of the hypotheses in many different attempts, particularly in "least likely" cases (i.e. in instances in which B could be expected to occur anyway, even without A) provides some confidence that the proposition might be correct for the domain in which it was tested.

The survey might be used to test a necessary condition as well. For a test in a survey, a population can be selected in which the necessary condition A is known to be absent or the dependent concept B is known to be present. If the values of the concepts are unknown, any population could be selected from the domain. It is tested in this population whether the frequency of occurrences of instances with the values A absent/B present is zero (as expected if the proposition is true in the population) or is very small (according to a "pragmatic determinist" criterion, as discussed in Box 8). The hypothesis is rejected if the proportion of instances with the values A absent/B present is larger than zero or larger than the proportion specified. The same argument about inefficiency of the survey as discussed above for the use of the survey for testing a sufficient condition applies here as well.

4.4.3 Strategy for testing a proposition that expresses a deterministic relation

A proposition that expresses a deterministic relation implies that for *each* single instance in the domain the proposition is true according to the theory. This means that the proposition can be tested in a single instance.

The preferred strategy for testing a deterministic relation is the experiment. In such an experiment it must be demonstrated that each change in the value of the independent concept results in a predicted change in the value of the dependent concept. Depending on whether condition A can be administered in different dosages, the experiment could either be cross-sectional (in which different values of A are administered to different groups) or longitudinal (in which the value of A is, for instance, gradually increased over time). The hypothesis is confirmed if the effect B increases according to the prediction.

If an experiment is not feasible, the longitudinal single case study or the comparative case study is the second-best strategy. In the longitudinal single case study one instance is selected for measurement of both the independent and the dependent concept over time. It is assessed for each measurement point separately whether the value of dependent concept corresponds to the expected value. In the comparative case study, two (or more) instances are selected (each with a different value of the independent concept) and the value of the dependent concept is observed, or one instance is selected for measurement of both the independent and the dependent concept over time. It is assessed for each measurement point separately whether the value of the dependent variable corresponds to the expected value.

The survey might be used to test a deterministic relation as well. For a test in a survey, any population can be selected from the domain. The statistical analysis could compute for each pair of instances in the sample or in the population whether an observed difference in the values of the dependent concept B in the two instances of the pair corresponds (in the way predicted by the proposition) with the difference in the values of the independent concept A. It is tested in this population whether the frequency of occurrences of pairs of instances in which B does not follow A in the predicted direction is zero (as expected if the proposition is true in the population) or is very small (according to a "pragmatic determinist" criterion, as discussed in Box 8). The hypothesis is rejected if the proportion of instances with the values A absent/B present is larger than zero or larger than the proportion specified. The same argument about inefficiency of the survey as discussed above for the use of the survey for testing a sufficient or a necessary condition applies here as well.

4.4.4 Strategy for testing a proposition that expresses a probabilistic relation

The experiment is the preferred research strategy for testing a probabilistic relation. The effect of an independent concept (causal factor A) is investigated by comparing the change in value of a dependent concept (effect B) in an experimental group (which was exposed to the causal factor A) with the change in value of B in a control group (which was in the same condition as the experimental group but without the independent concept A (causal factor)). Different experimental conditions, with different values of A, might be created and the range of values of B in each of these conditions is measured. Differences in the values of B between the different experimental groups are analysed, usually statistically, in order to draw a conclusion about how the values of B co-vary probabilistically (i.e. on average) with the values of A.

If such an experiment is not feasible, the survey is the next best strategy for testing a probabilistic relation. In a survey, the co-variation between the values of two or more concepts is observed in a group of real life (non-experimental) instances. These are usually cross-sectional measurements (i.e. at one point in time), but sometimes it is possible to design a prospective and longitudinal survey, allowing the researcher to observe how changes in the dependent concept follow (in time) upon changes in the independent concept.

If a survey is not feasible, a comparative case study is the next best option (see Box 9). In this type of case study the principles of a good survey are followed as closely as possible ("**quasi-survey case study**"). This implies that a population is specified in which the proposition is tested, and that the sample is representative for that population and should be selected randomly.

Box 9 How the survey can become a case study

An essential characteristic of any survey is **probability sampling**, e.g. **random sampling** of instances from the population in which each instance of the population has an equal chance of being selected. This is the only guarantee that a co-variation that is observed in the group of observed instances in the sample also exists in other instances than those included in the sample. Probability sampling is only possible if the **sampling frame** is specified, i.e. if there is a list of members of a population or a set of directions for identifying each of them. Because there is never (or very rarely) a sampling frame for all members of an entire theoretical domain, a theory-testing survey is always conducted in a specified population of instances from within that domain. The proposition is tested in that population and this test will be followed by other tests in other populations in a replication strategy, in order to achieve generalizability to other parts of the domain.

If no population of instances can be identified in the domain (no sampling frame is available), it is not possible to test the proposition with a survey. However, this problem can be solved by specifying a smaller population within a domain for which a frame for probability sampling can be defined. It is, for instance, not likely that there is a sampling frame (list) of innovation projects in general, or of such projects in Europe, or in an economic sector in a country, but it is likely that there is a list of projects for which an EU subsidy was requested or a list of projects within a large company. Such (often small) populations are not "representative" of the domain, but no population ever is. A consumer behaviour theory, for instance, is always tested in a specific population of consumers (say Rotterdam housewives or Toronto students) and then replicated in other populations (see Chapter 3.2.3).

Another problem may then arise with such strategy: the number of available instances from the domain is too small for conducting a statistical analysis of the data, which is the main characteristic of a survey. This problem exists, for instance, in the field of comparative politics research when propositions about nations with specific characteristics (e.g. "Islamic states" or oil-producing states) need to be tested. The number of cases may also be small for practical reasons, e.g. if the measurement of the concepts is so time- and labour-intensive that measurements can be conducted in only a limited number of instances. In such situations, in which the number of instances is too small to conduct a statistical analysis, a qualitative analysis of the few instances available can be conducted. The survey has become a quasi-survey case study.

Case selection is different in the two conditions mentioned. On the one hand, if statistical analysis is not possible because the population is too small, case selection is not necessary. The quasi-survey comparative case study will include all instances in that small population. The outcome of the study concerns that small population and generalization will be sought by replication in other (possibly equally small) populations from the domain. On the other hand, if a quasi-survey comparative case study is conducted because of limitations caused by intensive measurement procedures, instances must be selected from the population. In principle this should be done with probability sampling, which in practice usually is very difficult to achieve. A test in a quasi-survey, however, is not useful if an outcome in the sample cannot be generalized to the population. This is the main reason why we advise for all quasi-survey comparative case studies (i.e. for all tests of probabilistic propositions) to select very small populations in each of which a census can be conducted. The outcome of a test of a probabilistic proposition in a very small population is useful as one test in a series of replications (in other small and large populations in the domain), whereas the outcome of a test in a non-probability sample has no significance at all.

4.4.5 Testing more complex conceptual models

Our book focuses on relatively simple causal relations in which one concept causes another concept, which is the effect, as shown in Figure 3.1 of section 3.2 "Principles of theory-testing research". More complex models can be tested as well, as shown in Box 10. One more complex and frequently used conceptual model is a model with several independent concepts (causes), and one dependent concept (effect). Such a model could represent a theory that all causes have, separately, a probabilistic relation with the effect, for example as shown in previous (survey) research. A further exploration of theory and practice could result in a belief that some factors, when present together, are more important for having the effect, than other combinations of factors.

Then the proposition could be formulated, for example, as a deterministic condition (e.g. a necessary condition), and the combination of factors is then the independent concept, which is a necessary condition for the effect. The complex model is reduced to again the simple model and testing the propositions is straightforward.

Box 10 More complex conceptual models

Our book focuses on relatively simple causal relations in which one concept causes another concept, as shown in Figure A below.

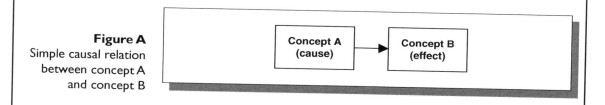

Figure A
Simple causal relation between concept A and concept B

However, more complex models are possible as well. For example, it is possible that concept A has an effect on B via another "intervening" or "mediating" concept. A **mediating** concept is a concept that links the independent and the dependent concept in a proposition and which is necessary for the causal relation between the independent and the dependent concept to exist. This is shown in Figure B. First A affects C and then C affects B. Separate propositions can be formulated and tested about the relation between A and C, C and B, and A and B.

consumer behavior

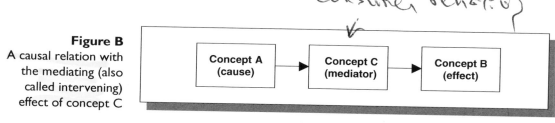

Figure B
A causal relation with the mediating (also called intervening) effect of concept C

It is also possible that a concept C has a moderating effect on the relation between A and B. A **moderating** concept is a concept that qualifies the relation between the independent and the dependent concept in a proposition. For example, the relation between A and B only exists (or is stronger) if C has a certain value. This is shown in

Figure C. The propositions can be formulated and tested in terms of the effect of A on B for different values of C.

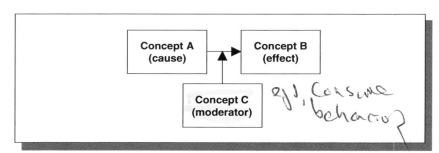

Figure C
A causal relation with the moderating effect of concept C on the relation between A and B

Other possible conceptual models have more than one causal factor or more than one effect. This is shown in Figures D and E, respectively. If there are more causal factors, the proposition can be formulated in terms of combinations of factors that must be present in order to have an effect. If there are more effects, the proposition can be formulated such that the causal factor(s) can have more than one effect.

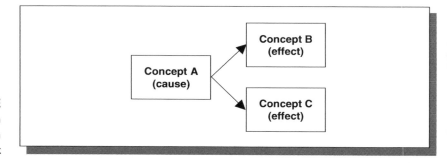

Figure D
A causal relation with more than one causal factor

Figure E
A causal relation with more than one effect

4.5 Outcome and implications

Testing consists of comparing the "facts as observed" in the instances studied with the expectations formulated in the hypothesis, which is derived from the proposition. This "observation of facts" is called measurement, which itself consists of the collection of data and the coding of these data. The result of these two procedures is a score that represents the value of a concept in the observed instance of the object of study (see Appendix 1 "Measurement" for a further discussion).

In this book we do not discuss how a hypothesis is tested in a statistical analysis. We will discuss qualitative analysis as applied in theory-testing case study research in Chapters 5–7. The result of a test is either a **confirmation** of the hypothesis or a **rejection**. Both a confirmation and a rejection require an interpretation of what is the most likely explanation of the outcome.

- Is it possible that the outcome is not correct because of methodological or practical limitations and errors?
- Does the outcome require rethinking (and possibly reformulation) of the proposition?
- Does the outcome require a reformulation of the boundaries of the domain of the theory?

A common-sense idea of a scientific test is that the desired **outcome** is always a *confirmation* of the expectation, meaning that the theory is correct. This is true in the sense that the aim of theory development is to build correct statements about the object of study and that, therefore, it is hoped that the theory is able to produce correct expectations, particularly when it is fully established and specified after a long process of development. However, from the viewpoint of theory development, a confirmation of a hypothesis is not stimulating for further improvement and specifying of the current theory, particularly in "most likely" instances in which it was expected to find a confirmation anyway. If the theory is not yet fully developed, it is hoped that new instances of the object of study will be found, in which the theory does not seem to hold, because such rejections of the theory stimulate revisions.

Theory-testing, thus, is not only a strategy for confirming a hypothesis but is also a way by which one aims to learn more about the object of study by identifying instances in which the hypothesis (as presently formulated) is rejected. This means that one purposively tries to find confirmations in "least likely" instances in which an outcome (either a confirmation or a rejection) is expected to be productive in terms of theory development.

After a hypothesis is confirmed or rejected in one study ("one-shot"), replications are needed in order to enhance the robustness and the generalizability of the proposition. A **replication strategy** must be formulated in accordance with the researcher's answers to such questions as listed above regarding the outcome of the previous test. Testing of propositions by replication follows the same procedures as initial testing of propositions discussed above.

4.6 Summary

Theory-testing research is testing a proposition of a theory by confirming or rejecting a hypothesis that is derived from that proposition in an instance of the object of study (or in a group of instances or a population). After a hypothesis is confirmed or rejected in one study ("one-shot"), replications are needed in order to enhance the robustness and the generalizability of the proposition.

Four types of proposition can be distinguished: a sufficient condition (*If there is A, then there will be B*), a necessary condition (*B exists only if A is present*), a deterministic relation (*If A is higher, then B is higher*), and a probabilistic relation (*If A is higher, then it is likely that B is higher*). Many business and management problems are formulated as necessary conditions, but most business research tests probabilistic relations.

We argue that the *experiment* is the preferred research strategy for testing all types of proposition. In an experiment the independent concept A is manipulated and its effect on the dependent concept B is investigated. Confirmation in a well-conducted experiment is strong evidence for the existence of a causal relation. However, in the actual practice of business research, it is often not possible to create experimental conditions. If experimental research is not feasible, survey research is a good alternative for testing a probabilistic relation and case study research is a good alternative for testing deterministic conditions or relations.

The *survey* is the second-best research strategy for testing a probabilistic relation. In the survey, a (sample of a) population is selected for the test, and a statistical analysis is conducted in order to test for probabilistic relations between the independent and dependent concepts. The survey is the third-best strategy for testing deterministic relations.

Despite the widespread belief that *case study* research is not an appropriate research strategy for theory-testing, we show that the case study is the second-best research strategy for testing deterministic relation. The *single* case study is the second-best strategy for testing a sufficient condition, or a necessary condition. The *longitudinal* single case study or the *comparative* case study is the second-best strategy for testing a deterministic relation.

We will discuss in detail how to design and conduct a theory-testing case study in Chapters 5–7.

4.7 References

Goertz, G. 2003, The substantive importance of necessary conditions, Chapter 4 (pp. 65–94) in Goertz and Starr (2003), *Necessary conditions, theory, methodology, and applications*. Oxford: Rowman & Littlefield.

Goertz, G. and Starr, H. (eds) 2003, *Necessary conditions: theory, methodology, and applications*. Oxford: Rowman & Littlefield.

Ragin, C. 2000, *Fuzzy-set social science*. Chicago: University of Chicago Press.

Van de Ven, A.H. 1989, Nothing is quite so practical as a good theory. *Academy of Management Review*; 14(4): 486–489.

CHAPTER 5

Testing sufficient and necessary conditions with a case study

As discussed in Chapter 4 "Theory-testing research", case studies can be used to test theory by testing propositions. A test of a proposition is determining whether a hypothesis that is derived from the proposition is confirmed or rejected in an instance of the object of study. A hypothesis is confirmed if the observed pattern of scores is the same as the pattern predicted by the hypothesis, and rejected if the scores are not the same. Depending on the outcome of the **test**, the proposition from which it is derived will be **supported** or not supported.

This chapter discusses how to design and conduct a case study in which a proposition with a **sufficient condition** or a **necessary condition** is tested. The case study methodology for testing a sufficient condition is in almost all respects the same as for testing a necessary condition. The only difference is how a case is selected for the test. In all other respects, the way in which the case study is designed and conducted is the same in testing both types of conditions.

In this chapter we first present a "How to do" guide to the testing of a sufficient condition or a necessary condition. We then present two examples of actual case studies, which are both presented in the same format as the "How to do" guide. Each example is followed by a "methodological reflection" in which the case study is discussed in detail and evaluated.

Thus, the contents of Chapter 5 are as follows:

- 5.1 How to test a sufficient or a necessary condition with a case study;
- 5.2 Case Study 1: Testing a theory of collaboration characteristics of successful innovation projects (by Koen Dittrich);
- 5.3 Methodological reflection on Case Study 1;
- 5.4 Case Study 2: Testing a theory of ideal typical organizational configurations for successful product innovations (by Ferdinand Jaspers and Jan Van den Ende);
- 5.5 Methodological reflection on Case Study 2.

5.1 How to test a sufficient or a necessary condition with a case study

5.1.1 Introduction

This chapter deals with theory-testing case study research for testing two types of propositions with a single case study:

- Sufficient condition:*If there is A, then there will be B.*
  Alternative ways to express that A is a *sufficient* condition for B are:
  - "If A then B"
  - "If there is A there must be B"
  - "There is only B if there is A"
  - "A is enough for B".

- Necessary condition: *B exists only if A exists.*
  Alternative ways to express that A is a *necessary* condition for B are:
  - "B does not exist without A"
  - "If there is B there is A"
  - "A is needed for B"
  - "There must be A to have B"
  - "Without A there cannot be B"
  - "If there is no A there cannot be B".

The sufficient condition "If there is A, then there will be B" can also be expressed as the necessary condition "non-B exists only if non-A exists". Similarly, the necessary condition "B exists only if A exists" can also be expressed as the sufficient condition: condition "If there is non-A, then there will be non-B".

5.1.2 Candidate cases

A **candidate case** is a member of a set of cases from which the researcher will select one case or a small number of cases for a case study. For a single case study only one single instance of the object of study must be selected from the domain to which the theory is assumed to apply. This selection is essentially an arbitrary choice, which is only marginally regulated by theoretical considerations. In this respect, the selection of a case for a single case study is similar to the choice of a population for a theory-testing survey. For a specific study, candidate cases could be selected from the entire domain, from a defined subset of the domain, or even from outside the domain (e.g. to find the boundaries of the domain to which the theory applies).

The exploration of "practice" at the very beginning of the research project may have provided information about where specific cases could be found. Experts and practitioners could be asked to help to make a list of candidate cases. Usually such a list is bound by regional or national boundaries and the information collected will apply to, for instance, Dutch or European instances of the object of study, whereas the domain that is specified is not defined by such geographical or political boundaries. Confining the identification of potential cases to a limited geographical domain (or to another domain that is "convenient", which could be a worldwide virtual domain as well) does not matter much if the findings will be replicated in later studies.

5.1.3 Case selection

Case selection is the selection of a case from the candidate cases. As discussed in Chapter 4 "Theory-testing research", the case for the single case study must be selected on the basis of the presence or absence of the dependent concept or independent concept.

For testing whether A is a *sufficient* condition for B, there are two possibilities for selecting the case:

- selection on the basis of the *presence of the independent concept* "If there is A, then it is tested if there is also B";
- selection on the basis of the *absence of the dependent concept* "If there is no B, then it is tested if there is also no A" (non-A is a necessary condition for non-B).

For testing whether A is a *necessary* condition for B, there are also two possibilities for selecting the case:

- selection on the basis of the *presence of the dependent concept* "If there is B, then it is tested if there is also A";
- selection on the basis of the *absence of the independent concept* "If there is no A, then it is tested if there is also no B" (non-A is a sufficient condition for non-B).

Depending on the objective of the research a "most likely" or a "least likely" case can be selected. A "most likely" case is an instance of the object of study in which confirmation of the hypothesis is likely. Such selection strategy can be used when the proposition is tested for the first time ("initial theory-testing research"). This strategy is also possible when the outcomes of earlier tests result in doubts about the support for the proposition in the domain where it was tested. The researcher may then want to select a "most likely case" to find parts in the domain where the proposition could be supported. A "least likely" case is an instance of the object of study in which support for the proposition is not likely. This strategy may be used when the outcomes of earlier tests indicate support for the proposition, and the researcher wants to know what the boundaries of the domain are. This is important for determining the generalizability of the theory.

For case selection, as it is described here, it is necessary to measure the value of the independent or dependent concept before the actual test is conducted, i.e. before "measurement" has occurred. However, it might not be feasible to measure the value of the relevant concept at this stage of the research. In this case, an alternative strategy for case selection is that a candidate case is selected and that it is verified in the measurement phase of the research whether the concept is indeed present. If not, then the case cannot be used for testing the hypothesis and another case must be selected.

5.1.4 Hypothesis

A proposition is a statement about a relation between concepts. For testing, a proposition must be reformulated into a hypothesis. A hypothesis is a statement about a relation between variables in which the variable is a measurable indicator of the concept.

In this type of theory-testing the hypothesis can be formulated quite easily. If the proposition specifies a *sufficient* condition and a case is selected in which the condition is present, the hypothesis is that the effect is also present in that case. If a case is selected in which the effect is absent, the hypothesis is that the condition is also absent in that case. If the proposition specifies a *necessary* condition and a case is selected in which the effect is present, the hypothesis is that the condition is also present in that case. If a case in which the condition is absent is selected, the hypothesis is that the effect is also absent in that case.

5.1.5 Measurement

In order to compare the prediction expressed in the hypothesis with the facts of the case, these facts must first be measured. Measurement is a process in which a score or scores are generated for analysis. Measurement consists of (a) data collection, and (b) coding. Measurement issues are discussed in Appendix 1 "Measurement".

As mentioned above, a complication regarding the case selection in this specific type of theory-testing case study is that the value of one of the concepts must be known before case selection. Otherwise it is not possible to identify and select this specific case in the first place. Hence, the principles of measurement as discussed in Appendix 1 also apply to the procedures of case selection.

5.1.6 Data presentation

For testing a *sufficient* condition it must first be shown that the *condition A* was present (or effect B was absent) in the case, so that the case can be accepted for the test. Next, the observed score of *effect B* (or the score of condition A) must be present.

For testing a *necessary* condition it must first be shown that the *effect B* was present (or the condition A was absent) in the case, so that the case can be accepted for the test. Next, the observed score of *condition A* (or the score of effect B) must be present. (In a serial or parallel single case study, the data must be presented for each case separately.)

5.1.7 Data analysis

Data analysis is the interpretation of scores obtained in a study in order to generate the outcome of the study. After having measured the actual score of either effect B or condition A, data analysis consists of testing the hypothesis. Hypothesis-testing is comparing the observed pattern of scores with the pattern predicted by the hypothesis. The test result is either a confirmation or a rejection of the hypothesis. The rules for this decision should be very precise and their application should be rigorous. These rules should aim at avoiding type 1 error (confirming the hypothesis in an instance in which it actually should not have been confirmed) and, therefore, allow for the possibility that type 2 error (rejecting the hypothesis in an instance in which it actually should not have been rejected) may occur. In operational terms, this means that rules must be formulated in such a way that it cannot be easily concluded that there actually is a presence/absence of A or B.

Data analysis in case study research is qualitative. **Qualitative analysis** is called "pattern matching". **Pattern matching** is comparing two or more patterns by visual inspection in order to determine whether patterns match (i.e. that they are the same) or do not match (i.e. that they differ). Pattern matching in theory-testing is comparing an **observed pattern** with an **expected pattern**. It is a non-statistical test of the correctness of the hypothesis.

For testing a necessary or sufficient condition the test itself is straightforward. The expectation is that A or B is present or absent. If the observations indicate that the predicted condition or effect is indeed present or absent, then the hypothesis can be confirmed. If the observations indicate that this is not true, the hypothesis must be rejected.

5.1.8 Implications for the theory

In any theory-testing research, both the confirmation and the rejection of a hypothesis can be artefacts produced by research errors, even if the procedures have been conducted correctly.

Assuming that the study was conducted adequately, a *confirmation* of the hypothesis shows that the proposition is true in one case (namely the one that was studied) and this might be taken as an indication of the likelihood that the proposition is also supported in other cases. It can, however, not be concluded that the proposition is correct for all cases in the domain to which the theory is assumed to apply. Only after many failures to reject the proposition in different "least likely" instances, can we begin to accept the "generalizability" of the proposition.

Assuming that a study was conducted adequately, a *rejection* of the hypothesis can mean (a) that there is something wrong with the proposition (i.e. that A is not a sufficient condition for B or that it is not a necessary condition for B), or (b) that something is wrong with the domain that was specified in the theory (i.e. A may be a sufficient or a necessary condition for B in other instances of the domain). The researcher must try to explain the result of the test on the basis of other information about the case. This information may help to develop an improved version of the original proposition or of the specification of the boundaries of its domain.

If the hypothesis is rejected in the first test, then the researcher can interpret the rejection as meaning that the proposition is not correct. Such a conclusion cannot be drawn lightly, presuming that the exploration at the beginning of the research was conducted seriously and that, thus, the proposition that was formulated and tested was based on sound practical and theoretical insights. However, if it is decided that the proposition should be changed, then the reformulated proposition needs to be tested in new theory-testing research.

5.1.9 Replication strategy

Any rejection or confirmation of a hypothesis needs to be replicated in further tests. If the hypothesis was tested for the first time, we recommend a strategy of replication in which the same proposition is tested again in similar cases. If the hypothesis is confirmed in such replications, then it can be concluded that the proposition is supported for at least a part of the domain. Before continuing with further replications in less similar cases, in order to determine whether the proposition holds also in other parts of the domain, we recommend with necessary conditions first to conduct a test for *trivialness*.

A necessary condition is trivial if there is no variation in either the dependent or the independent concept, or in both. An example is a proposition that states that globalization is a necessary condition for the success of off-shoring projects, which is trivial because globalization is present for all off-shoring projects, both unsuccessful and successful ones. A simple way of testing for trivialness consists of selecting a case in a different manner from that used in earlier tests. If initial tests were conducted in cases that were selected on the basis of the *presence of the dependent concept*, a next case should be selected on the basis of the *absence of the independent concept* (or the reverse). In our example, it would immediately become clear that no off-shoring projects without globalization could be found.

After having found initial support for the proposition and, in case of necessary conditions, having found that it is not trivial, we recommend a replication strategy to test the proposition in instances that are "less similar". The replication strategy in such a further series of tests depends on the outcome of each test. If the proposition is supported again and again, then we recommend a replication strategy in instances in which confirmation of the hypothesis is increasingly "less likely".

If the proposition is not supported in a number of instances, and researchers think that the proposition itself is correct, though only for a more limited domain, then a replication in "most likely" cases is recommended. The contrast between an instance in which the proposition is confirmed and one in which it is not might indicate the boundary of the domain to which the proposition applies.

The number of replications is virtually unlimited. A theory can always be developed further. The only limitations are practical, such as resource constraints.

Box 11 An example of a theory-testing single case study

Sarker and Lee (2002) tested three "theories-in-use" of business process redesign using what they call "a positivist case study". These three theories are the technocentric (TC), the sociocentric (SC), and the sociotechnical (ST) theories of redesign. Based on the literature, they formulated statements for each of these three theories in which their core beliefs regarding effective business process redesign are expressed:

TC statement 1: Effective business process redesign can occur only if the redesigning is IT-driven.

TC statement 2: Successful design (and installation) of enabling IT guarantees the effectiveness of business process redesign (and the effectiveness of the implementation of redesigned business processes).

SC statement 1: Effective redesign of processes can be accomplished only if the redesign is driven by leadership's vision regarding the reengineered processes.

SC statement 2: Effective redesign of processes can be accomplished only if a balanced team undertakes redesign.

ST statement 1: Effective redesign of processes can be accomplished only if an understanding of both the IT and the business processes within the social context is used during redesign.

ST statement 2: Effective redesign of a process can occur only if the redesigners seek to enhance the functional coupling in the business process through the use of technological as well as social enablers.

Five of these statements (namely TC1, SC1, SC2, ST1, and ST2) express a necessary condition. One statement (TC2) expresses a sufficient condition. These statements were tested in a single instance of successful business process redesign.

- TC2 *could not be tested* because enabling IT was not successfully designed in this case.
- TC1 was *rejected* because redesigning in this case had not been IT-driven.
- SC1 was *rejected* because the redesign was not based on the leadership's vision of the process flows.
- SC2 was *rejected* because there was no evidence of the existence of a balanced team.
- ST1 was *confirmed*. The redesign effort involved a sequential-recursive design process in which the relation between the social and the technical was taken into account.
- ST2 was *confirmed* as well. Redesigners used technological as well as social enablers as described in this statement.

It is interesting that the authors do not use the word "confirmed" but state instead that they "failed to reject" the ST statements. They state that this study has successfully challenged the technocentric theory regarding business process design and also invalidates the socio-centric theory, "thereby demonstrating the lack of survivability of both these perspectives". This is in accordance with our view that the development of a theory primarily entails seeking rejections of propositions in "most likely" cases rather than seeking confirmation.

5.2 Case Study 1: Theory-testing research: testing a necessary condition

Testing a theory of collaboration characteristics of successful innovation projects[1]

by Koen Dittrich

5.2.1 Introduction

Because companies need to be innovative in order to survive in a turbulent environment (Hamel and Prahalad, 1994), the management of innovation (projects) is of paramount importance. One way to organize innovation projects is to collaborate with partners in alliances. This chapter describes testing a theory of collaboration characteristics of successful innovation projects.

[1] This chapter is based on: Dittrich, K., 2004. *Innovation Networks: exploration and exploitation in the ICT industry.* Delft, Delft University of Technology. ISBN: 90-5638-126-1.

5.2.2 Theory

5.2.2.1 Object of study

The object of study in this chapter is an *alliance project* in which two or more firms collaborated on product innovation. We will call this type of alliance project an "innovation project".

5.2.2.2 Concepts

The concepts of interest in this study are:

- type of innovation;
- success of the project;
- collaboration characteristics.

Generally two main *types of innovation* are distinguished: radical innovation in which both the technology and the market are new and customer needs are unknown, and incremental innovation, consisting of the improved use of existing technologies to meet known customer needs (Henderson and Clark, 1990). The literature on these different types of innovation suggests that for the success of the project, different kinds of collaboration in alliances are needed. *Success* in this study is defined as a successful product launch: *not* in terms of high revenues or sales of a new product after its launch. This new product can also be a new service or new software.

Three *collaboration characteristics* seem to be particularly important: collaboration history, technological capabilities, and level of commitment. It is claimed, for instance, that successful incremental innovation projects need partners that are committed to long-term collaboration, whereas such long-term commitment is not considered necessary for radical innovation projects. *Collaboration history* here means whether or not firms have collaborated in an innovation project before. A new partner firm is a firm with which the company has not previously engaged in an innovation project. *Technological capabilities* are determined based on the line of business that firms are in. A collaboration with a high *level of commitment* is an alliance that is explicitly oriented to a long-term relationship such as, for instance, a joint venture that is also targeted at developing other new products or technologies in the future. In contrast, we considered explicit limitations to the *scope* of the collaboration (such as confining the collaboration only to joint *research* or only the *development* of new technology or products), or to the *duration* of the project as indications of low(er) commitment.

5.2.2.3 Propositions

Collaboration history

Radical innovation is associated with searching for new possibilities and ideas, experimentation, and risk taking (March 1991). If we apply Granovetter's (1973) finding that new ideas often come from people outside the circle of family and friends ("weak ties"), it is hypothesized that new ideas and business opportunities will come from "new" partners, i.e. partners with which a company has no collaboration history. Incremental innovation, on the other hand, consists of strengthening and broadening knowledge of established technologies and products. It is hypothesized that this requires that partners are already part of the "family". This leads to the following propositions.

> *Proposition 1a*: Success in radical innovation projects requires collaboration with new partners.

> *Proposition 1b*: Success in incremental innovation projects requires collaboration with existing partners.

Technological capabilities

Based on the same principle formulated by Granovetter (1973), it is hypothesized that new ideas and possibilities will come from partners that are involved in the production of other types of products, since these companies will have a different knowledge base. Thus, for success in radical innovation projects a company needs to establish alliances with companies that have different capabilities, preferably in a different subsector of the industry (Gilsing and Nooteboom, 2006). Because, on the other hand, incremental innovation projects must make use of existing knowledge and capabilities, they will require collaboration with partners that have similar technological capabilities (Granovetter, 1973; Gilsing and Nooteboom, 2006). These assumptions lead to the following propositions.

> *Proposition 2a*: Success in radical innovation projects requires collaboration with partners that have different technological capabilities.

> *Proposition 2b*: Success in incremental innovation projects requires collaboration with partners that have similar technological capabilities.

Level of commitment

It has been assumed that radical and incremental innovation projects do not only need different types of partners but also different structures of collaboration. A firm's choice to enter into an alliance can be distinguished in terms of its motives to explore for new opportunities, i.e. radical innovation, or to exploit existing capabilities, i.e. incremental innovation (Koza and Lewin, 1998). The intent behind entering joint radical innovation projects involves the desire to discover new opportunities. Partners in such a project seek to maintain their independence and typically do not engage in joint equity relations (Koza and Lewin, 1998). This means that joint radical innovation projects require only a low level of commitment to be successful.

Conversely, the most common way to organize joint incremental innovation projects involves the joint maximization of complementary assets by sharing in the residual returns from a business activity. The structure of such a joint effort usually takes the form of establishing a daughter company in which the parents have equity positions (Koza and Lewin, 1998). This means that joint incremental innovation projects need a high level of commitment to be successful. These two assumptions lead to the following propositions.

> *Proposition 3a*: Success in radical innovation projects requires that partners establish alliance contracts with a low level of commitment.

> *Proposition 3b*: Success in incremental innovation projects requires that partners establish alliance contracts with a high level of commitment.

5.2.2.4 Domain

Our theory does not specify any restriction regarding the domain of innovation projects. It follows that the domain covered by the theory is the universe of all instances of innovation projects in which two or more firms collaborate on product innovation, without any restriction in terms of geography, economic sector, time, etc.

5.2.2.5 Conceptual model

The theory specifies, for two types of innovation projects (radical and incremental), the relation between collaboration characteristics (independent concepts), and success (dependent concept).

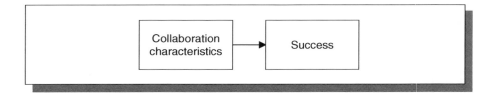

In the theory it is assumed that the success of radical and incremental innovations depends on a different set of collaboration characteristics, as formulated in the six propositions.

5.2.3 Research objective

The *objective* of this research is to contribute to the theory about the relation between collaboration characteristics of incremental and radical innovation projects and the success of these projects, by testing the following new propositions.

> *Proposition 1a*: Success in radical innovation projects requires collaboration with new partners.
>
> *Proposition 1b*: Success in incremental innovation projects requires collaboration with existing partners.
>
> *Proposition 2a*: Success in radical innovation projects requires collaboration with partners that have different technological capabilities.
>
> *Proposition 2b*: Success in incremental innovation projects requires collaboration with partners that have similar technological capabilities.
>
> *Proposition 3a*: Success in radical innovation projects requires that partners establish alliance contracts with a low level of commitment.
>
> *Proposition 3b*: Success in incremental innovation projects requires that partners establish alliance contracts with a high level of commitment.

5.2.4 Research strategy

The propositions specify *necessary* conditions for success. Because these conditions cannot be manipulated experimentally, the case study strategy is the preferred strategy (Chapter 4). The propositions predict that success only will occur if the condition stated in the proposition is present. This means that these propositions can be tested by assessing whether the assumed necessary condition has indeed been present in successful projects. The proposition will be rejected if success also occurs in the absence of this condition. A single such case would be sufficient for such a rejection, in principle.

5.2.5 Candidate cases

Because it is sufficient for our test to find *a single* innovation project that was successful in the absence of the conditions specified by our propositions, any such case would suffice. It could be a project from any company and in any sector. Because we have been investigating certain aspects of Nokia's innovation projects anyway (see Dittrich, 2004) and, therefore, knew how to find the information about these projects that was relevant to this study, it was convenient for us to select some of Nokia's innovation projects for this study.

We have made use of the alliance database of the Centre for Global Corporate Positioning (CGCP) (see www.cgcpmaps.com). The CGCP database contains information on alliances of a large number of firms. Alliance agreements in this database are defined as common interests between independent industrial partners, which are not connected through majority ownership. Only those collaborative agreements containing some arrangements for technology transfer or joint research have been collected for this database. The information in the database includes the starting date of the alliance as well as its form and its goal. If available, financial details have been included in the database as well. These data have been systemically collected from Internet resources, such as press releases on corporate websites and online professional journals. The database has been maintained continuously. The definition of innovation projects used to build the database is the same as was used in this case study. From this database we only analysed those innovation projects that had as an explicit goal the market introduction of a new product.

5.2.6 Case selection

First we identified in the CGCP database all alliances in which Nokia was a partner.

Second, we identified the *radical* and *incremental* innovation projects within this selection. We used the following two criteria, derived from Henderson and Clark (1990):

- whether the *technology* developed in the project was new or already available;
- whether the *market* for the new product was new or a current one.

An innovation project was categorized as radical if both the technology and the market were new, and an innovation was considered to be an incremental one if both the technology was already available and the market was current. For our purposes we could dismiss all projects that were not clear-cut cases of radical or incremental innovations, such as projects in which the technology was new but not the market.

Third, we assessed which projects had been successful, i.e. which projects had resulted in the market launch of a new product. This was assessed through inspection of press releases.

Finally, we selected five radical and five incremental successful innovation projects from the two lists of radical and incremental successful innovation projects in which Nokia had been a partner. We did this in a rather arbitrary way, without using any criterion in particular.

5.2.7 Hypotheses

For the five successful *radical* innovation projects, we specified the three propositions in this study as follows.

Hypothesis 1a: All five projects are alliances with new partners.

Hypothesis 2a: All five projects are alliances with partners that have different technological capabilities.

Hypothesis 3a: All five projects are alliances with contracts with a low level of commitment (short-term).

For the five successful *incremental* innovation projects, we specified the three propositions in this study as follows.

Hypothesis 1b: All five projects are alliances with existing partners.

Hypothesis 2b: All five projects are alliances with partners that have similar technological capabilities.

Hypothesis 3b: All five projects are alliances with contracts with a high level of commitment (long-term).

5.2.8 Measurement

In order to test the hypotheses, we needed to measure the three collaboration characteristics; collaboration history, technological capabilities, and level of commitment. We needed to determine, for each case, the newness of the partners for Nokia, similarity of technological capabilities between Nokia and the partner, and level of commitment in the alliance. These three characteristics were measured in the following ways.

1. The CGCP database contains data regarding all innovation projects in which Nokia was engaged since 1985. A partner in an alliance was considered to be a *new partner* for Nokia if that partner had not collaborated with Nokia in a previous alliance in the database since 1985. *Old partners* were partners with which Nokia had engaged in at least one innovation project in the database since 1985.

2. A partner's *technological capabilities* were mainly determined by its code in the SIC (Standard Industrial Classification). The SIC is a four-digit code developed by the US Office of Management and Budget to identify industrial sectors. Nokia is classified as a manufacturer of "telephone and telegraph apparatus" (SIC 3661). Partners with code 3661 were considered to have similar technological capabilities, whereas partners with other codes were considered to have different capabilities.

3. *The level of commitment* is determined by the type of alliance agreement that the firms engaged in, in terms of investments made in the innovation project and innovation project duration. This was done based on Hagedoorn (1990), who presents a classification of alliance agreements and their organizational interdependence. The largest organizational interdependence can be found in joint ventures and the smallest in licensing agreements. The organizational interdependence refers to the intensity of the relation, which we refer to as "commitment".

5.2.9 Data presentation

5.2.9.1 Radical innovation projects

Case 1 is a project to create a new pen-based product category. It was organized as a joint development and licensing agreement between

Nokia and Palm Computing Inc., which was announced in 1999. Nokia has introduced its first pen-based products in the American market and subsequently on a worldwide basis.

New partner? Nokia and Palm Computing are collaborating for the first time on this project.

Capabilities. Since Palm Computing Inc. is a provider of handheld computing solutions, the company can be said to have *different capabilities* from Nokia.

Commitment. This joint development and licensing agreement is *not a long-term* commitment.

Case 2 is a project to develop Internet-enhanced television solu-tions. It was organized as a joint development agreement between Nokia and Intel and was announced in 1999. The solutions developed in this alliance allowed broadcasters to provide consumers with access to new, Internet-enhanced television services, as well as to the extensive range of services already available on the Internet. The product is based on Nokia and Intel technology, open standards, and specifications, including Digital Video Broadcast (DVB), Internet protocols, the Advanced Television Enhancement Forum specification (ATVEF), as well as open source, including Linux and the Mozilla browser. The first products were introduced in the second half of 2000.

New partner? This is the *first time* that Nokia and Intel collaborated in a joint R&D project.

Capabilities. Intel, the world's largest chipmaker, is also a lead-ing manufacturer of computer, networking, and communications products, though it does not develop telecommunication products. Nokia and Intel work in different industries and have *different capabilities.*

Commitment. This joint development agreement is *not a long-term* commitment.

Case 3 is a project to deliver enterprise-class intrusion detection for effective information protection. It was organized as a joint develop-ment agreement between Nokia and Internet Security Systems (ISS) signed in 2001. This agreement broadened the scope of the existing ISS/Nokia relation encompassing continued development of the indus-try's first enterprise-class intrusion detection appliance, RealSecureI for Nokia. In addition, the agreement covered offerings, and joint channel, and marketing activities that would broaden each company's reach in delivering simplified security solutions to partners and cus-tomers worldwide.

New partner? Nokia and ISS have collaborated before, so ISS is *not a new partner* for Nokia.

Capabilities. Internet Security Systems is a leading global provider of security management solutions for the Internet, protecting digital assets and ensuring safe and uninterrupted e-business. This requires *different capabilities* from Nokia's know-how in telecommunications.

Commitment. This joint development agreement is *not a long-term* commitment.

Case 4 is a project to produce and market software for mobile and online financial services. It is a combined venture between 3i Group plc, Accenture, Nokia, and Sampo, established in 2001, called Meridea Financial Software. The new company, Meridea, showcased in 2001 its first, next-generation software solution for financial institutions, which enables consumers to access electronic and mobile financial services through multiple channels including mobile devices, the Internet, telephones, IVRs (Interactive Voice Response systems), and digital TV. Meridea employed more than 100 people in Finland by the end of 2002.

New partner? For Nokia, all partners in this combined venture are new.

Capabilities. 3i is a provider of venture capital and brings capital, knowledge, and connections to the creation and development of businesses around the world. It invests in a wide range of opportunities from start-ups to buy-outs and buy-ins, focusing on businesses with high growth potential and strong management. Accenture is the world's leading management and technology consulting organization. Sampo is Finland's first full-service financial group providing financial, investment, and insurance services. It has one of the world's highest e-banking penetrations. Thus, all four companies in the combined venture have *very different capabilities.*

Commitment. This joint venture *is a long-term* commitment.

Case 5 is a project targeted on the integration of the Macromedia Flash Player into the Nokia Mediaterminal, an innovative infotainment device that seamlessly combines DVB, full Internet access, personal video recorder (PVR) technology, and gaming. This project was organized as a joint development agreement between Nokia and Macromedia, and announced in 2002.

New partner? The partnership between Nokia and Macromedia is *new.*

Capabilities. Macromedia is a company that facilitates content delivery of designers and developers on the web, and enables innovative Internet business applications. Nokia and Macromedia have *quite different capabilities.*

Commitment. This joint development agreement is *not a long-term* commitment.

These data are summarized in Table 5.1.

Table 5.1

Radical innovation projects

	Collaboration history	Technological capabilities	Level of commitment
Case 1	New	Different	Short-term
Case 2	New	Different	Short-term
Case 3	Not new	Different	Short-term
Case 4	New	Different	Long-term
Case 5	New	Different	Short-term

5.2.9.2 Incremental innovation projects

Case 6 is an operating system solution for the Nokia 9000 Communicator and intelligent mobile devices. The innovation project was a joint development agreement signed in 1997 between Nokia and Geoworks to develop new software. The Nokia 9000 Communicator, which integrates the Geoworks' GEOS operating system, was the world's first all-in-one communications device that combined wireless voice and data services with personal organizer functionality.

New partner? This alliance continues the strong relationship that the two companies formed during the development of the Nokia 9000 Communicator. In addition, Nokia and Geoworks are working on delivering wireless content and services solutions that provide value-added services including remote shopping, telebanking, and access to Internet information and entertainment. Since Geoworks and Nokia collaborated before, they can be said to have formed *strong ties.*

Capabilities. Geoworks Corporation's principal activity is to provide software design and engineering services to the mobile and handheld device industry. It develops operating systems, related applications, and wireless server technology. Geoworks Corporation operates in the mobile telecommunications industry and can be said to have *similar capabilities.*

Commitment. The joint development agreement between Nokia and Geoworks is *not a long-term* commitment.

Case 7 is an innovation project to develop TETRA-switches technology and TETRA applications for a nationwide network in Austria, based on IP Telephony. It was organized as a joint development agreement between Nokia and Frequentis announced in 2000.

New partner? Frequentis and Nokia have not collaborated before, so they are *new partners.*

Capabilities. Frequentis develops communication and information systems for safety critical areas. Frequentis operates in the telecommunications industry and can be said to have *similar capabilities* to Nokia.

Commitment. The joint development agreement between Nokia and Frequentis is *not a long-term* commitment.

Case 8 is a project targeted at the design, development, and marketing of the value-added mobile applications for clients of Telefónica Móviles. It was organized as a joint development agreement between Nokia and Telefónica Móviles, signed in 2001. The two companies established a joint Services Creation Center, which has the latest Nokia infrastructure and technology to execute the new developments.

New partner? Telefónica Móviles and Nokia are *new partners*.

Capabilities. Telefónica Móviles is a leading mobile telephone operator and so it can be said to have *similar* capabilities to Nokia.

Commitment. The joint development agreement between Nokia and Telefónica Móviles is *not a long-term* commitment.

Case 9 is a project for delivering network operations services to operators. It was organized in a co-production contract between Nokia and Primatel, signed in 2001. This non-exclusive cooperation reinforced Nokia's capability to support network operations for advanced 2G and 3G networks. Working with Nokia, Primatel built on its extensive previous experience with mobile networks to support the development, management, integration, and optimization of network operations for 3G and 2G.

New partner? This is the *first time* that Nokia and Primatel work together.

Capabilities. Primatel Ltd is Finland's leading provider of telecommunication solutions. Primatel specializes in comprehensive design, implementation, and maintenance of telecommunication networks and has similar capabilities to Nokia.

Commitment. The co-production contract between Nokia and Primatel is *not a long-term* commitment.

Case 10 is a project targeted at the development of 3G wireless communications products in China. It was a combined venture of Nokia, Texas Instruments (TI), China PTIC Information Industry, China Academy of Telecommunications Technology (CATT), and Korea's LG Electronics, established in 2002. LG, Nokia, and TI have each taken a 13.5 per cent equity stake in the company, which was founded with an initial investment of $28 million.

New partner? This is the *first time* that Nokia has collaborated with any of the partners in this combined venture.

Capabilities. China PTIC Information Industry and CATT have *similar capabilities* to Nokia. But, in contrast, TI and LG Electronics are

Table 5.2

Incremental innovation projects

	Collaboration history	Technological capabilities	Level of commitment
Case 6	Not new	Similar	Short-term
Case 7	New	Similar	Short-term
Case 8	New	Similar	Short-term
Case 9	New	Similar	Short-term
Case 10	New	Similar	Long-term

major players in the microelectronics industry, which means that they have quite *different capabilities* from Nokia, which specializes in mobile telecommunications.

Commitment. This joint venture is an example of *a long-term* commitment. These data are summarized in Table 5.2.

5.2.10 Data analysis

Hypothesis 1a predicts that in each of the five radical innovation projects an alliance was formed with new partners. If we match this expected value (new) with the one that is actually observed in each case (new or not new), as in Table 5.1, we see that the observed value matches with the predicted one in cases 1, 2, 4, and 5, but does not match in case 3. Case 3, thus, is a "black swan", which demonstrates that the proposition that newness of the partner is a necessary condition for success in a radical innovation project is *not true* for all cases.

Hypothesis 1b predicts that in each of the five incremental innovation projects an alliance was formed with existent partners ("not new"). If we match this expected value (not new) with the one that is actually observed in each case (new or not new), as in Table 5.2, we see that there are many cases in which the observed value does not match with the expected one, indicating that the proposition is *not true*.

Hypothesis 2a predicts that in each of the five radical innovation projects an alliance was formed with partners with technological capabilities that differ from Nokia's. If we match this expected value (different) with the one that is actually observed in each case (different or similar), as in Table 5.1, we see that the observed value matches with the predicted one in all cases. No "black swan" has been found.

Hypothesis 2b predicts that in each of the five incremental innovation projects an alliance was formed with partners with technological capabilities that are similar to Nokia's. If we match this expected value (similar) with the one that is actually observed in each case (different or similar), as in Table 5.2, we see that the observed value matches with the predicted one in all cases. No "black swan" has been found.

Hypothesis 3a predicts that in each of the five radical innovation projects a short-term commitment between partners will exist. If we match this expected value (short-term) with the one that is actually observed in each case (short-term or long-term), as in Table 5.1, we see that the observed value matches with the predicted one in cases 1, 2, 3, and 5, but does not match in case 4. Case 4, thus, is a "black swan", which demonstrates that the proposition that short-term commitment of partners is a necessary condition for success in a radical innovation project is *not true* for all cases.

Hypothesis 3b predicts that in each of the five incremental innovation projects a long-term commitment between partners will exist. If we match this expected value (long-term) with the one that is actually observed in each case (long-term or short-term), as in Table 5.2, we see that there are many cases in which the observed value does not match with the expected one, indicating that the proposition is *not true*.

5.2.11 Implications for the theory

The two hypotheses on technological capabilities (2a and 2b) were confirmed in all cases. This is an indication that the propositions from which these hypotheses were derived are correct, at least for the Nokia cases.

The other hypotheses were rejected. The hypothesis that a successful radical innovation project requires an alliance with new partners (1a) was rejected in one of the five radical innovation projects. This suggests that building an alliance with a new partner is not a necessary condition for a successful radical innovation project. The hypothesis that a successful incremental innovation project requires an alliance with existent partners (1b) was rejected in four of the five incremental innovation projects. This suggests that the proposition from which this hypothesis was derived is not correct. The two hypotheses (3a and 3b) about the level of commitment that would be found in each successful innovation project were rejected in five of the ten innovation projects.

The rejections of these hypotheses can mean that the propositions from which these hypotheses were derived are not correct, or that they do not apply to certain Nokia projects. Since we also found single cases in which hypotheses were accepted, we do not conclude that the propositions are definitively incorrect; the proposition might be correct for a smaller domain.

5.2.12 Replication strategy

Although two hypotheses were confirmed, we cannot be sure that the underlying proposition is correct in the entire domain that is covered by the theory. We therefore propose a replication strategy to study innovation projects that are different from the ones studied here, i.e. innovation projects in different fields from telecommunication, and involving other companies than Nokia.

We do not think that the rejection of the other hypotheses means that the underlying propositions are definitely not true. The proposition might be true for certain innovation projects but not for all Nokia's (and perhaps other) projects. To assess this possibility we propose that the proposition be tested in different cases from the domain that is covered by the theory. Other innovation projects, which are different from the ones studied here, could be selected, i.e. innovation projects in other fields than telecommunication and involving other companies than Nokia.

5.3 Methodological reflection on Case Study 1

5.3.1 Theory

In Case Study 1, the *object of study* was innovation projects in which two or more firms collaborated on product innovation. Two main types of innovation are distinguished: radical innovation in which both the technology and the market are new and customer needs are unknown, and incremental innovation, consisting of the improved use of existing technologies to meet known customer needs.

It is theorized that radical and incremental innovations require different collaboration characteristics, and two sets of *propositions* were formulated, one for radical and one for incremental innovations. Each proposition described a *necessary* relation: success was not possible without a specific value for the independent concept ("necessary condition").

The literature suggests that certain collaboration characteristics are important for achieving success. However, it does not suggest that they are necessary for success. The propositions, therefore, could also have expressed probabilistic relations. The choice for the necessary condition can be justified, because probabilistic propositions (if confirmed) would only give an indication of the *probability* of success, whereas the necessary condition propositions would give deterministic knowledge about success factors, which, under certain conditions, could be more significant for managerial practice.

The theory does not set a restriction regarding the *domain* of innovation projects aimed at product innovation. The domain covered by the theory is the universe of all instances of such alliances, without restrictions in terms of geography, economic sector, time, etc. This implies that the theory is assumed to be applicable in a large domain of different types of innovation projects, requiring a large number of replications.

5.3.2 Research objective

The objective of the research was to test a set of new propositions. Hence the study could be characterized as initial theory-testing research.

5.3.3 Research strategy

The propositions specified necessary conditions for success. The preferred research strategy for testing necessary conditions is the experiment. The second-best research strategy is the *single case study*. The preferred replication strategy is a serial one in which each proposition is tested in a single case before the next case is selected.

The research strategy chosen was the **parallel single case study**, in which each proposition is tested in five cases at the same time. An advantage of the parallel approach is that the chance of finding a rejection of the proposition in one round of (parallel) testing is considerably higher than with a test in a single case. A disadvantage is that more tests are conducted than strictly necessary, and that outcomes from one case cannot be used for the selection of the next case (e.g. in a case from a more narrow domain if the hypothesis is rejected). Additionally, there is a danger that a probabilistic approach will unwittingly creep into the analysis (comparative case study).

We will expand here upon the advantage, disadvantage, and danger of parallel replication.

The testing of propositions 1b, and 2b in incremental innovation projects (see Table 5.2) can illustrate the *advantage* of the parallel single case study. The corresponding hypotheses predict *not new* partners, and *similar* technical capabilities in these projects. If it is assumed that in a serial case study, case 6 would have been selected for the first test, the test would have confirmed the two hypotheses. After this first confirmation, a second case would have been selected for replication.

The replication strategy after a confirmation could be to select a case from a very different part of the domain from which the theory is considered applicable. Then the new case in a serial case study would *not* have been a case from Nokia, but a case from, for example, another economic sector. This would continue until cases were found that were rejected, and then the boundaries of the domain to which the theory applies would be determined.

However, by using the parallel case study, rejections of hypothesis 1b were found immediately, indicating that proposition 1b for the small domain of the Nokia cases cannot be supported. The parallel single case study, thus, appears to be an effective and relatively fast way to discover cases in which the proposition is not supported.

The replication strategy, after a confirmation, could also be to select a case from the same part of the domain: the new case in a serial case study would be another case from Nokia. Then, after the second test (say case 7) or third test (say case 8), the conclusion would be justified that proposition 1b could not be supported for Nokia cases, and replications with cases 9 and 10 would not have been needed. This illustrates the *disadvantage* of the parallel single case study approach, i.e. the potential to waste time and effort on measurement and hypothesis-testing.

The *danger* of the parallel case study can be illustrated with the results of testing propositions 1a and 3a with respect to radical innovation projects (see Table 5.1). The test result of case 3 is enough to conclude that proposition 1a (which formulates a deterministic relation) is not correct, and the test result in case 4 is enough to conclude the same regarding proposition 3a. The danger is that inspection of all five tests together results in conclusions such as "but ... the hypothesis is confirmed in the large majority of cases (four out of five)". Such a conclusion could only be made after many replications when the hypothesis is rejected in only one case but is confirmed in all other cases, and if one accepts a "pragmatic determinism" view. Normally, a rejection of the hypothesis in a single case (from the domain to which the theory is assumed to be applicable) is sufficient to reject the hypothesis for that domain (although it might be true for a smaller domain).

The fact that the hypothesis could be confirmed in the majority of tests but that there are also instances in which the hypothesis was rejected can also be an indication of the correctness of *another* proposition, a probabilistic one.

5.3.4 Candidate cases

The domain covered by the theory is the universe of all instances of innovation projects in which radical and incremental innovation was pursued, without restrictions in terms of geography, economic sector, time, etc. It was enough for this initial test of new propositions to find a single innovation project (for each of two types of product innovation) that was successful in the absence of the conditions specified by the propositions, and this could be a project from any company and in any sector.

Cases were selected from the CGCP database. The advantage of using this database was that it is not only a (partial) list of instances of the object of study (from which cases can be selected) but also contains the data that are needed for the testing. It was a commendable strategy to test the propositions in this database initially and, after a series of replications, to draw conclusions regarding the support or non-support of these (or altered) propositions for the sub-domain of instances in this database. In a next series of replications, these conclusions could be tested in instances of the object of study that are not covered by the database.

5.3.5 Case selection

Because a new proposition must be tested, any instance will do for a first test. It could be a project from any company and in any sector. Therefore the Nokia cases selected were as good for this purpose as innovation projects undertaken by any other company. This reasoning, however, applies to the first case in a serial case study. A second case and later cases of the series could be selected on the basis of a replication strategy that is based on the test result in the preceding case.

The selected cases should be instances of either a *radical* or an *incremental* innovation project. An innovation project was categorized as radical if both the technology and the market were new, and an innovation was considered to be an incremental one if both the technology was already available and the market was current. It should be specified how in the set of candidate cases, differences between new and already available technology, and between new and current markets could be recognized.

Because the propositions in this study specified *necessary* conditions, successful cases were selected (selection on the presence of the dependent concept), i.e. projects that had resulted in the market launch of a new product. Product launch was identified through press releases.

5.3.6 Hypothesis

Because the propositions in this study specified *necessary* conditions and the selection was done on the basis of the presence of the dependent concept, the hypothesis was that the condition was present in each case that was studied.

5.3.7 Measurement

In order to test the hypotheses, the three collaboration characteristics (collaboration history, technological capabilities, and level of commitment) had to be measured in each case.

A partner in an alliance was considered to be a *not new partner* for Nokia if that partner had collaborated with Nokia in a previous alliance in the database since 1985 and *new* if it had not collaborated before. The year 1985 was arbitrary and it is possible that partners that had collaborated with Nokia before 1985 were incorrectly classified as new. This measurement procedure was precisely specified and, therefore, likely to result in reliable scores.

A partner's *technological capabilities* were mainly determined by its code in the SIC. Partners with the same code were considered to have similar technological capabilities, whereas partners with other codes were considered to have different capabilities. An industrial classification such as SIC is not a classification of technological capabilities and the measurement validity of this operationalization of similarity in capabilities, therefore, depends on the likelihood that companies with the same capabilities get the same SIC code. It is unknown whether or not companies with the same capabilities do indeed have the same SIC code. This method for measuring similarity of technological capabilities is likely to be very reliable because the coding rule – is it SIC code 3661 or is it not code 3661? – is precise.

A high *level of commitment* is the "intensity of the relation" between the partners in the alliance and is determined by the type of alliance agreement, referring to the classification by Hagedoorn (1990). The greatest intensity of the relation can be found in joint or combined ventures, and the smallest in licensing agreements. Regarding measurement validity, it is not known whether "intensity of the relation" was as good a descriptor of level of commitment as it was meant to be. The method for measuring commitment using agreements and contracts is likely to be reliable.

5.3.8 Data presentation

All relevant data of each individual case were provided: whether the project was an incremental or a radical innovation project; why it was considered successful; and what the score of the three collaboration characteristics were.

5.3.9 Data analysis

Hypothesis-testing was straightforward: comparing the "observed" scores for the collaboration characteristics (in the tables) with the predicted ones (in the hypotheses). This test was conducted for each hypothesis and for each case separately, and each test result (rejection or confirmation) was evaluated on a case-by-case basis.

5.3.10 Implications for the theory

The two hypotheses on technological capabilities (2a and 2b) were confirmed. This gave support to the corresponding propositions in the theory, at least for the domain of the test (Nokia).

The two hypotheses on collaboration history (1a and 1b) were rejected. Case Study 1 does not conclude that the corresponding propositions in the theory are incorrect, but rather that they might be true for a more limited domain.

The two hypotheses on level of commitment (3a and 3b) were rejected. This is considered as evidence that the proposition is not correct at all.

Case Study 1 does not suggest a reformulation of a proposition that was not confirmed. A probabilistic proposition agrees with the test results, and it would be defensible to reformulate propositions 1a and 3a as probabilistic relations.

5.3.11 Replication strategy

Because the two hypotheses on technological capabilities (2a and 2b) were confirmed (for all cases) it is concluded that a replication strategy should be applied in which the confirmed hypotheses are tested for cases that are very different from the ones studied here, i.e. innovation projects in other fields than telecommunication, and involving other companies than Nokia. With each new test, the researcher should put more energy into identifying and selecting a case that is less "typical" in order to increase the likelihood of a rejection of the proposition and (which boils down to the same) to try to get a sense of the boundaries of the domain to which the proposition applies.

For the other propositions, the hypotheses were rejected. Then the researcher has two options for replication:

1. The researcher might interpret the proposition itself as correct, but only in a *more limited domain*. Then a replication must be done with cases from a more limited domain, in which the theory points to a higher chance of its confirmation. This replication strategy was adopted for the two propositions on collaboration history (1a and 1b). It stated that these propositions, though not true for all projects undertaken by Nokia, might be true for a domain of innovation projects that does not include Nokia's (and perhaps some more) projects.

2. The researcher might interpret the rejection of a hypothesis as evidence that the proposition could not be correct at all. Case Study 1 adopted this strategy for the two propositions on level of commitment (3a and 3b).

A very different strategy could be to reformulate the propositions on the basis of the test results as probabilistic ones. This strategy would be defensible for propositions 1a and 3a. If such a strategy were adopted, the newly formulated propositions should be tested in a new study. If an experiment was not possible, this study could be a survey, either of newly collected data or by using the CGCP database. It is, however, advisable not to abandon a deterministic proposition too soon and to wait for further test results before it is concluded that a proposition in its current form definitely cannot be maintained. This is the strategy proposed in Case Study 1.

5.4 Case Study 2: Theory-testing research: testing a necessary condition

Testing a theory of ideal typical organizational configurations for successful product innovations[2]

by Ferdinand Jaspers and Jan Van den Ende

5.4.1 Introduction

Product innovation is an important strategy for the growth and survival of firms. Innovation is an inherently uncertain exercise, however, requiring firms to organize their innovative activities to deal with the challenges of innovation projects as much as possible.

In this section we test a theory that considers multiple dimensions of the organizational form for innovation projects. In contrast to "traditional" univariate or interaction models, this type of theory provides the possibility of testing the explanatory power of a group of concepts holistically. Such typological theories are more in line with managerial practice, as multiple decisions have to be made simultaneously and not in isolation.

5.4.2 Theory

5.4.2.1 Object of study

The object of study in this case study is *product innovation projects*.

---

[2] This chapter is based on: Jaspers, F. and Van den Ende, J. (2005), Organizational Forms for Innovation in System Industries: A Typology Test with Case Studies on the Development of Mobile Telecom Applications, In: Wynstra, J.Y.F., Dittrich, K. and Jaspers, F.P.H. (Eds.), 2005, *Dealing with dualities*, Proceedings of the 21st IMP Conference, 1–3 September 2005, Rotterdam. Rotterdam: RSM Erasmus University. ISBN: 90-9019-836-9.

5.4.2.2 Concepts

The concepts of interest in this study are:

- type of product innovation;
- success;
- organizational configuration.

In this study we consider six *types of innovation* to components of a larger product (e.g. Henderson and Clark, 1990; Teece, 1996):

1. incremental innovation for core components;
2. incremental innovation for peripheral components;
3. modular innovation;
4. architectural innovation for core components;
5. architectural innovation for peripheral components;
6. radical innovation.

These types of innovation are defined by the extent of component change (incremental or radical), the extent of change to the interface between the component and the rest of the product (incremental or radical), and the distinction between core and peripheral components for innovations that involve incremental component change. Table 5.3 shows how we define the six types of innovation.

The extent of *component change* reflects the level of uncertainty regarding the component's underlying technologies. Radical component change pertains to a component based on entirely new technologies. This causes a high level of uncertainty since it is very likely that many technical problems need to be solved. In contrast, incremental

Table 5.3

Six types of innovation that change a product's components and interfaces

		Component change		
		Incremental, core	**Incremental, peripheral**	**Radical**
Product interface change	Incremental	Incremental innovation for core components	Incremental innovation for peripheral components	Modular innovation
	Radical	Architectural innovation for core components	Architectural innovation for peripheral components	Radical innovation

component change reinforces the existing technologies underlying a component and is therefore surrounded by a low level of uncertainty.

The extent of *interface change* reflects the level of interdependence between the component and other components of the product. Radical interface change pertains to the creation of entirely new linkages between components. This causes a high level of interdependence since it is very likely that this affects all interrelated components. In contrast, incremental interface change reinforces a component's existing interfaces, and is hence characterized by a low level of interdependence. The distinction between *peripheral* and *core components* as made by Gatignon *et al.* (2002) shows that core components are strategically important to the company and/or tightly coupled with other components. In contrast, peripheral components are loosely coupled and/or their strategic importance is limited.

Success is defined relative to the project's aims and expectations. It is defined as a result that is as initially expected, or better.

In our theory, the *organizational configuration* for product innovation projects is built from four building blocks or organizational dimensions (Jaspers and Van den Ende, 2006):

1. *coordination integration*: the extent that the firm coordinates the innovation project;
2. *ownership integration*: the extent that the firm controls the innovation project;
3. *task integration*: the extent that the firm performs the tasks in the innovation project; and
4. *knowledge integration*: the extent that the firm acquires in-depth knowledge about the innovation.

These organizational building blocks can be combined into a wide range of organizational configurations. At one extreme, *complete integration* is characterized by a high value on each organizational dimension. This resembles an organizational form in which the firm performs and controls the innovation project on its own, extensively coordinates the innovation process, and absorbs all new knowledge that is being generated in the innovation project. At the other extreme, *no integration* is characterized by a low value on each dimension and means that the innovation project is performed and owned by one or more firms external to the focal firm. In addition, there is no coordination between the firm and the external firm(s) that perform the innovation project. Neither does the firm acquire knowledge about this project. Because, in principle, the four dimensions are to a large extent independent of each other, many more configurations exist besides these two extreme configurations.

5.4.2.3 Proposition

Based on a review of the innovation management literature, we theoretically constructed a typology of six organizational configurations, each of which corresponded to one type of innovation (for more details see Jaspers and Van den Ende, 2005). Table 5.4 presents the typology.

Table 5.4

Typology of ideal organizational configurations for product innovation success

	Incremental core component change		**Incremental peripheral component change**		**Radical component change**	
Incremental interface change	Coordination:	L	Coordination:	L	Coordination:	L
	Task:	H	Task:	L	Task:	L
	Ownership:	H	Ownership:	L	Ownership:	L
	Knowledge:	H	Knowledge:	L	Knowledge:	H
Radical interface change	Coordination:	H	Coordination:	H	Coordination:	H
	Task:	H	Task:	L	Task:	M
	Ownership:	H	Ownership:	L	Ownership:	H
	Knowledge:	H	Knowledge:	H	Knowledge:	H

(L = low, M = medium, H = high)

In our theory each ideal typical configuration of coordination integration, ownership integration, task integration, and knowledge integration is assumed to be a *necessary* condition for the success of each respective type of innovation. In other words, we assume that successful projects need to have, at the very least, the predicted organizational configuration. Deviation from this ideal type is unlikely to result in a high performing innovation project. Reflecting a necessary condition, the proposition that we want to test in this study is the following.

> *Proposition*: A product innovation project can only be successful if the project has its ideal typical organizational configuration.

5.4.2.4 Domain

We claim that our theory applies to all product innovation projects. It follows that the domain covered by the theory is the universe of all instances of product innovation projects, without any restriction in terms of geography, economic sector, time, etc.

5.4.2.5 Conceptual model

The theory specifies, for each of the six types of product innovation projects, the relation between the organizational configuration (independent concept) and success (dependent concept).

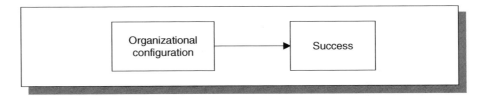

In the theory, it is assumed that the success of each type of product innovation depends on the organizational configuration, as formulated in the proposition.

5.4.3 Research objective

The objective of this research is to contribute to the development of theory about the relation between the organizational configuration of product innovation projects and the success of these projects by testing the following new proposition.

> *Proposition*: A product innovation project can only be successful if the project has its ideal typical organizational configuration.

5.4.4 Research strategy

The proposition specifies a *necessary* condition for success. Therefore the case study strategy is the preferred strategy. The proposition predicts that success will only occur when the condition stated in the proposition is present. This means that this proposition can be tested by assessing whether the assumed necessary condition has indeed been present in successful projects. The proposition will be rejected if success also occurs in the absence of this condition. A single such instance would be sufficient for such a rejection, in principle.

5.4.5 Candidate cases

The object of study to which our theory applies is product innovation projects. Hence, in order to test our typology we need to identify instances of product innovation projects. Because it is sufficient for our purposes to find *a single* innovation project (of a specific type) that was successful in the absence of the conditions specified by our typology, any such instance would suffice. It could be a project from any company and in any sector.

5.4.6 Case selection

For reasons of convenience, we conducted a first test of our theory in one industry (mobile telecommunications) in one country (the Netherlands). In 2002 and 2003 we studied 30 innovation projects of mobile telecommunications applications. We identified these cases through news articles and websites and also by contacting key industry participants, such as all Dutch mobile network operators. Examples of new products or services in this industry are mobile games, location-based services, mobile office solutions, and mobile commerce applications. These projects were selected in such a way that variation in the type of innovation was obtained. In particular we wanted to make sure that a number of radical innovation projects was included, because these are relatively rare.

For testing our necessary condition proposition we needed to select cases on the basis of the dependent concept (success of the product innovation project). *Before* we could know which projects eventually would be included as cases, we had to determine which projects were successful. Successful projects were then categorized according to innovation type, and it was hoped that in each category there would be at least one successful project.

5.4.7 Hypothesis

For all selected innovation projects we specified the hypothesis as follows.

> Hypothesis: In all selected successful projects the ideal typical organizational configuration is present.

5.4.8 Measurement

For checking whether the case (innovation project) was successful and therefore could be included in the study, *success* was determined with a questionnaire that was filled out by the project manager of that project. Items on project performance in our questionnaire asked for specific judgements regarding: meeting the time-to-market deadline; adherence to interim project deadlines; quality of the project; and budget performance of the project. A control item asking for an overall judgement of project performance was also included. For each indicator we measured actual performance relative to expectations as perceived by the project managers on a five-point scale (ranging from "very disappointing performance" to "a performance level well beyond expectations"). First, the average score for the first four items was calculated. Next, to reduce measurement error even further, we averaged the score for "overall project performance" with the average for the four items. Successful projects were defined as projects with a score of three (which means that the project performed in line with expectations) or higher. From the 30 projects that we analysed, we identified 15 successful projects; hence, our cases.

For each case, the *type of innovation* was determined based on the qualitative project descriptions that we had collected. Additionally, the project manager filled out a questionnaire to determine a project's *degree of interface change* using a four-point rating scale about "the degree of uncertainty regarding the interfaces to connect the application to the network" and "the degree of standardization of the platform to which the application was connected". This latter scale ranged from "no standards" to "highly standardized". Usually, newly introduced networks employ tailor-made platforms, whereas over time standardized platforms emerge that manage the development and interconnection of applications. To rate a project's *degree of component technology change*, we used a rating scale for "the uncertainty regarding the costs to develop this application". For the *distinction between core and peripheral projects* we also primarily drew on the interview data with the project manager. We followed Gatignon *et al.* (2002) who characterize core components as strategically important to the firm and/or tightly coupled to the larger system. During the interviews, we assessed the strategic importance of the application to the operator. We could corroborate these findings using data on the questionnaire item asking for "the urgency felt by the network operator to introduce this application quickly". We hypothesized that operators experience high urgency for strategically important applications in order to build

quickly a customer base. The extent of coupling, the number of interfaces between an application and the network, was determined based
on the technical characteristics of the project. Some applications, such
as voice services or person-to-person text messaging, involve applications that are integral parts of the mobile network, i.e. interconnected
with many network elements. In contrast, peripheral applications are
often connected to the mobile network, or in many cases to an application platform, through a single interface.

For each case (i.e. for each successful project) we determined the
organizational configuration by assessing the four dimensions of the
organizational form (coordination integration, ownership integration, task integration, and knowledge integration) using a qualitative
interview with the project manager. Based on the interview data, we
characterized each dimension as a low, medium, or high level of integration. To check the measurement validity of our ratings, we compared the researcher's ratings of ownership integration and task
integration with the ratings by the project manager for these dimensions. The project manager rated these dimensions on a five-point
scale using a questionnaire with the statements "the extent that the
operator invested in the mobile application development project"
and "the extent that the operator performed the project tasks". No
major deviations were found between the assessment of the
researcher based on the interview data and the assessment of the project manager in the questionnaire.

We performed the following procedures to collect the data. As indicated above, the project managers of the different projects were our
key informants for both the dependent and the independent concept
and the classification of the project into one of the six types of innovation. From each project performed in a single firm, the project
manager was interviewed. If multiple firms were involved in the project, we interviewed only the project manager from the most important
firm (in some cases we did interview project managers from multiple
firms though). At the project manager's company, each project
manager first completed a questionnaire in the presence of the
researcher. Our presence allowed us to clarify the questionnaire if necessary and also might have acted as a barrier to self-report bias. The
questionnaire contained not only questions about the organizational
dimensions of the project but also about (the respondent's opinion
on) the performance of the project. After having completed the questionnaire, respondents were interviewed in a semi-structured way, covering the same topics as in the questionnaire and in the same order.
The researchers' prior experience in the mobile telecommunications

industry facilitated the interviews and increased the richness of the data and also enabled us to build the questionnaire using wording familiar to the respondents. The interviews enabled us to validate the answers we obtained with the questionnaire, ensuring measurement validity. We found no serious problems or diverging interpretations of key constructs. The field notes obtained during the interviews were converted into a detailed summary immediately after the interview. In some cases we contacted respondents afterwards to seek clarifications on data that appeared unclear. Letting informants review the case reports was not a standard procedure, however, because the congruence between the questionnaire data and the interview data was considered sufficient to ensure measurement validity. A single researcher mostly conducted the interviews. To improve reliability of the collected data, the first interviews were conducted by the two researchers together to become experienced with the method and to develop an agreed-upon approach to follow. To achieve participation of all firms in our research and to achieve good quality of the data they would provide, we promised all involved firms that we would keep their data confidential. Therefore, we will here present the collected data in such a way that individual projects are "anonymous" and cannot be identified.

5.4.9 Data presentation

The data that we collected are represented in Table 5.5 in the column beneath the case number. It turned out that for each of the six types of innovation we had at least one successful project.

5.4.10 Data analysis

The hypothesis states that each successful product innovation project has an ideal typical organizational configuration. We tested this hypothesis in all 15 cases by comparing the "observed" pattern (presented in Table 5.5 in the column beneath the case number) with the "predicted" pattern (as specified in the column "Ideal type"). We considered the hypothesis confirmed if the observed configuration is a perfect match with the predicted configuration, i.e. if all four values are exactly the same. The hypothesis is rejected if the observation does not perfectly match the predicted configuration. We conducted 15 tests and in each of them the proposition was rejected.

Table 5.5
Data for 15 successful product innovation projects

Incremental interface change

	Incremental change for core application		Incremental change for peripheral application					Radical application change			
	Ideal type	Case 1	Ideal type	Case 2	Case 3	Case 4	Case 5	Ideal type	Case 6	Case 7	Case 8
Coordination	L	L	L	H	H	H	H	L	H	H	L
Task	H	L	L	L	H	M	M	L	L	L	L
Ownership	H	L	L	L	H	M	L	L	L	L	L
Knowledge	H	M	L	L	H	M	M	H	L	L	L

Radical interface change

	Incremental change for core application		Incremental change for peripheral application		Radical application change					
	Ideal type	Case 9	Ideal type	Case 10	Ideal type	Case 11	Case 12	Case 13	Case 14	Case 15
Coordination	H	M	H	H	H	H	H	H	H	H
Task	H	M	L	L	M	M	L	L	L	L
Ownership	H	M	L	L	H	M	L	L	L	L
Knowledge	H	M	H	L	H	M	L	L	L	L

5.4.11 Implications for the theory

All 15 successful projects deviated from the ideal profiles on at least one of the four dimensions. Because we could not find an ideal typical configuration in a single successful project, our hypothesis that successful product innovation projects would have ideal typical organizational configurations was rejected in all cases. This could mean that:

1. the proposition was incorrect;
2. the theory does not apply to the domain that we investigated;
3. due to our research methods we could not show the possible correctness of the proposition.

With respect to the third option one could argue that we could not confirm the proposition because the test procedure that we employed in this study to accept the hypothesis was very strict: even a small deviation of one of the four organizational dimensions results in a rejection of that particular ideal type. However, a large number of the successful projects deviated not marginally but rather substantially from the predicted profile. Furthermore, a large number of cases (2, 6, 7, 10, and 12–15) all involved a similar profile. Since these cases were distributed across different types of innovation, this finding could indicate that our proposition was not correct. There may not be an ideal organizational configuration for each type of innovation, but rather one universally chosen "best way" to organize any innovation project. Hence, although our typological theory and its proposition are developed on the basis of a review of the literature, it may be that they are incorrect (option 1). Then the literature would need to be studied more thoroughly and confronted with our present findings, and, as a result, new propositions could be formulated. A possible new proposition would be to formulate the proposition as a probabilistic relation between ideal typical organizational configuration and success, instead of presuming that the ideal typical organizational configuration is a necessary condition for success. Our data could support such a proposition.

Another possibility is that the proposition could be still correct, but that the results from this study could be influenced by measurement problems (option 3). Obviously, self-response bias may have influenced the results. In addition, especially the dependent concept, i.e. success, could suffer from measurement error. The items for this concept asked for the extent that performance was "in line with expectations". Some project managers might not have formulated any *ex ante* expectations, however, or these might have been adjusted *ex post*.

So, assessing performance relative to some ill-defined expectation is risky and could have resulted in a wrong selection of cases to include in the analysis.

It might also be that our proposition is still correct, but only in a smaller domain (option 2). Our empirical setting in which the typological theory was tested was mobile telecommunications software applications. These software applications were considered "components" of the larger telecommunications product system. The literature that was reviewed to derive the configurational theory draws heavily on components of physical products, however, such as automobiles and computer hardware. Hence, we could argue that the current setting of software products is not suitable to test the model.

5.4.12 Replication strategy

Based on this last observation, we would suggest replicating the study and testing the present proposition for the domain of physical products, and then trying to extend the domain into other types of products.

5.5 Methodological reflection on Case Study 2

5.5.1 Theory

Case Study 1 and Case Study 2 present similar theories, both of which explain success from organizational characteristics. In Case Study 1 three different propositions, one for each relevant dimension, were proposed. In that theory, there was no link between the three propositions: one of the propositions could be rejected whereas, at the same time, another could be confirmed. In Case Study 2 four organizational dimensions were combined into a single ideal typical configuration for each innovation type. One *proposition* was formulated that predicted that successful projects must have a specific "typology" (an "ideal typical configuration"). The theory of Case Study 2 presumed interrelations between organizational dimensions, and therefore had claims that might have been more difficult to prove.

Case Study 2 originally stated that the theory did not set any restriction regarding the *domain* of product innovation projects to which the theory was assumed to be applicable. It follows that the domain covered by the theory is the universe of all instances of product innovation projects, without any restriction in terms of geography, economic sector, time, etc. Testing the theory for this large domain, therefore, would require a vast number of replications. Later in Case Study 2 it was suggested that the domain must be restricted to physical products and may not apply to software products.

In Case Study 2, the *concept* "success" was defined relative to the project's aims and expectations. It was defined as a result that is as expected, or better. Therefore, success is relative to the level of expectations or ambitions at the start of the project. Having a low level of expectations increases the chance of success. Test results are, therefore, only valid for this specific type of success. In order to avoid misunderstandings regarding the claims of the theory and the interpretation of test results, another label for this concept could be "satisfaction with result".

5.5.2 Research objective

The objective of the research was to test a new theory. The proposition to be tested was new and had never been tested before. Hence the study could be characterized as initial theory-testing research.

5.5.3 Research strategy

The proposition specified necessary conditions for success. The preferred research strategy for testing necessary conditions is the experiment. The second-best research strategy is the *single case study*. The preferred replication strategy is a serial one in which each proposition is tested before the next case is selected.

The study presented in section 5.4 Case Study 2 was a combined *single case study* and *parallel case study* (see below under "case selection" for explanation). See 5.3.3 for a discussion of the parallel single case study.

5.5.4 Candidate cases

News articles, website, and key industry participants, such as all Dutch mobile network operators, were used to identify projects in a sub-domain of the universe, i.e. in the mobile telecommunications industry in the Netherlands in two years (2002 and 2003). A set of 30 *candidate cases* was created in this way.

5.5.5 Case selection

From the pool of 30 candidate cases, 15 projects were successful and could therefore be included in the case study to test the necessary condition proposition. It further turned out that these cases were divided unequally amongst the six types of innovation projects (Table 5.6).

Table 5.6
Number of selected cases by product innovation type

Type of innovation	Number of cases
Incremental innovation for core components	1
Incremental innovation for peripheral components	4
Modular innovation	3
Architectural innovation for core components	1
Architectural innovation for peripheral components	1
Radical innovation	5

The result of this case selection procedure was that this study was partly a *single case study* (namely for projects aiming at products with incremental core component change as well as for projects aiming at architectural innovation of core or peripheral components), and partly a *parallel case study* for the other three types of product innovation.

5.5.6 Hypothesis

Because the proposition in this study specified *necessary* conditions and the selection was done on the basis of the presence of the dependent concept, the hypothesis was that the condition was present in each case that was studied.

5.5.7 Measurement

In order to select and classify cases, first the type of innovation was determined, and then the success of each case. Next, the organizational configuration was determined in order to compare the observed configuration with the expected ideal type.

Success of the product innovation project was determined with a questionnaire that was filled out by the project manager of that project. Project managers rated, for a number of success indicators on a five-point scale, whether there had been a "disappointing" performance or one "well beyond expectations". Successful projects were defined as projects with an average score of three (equal to expectations) or higher. The 15 successful projects in which the hypothesis was tested were selected according to this criterion: their performance had not disappointed the project managers. Several questions could be raised regarding the measurement validity of success, when success is measured by the "degree to which expectations have been met": the problem of measurement validity of success is briefly addressed in 5.4.11, where reasons for not confirming the hypothesis are discussed.

Case Study 2 also provides a quite detailed description of how *type of innovation* was determined. It is clear that this categorization was not achieved by a straightforward application of a set of clear-cut decision rules.

The values of the four dimensions of the *organizational configuration* (coordination integration, ownership integration, task integration, and knowledge integration) were derived from a qualitative interview with the project manager and, for two dimensions, compared with the project manager's rating on a five-point scale in a questionnaire. No major deviations were found between these two assessments.

5.5.8 Data presentation

Case Study 2 does not give detailed descriptions of the different projects (such as provided in Case Study 1), which would enable experts (who know one or more projects) to evaluate the correctness of, for example, the categorization of type of innovation or the estimation of success. For all 15 successful projects, all relevant data for testing are provided in Table 5.5, i.e. its type of innovation and the organizational configuration in terms of the values of the four organizational dimensions.

5.5.9 Data analysis

The hypothesis-testing consisted of comparing the "observed" typologies with the predicted ones (see Table 5.5). The four values for the organizational dimensions formed an observed "pattern" that could be compared with the ideal typical configuration. This test was performed for each case separately and each test result (rejection or confirmation) was evaluated on a case-by-case basis.

5.5.10 Implications for the theory

The hypothesis that successful product innovation projects possessed ideal typical organizational configurations was rejected. None of the six ideal types proved to be a necessary condition for initially expected project success in these 15 cases.

Case Study 2 suggests, as one possible implication for the theory, that the proposition itself might not be correct. However, assuming that the exploration phase at the very beginning of the research project was conducted in a serious manner and that, thus, the proposition that was formulated and tested was based on sound practical and theoretical insights, such a conclusion would be a significant one that cannot be drawn lightly, and other possible reasons for the rejection of the hypothesis in all 15 cases should be evaluated. Below we elaborate on the evaluation as presented in 5.4.11.

1. Case Study 2 rejects the likelihood that the test results were the result of a too-strict test procedure. The reason for this rejection was that "a large number of the successful projects deviate not marginally but rather substantially from the predicted profile". However, if something was wrong with the measurement of the four organizational dimensions, this would have had a direct effect on the test. If it is assumed that the measurement of these dimensions was too unreliable for justifying the middle value M and if, for that reason, the researchers would be forced to decide whether the value is H or L, it is possible that a number of tests would have resulted in a confirmation of the hypothesis. Repeating the same test on the same cases with different measurement procedures might yield different results.

2. It might be that the ideal type itself (not the test) was too strict. Why should it be necessary for a success to occur that an organizational configuration is exactly as prescribed on all four dimensions, and for all types of product innovation? Could it be possible that having an ideal typical organizational configuration consisting of only three dimensions is a necessary condition for success for one type of product innovation, and an ideal type consisting of specific values of another set of

three dimensions for another type of product innovation? Or, in other words, why must an ideal typical configuration have one and only one value on all four dimensions?

3. The theory on which the typology is based has been developed in specific industries (not the telecommunications industry). The typology might be correct for those other industries, as discussed in Case Study 2.

4. In the literature on success factors for innovation projects, other measures than "relative success" have been used. If success is defined in terms of a more stable criterion, it could be easier to show that success is influenced by organizational dimensions. Also, other cases could be identified as "successful" and the test could, therefore, involve other cases.

5. Although Case Study 2 is presented as a test of one typology, it is actually a test of six different ideal typical configurations. Test results could be evaluated for each ideal typical configuration separately, resulting in specific conclusions for types of innovation. We will expand on this point in the next section.

5.5.11 Replication strategy

Case Study 2 suggests a replication strategy in which the proposition is tested in another domain (physical products, rather than software products). This decision is based on an overall assessment of the test result of 15 cases. Another approach would be to have different strategies for different types of innovation. For three types of innovation (incremental innovation for peripheral components, modular innovation, and radical innovation) three to five parallel tests were performed, which all resulted in a rejection. This could mean that the proposition was not correct and new propositions need to be formulated. Case Study 2 suggests that a more thorough literature study is needed to find which results could be confronted with the present findings. However, the conclusion that the proposition must be reformulated seems to be premature for the other three types of innovation (incremental innovation for core components, architectural innovation for core components, and architectural innovation for peripheral components). For these types of innovation, only a single test was conducted in which the hypothesis was rejected. A proper strategy would be to replicate this test before the theory is abandoned. The aim of such a replication strategy is to find a "most likely" case (i.e. a case in which confirmation is thought to be likely). A rejection of the hypothesis in such a case, in which the theory points to a quite high chance of its confirmation, is more meaningful for the theory than a rejection in an instance in which confirmation is unsure. This implies a strategy in which a new successful project is identified and selected for other products than software. Case Study 2 therefore suggests selecting cases for replication from a part of the domain that is most discussed in the literature. This is the domain of physical products, from which experiences were used in building the theory that was used for the typology tested here. A rejection in such cases would indeed suggest that the theory itself is not correct.

5.6 References

Dittrich, K. 2004, *Innovation Networks: exploration and exploitation in the ICT industry*. Delft, Delft University of Technology.

Gatignon, H., Tushman, M.L., Smith, W., and Anderson, P. 2002, A structural approach to assessing innovation: construct development of innovation locus, type, and characteristics. *Management Science*, 48(9): 1103–1122.

Gilsing, V. and Nooteboom, B. 2006, Exploration and exploitation in innovation systems: the case of pharmaceutical biotechnology. *Research Policy* 35(1): 1–23.

Granovetter, M. 1973, The strength of weak ties. *American Journal of Sociology*, 78(6): 1360–1380.

Hagedoorn, J. 1990, Organizational modes of inter-firm co-operation and technology transfer. *Technovation* 10(1): 17–30.

Hamel, G. and Prahalad, C.K. 1994, *Competing for the future*. Boston (MA), Harvard Business School Press.

Henderson, R.M. and Clark, K.B. 1990, Architectural innovation: the reconfiguration of existing product technologies and the failure of established firms. *Administrative Science Quarterly*, 35: 9–30.

Jaspers, F. and Van den Ende, J. 2005, Organizational forms for innovation in system industries: a typology test with case studies on the development of mobile telecom applications, in: Wynstra, J.Y.F., Dittrich, K., and Jaspers, F.P.H. (eds), 2005, *Dealing with dualities*, Proceedings of the 21st IMP Conference, 1–3 September 2005, Rotterdam. Rotterdam: RSM Erasmus University.

Jaspers, F. and Van den Ende, J. 2006, The organizational form of vertical relations: dimensions of integration. *Industrial Marketing Management*, 35(7): 819–828.

Koza, M.P. and Lewin, A.Y. 1998, The co-evolution of strategic alliances. *Organization Science* 9(3): 255–264.

March, J.G. 1991, Exploration and exploitation in organizational learning. *Organization Science* 2(1): 71–87.

Sarker, S. and Lee, A.S. 2002, Using a positivist case research methodology to test three competing theories-in-use of business process redesign. *Journal of the Association for Information Systems,* 2(7).

Teece, D.J. 1996, Firm organization, industrial structure, and technological innovation. *Journal of Economic Behavior and Organization,* 31: 193–224.

CHAPTER 6

Testing a deterministic relation with a case study

In the preceding chapters we discussed how to design and conduct a case study that tests a proposition with a *sufficient condition* or a *necessary condition*. The methodology of testing a *deterministic relation* is different. This chapter discusses how to design and conduct a case study in which a deterministic relation is tested.

As in Chapter 5, we first present a "How to do" guide (6.1), followed by an example of an actual case study (6.2), which is presented in the same format as the "How to do" guide. The example is followed by a "methodological reflection" (6.3) in which it is discussed in detail and evaluated.

Thus, the contents of Chapter 6 are as follows:

- 6.1 How to test a deterministic relation with a case study;
- 6.2 Case Study 3: The influences of urban time access windows on retailers' distribution costs (by Hans Quak);
- 6.3 Methodological reflection on Case Study 3.

6.1 How to test a deterministic relation with a case study

6.1.1 Introduction

This chapter deals with theory-testing case study research for testing a **deterministic relation**. A deterministic relation presumes that if the value of the independent concept changes, the value of the dependent concept will always change in a predicted way. The proposition is formulated as follows:

"If A is higher then B is higher"

There are two ways to use the case study for testing a deterministic relation. The preferred way is to use a **longitudinal single case study**. In the longitudinal single case study the independent concept in the single case changes "naturally" with time, and the corresponding dependent concept for each moment in time is measured (either in *real-time* or *post hoc*). In the **comparative case study** two or more cases are selected, which have different values of the independent concept, but are otherwise similar, and the dependent concept in each case is measured.

6.1.2 Candidate cases

The issues regarding the universe for case selection are the same for all types of theory-testing case studies. See 5.1.2 for a discussion of this topic.

6.1.3 Case selection

In a *longitudinal single case study* a single case is selected that shows a relatively large variation in the value of the independent variable over time, whereas other variables that may also influence the effect should have stayed the same as much as possible. This would (a) allow multiple tests over time of the proposition within the same case, and (b) give information about the range of values of the independent concept in which the proposition is correct. In a *comparative case study* two or more cases are selected that are as similar as possible but that have different values of the independent concept.

Regarding the number of cases that must be selected, the general line of thought is first to select the minimum number of cases that is enough for doing the study. For a longitudinal case study one case is enough for the tests. For a comparative case study two cases are enough if the deterministic relation that is tested is continuously increasing or decreasing. For other deterministic relations (e.g. parabolic), the minimum number of cases depends on the specific relation. After the first test, a replication strategy must be formulated based on the outcome of the test, and other cases can be selected for additional tests. The number of replications usually is limited only by resource constraints. A theory can always be developed further.

6.1.4 Hypothesis

If the proposition states that the value of the dependent concept increases (or decreases) deterministically with an increase of the value of the independent concept, then the hypothesis in a *longitudinal case study* can be formulated as follows:

> *Hypothesis*: For each pair of measurement points in time, the value of the dependent variable at one point of the pair differs in the predicted direction from the dependent variable's value at the other point of the pair.

If the predicted relation between the independent and dependent variable is a *continuously* increasing or *continuously* decreasing relation or the predicted relation can be considered as a set of continuously increasing or decreasing separate relations, then for each separate continuously increasing or decreasing relation, the hypothesis can be formulated as follows:

> *Hypothesis*: The rank order of the measurement points in time, according to the observed values of the independent variable, is exactly the same as the rank order of the measurement points according to the observed values of the dependent variable.

If, for instance,

- the five measurement points were times t_1, t_2, t_3, t_4, and t_5, and
- A_1, A_2, A_3, A_4, and A_5 are the values of the independent variable at these points, and
- B_1, B_2, B_3, B_4, and B_5 are the values of the dependent variable at these points, and
- the independent variable is ranked according to increasing value (for example, A_4, A_5, A_3, A_1, A_2),

then, for a predicted continuously increasing or decreasing relation between the independent and the dependent variable, it is predicted that the dependent variable has exactly the same rank order (B_4, B_5, B_3, B_1, B_2), or the exact reverse order (depending on whether the proposition states that the value of the dependent variable increases or decreases deterministically with an increase of the value the independent variable).

If the proposition states that the value of the dependent variable increases (or decreases) deterministically (and continuously increasing or decreasing) with an increase of the value the independent variable, then the hypothesis in a *comparative case study* can be formulated as follows:

> *Hypothesis*: The rank order of cases, according to the observed values of the independent variable, is exactly the same as the rank order of the cases according to the observed values of the dependent variable.

This hypothesis can also be formulated as a sufficient condition, in the following form:

> *Hypothesis*: For all pairs of cases, if the value of the independent variable in case 1 is higher than the value of the independent variable in case 2 (condition), then the value of the dependent variable in case 1 will also be higher than the value of the dependent variable in case 2.

The logic of testing is the same as when we test a sufficient condition. If the condition is present, the hypothesis predicts that the effect is present as well, or if the effect is not present, the hypothesis predicts that the condition is not present as well.

6.1.5 Measurement

In a longitudinal case study it must be determined how many measurements of the two variables have to be conducted and on which moments within the longitudinal time frame. In a comparative case study there are similar cases with different values on the independent variable. This implies that the value of the independent variable was already measured in the earlier stage of case selection. Therefore the measurement in a comparative case study consists of measuring the value of the dependent variable in each case.

6.1.6 Data presentation

For a predicted continuously increasing or decreasing relation the measurement points (in the longitudinal case study) or cases (in the comparative case study) are ranked according to the value of the independent variable. Independently from this ranking, these points or cases are ranked according to the value of the dependent variable.

6.1.7 Data analysis

The data analysis for a predicted continuously increasing or decreasing relation consists of comparing the rank orders of the independent variable with the dependent variable. The hypothesis is confirmed if the two rank orders are exactly the same, assuming that both rank orders have been compared in the direction from low to high, or in the reverse direction, that is predicted by the hypothesis. If the rank orders differ, the hypothesis is rejected.

Rank orders might differ considerably or only slightly (e.g. when the rank orders differ only for two measurements out of a large number). If the rank order differs only slightly it is tempting to conclude that the hypothesis is *almost* confirmed. This is only acceptable if, in a large number of instances, only a few exceptions occur, and a pragmatic deterministic view is chosen. Normally the hypothesis is rejected if the predicted pattern does not match with the measured pattern.

6.1.8 Implications for the theory

The issues regarding the implications for theory are the same as for all theory-testing case studies. See 5.1.8 for a discussion of this topic.

6.1.9 Replication strategy

The issues regarding the replication strategy are the same as for all theory-testing case studies. See 5.1.9 for a discussion of this topic.

6.2 Case Study 3: Theory-testing research: testing a deterministic relation

The influences of urban time access windows on retailers' distribution costs[1]

by Hans Quak

6.2.1 Introduction

Urban freight transport is crucial to maintain the current urbanized way of living. It is vital to trade and leisure activities in cities as well as to the liveability in these areas. However, transport also causes noise, emissions, congestion, decreased city accessibility, fossil fuel use, visual intrusion, vibration, consequences of emissions on public health, injuries

---

[1] This chapter is based on: Quak, H.J. and De Koster, M.B.M., Exploring retailers' sensitivity to local sustainability policies, *Journal of Operations Management* (2007), doi:10.1016/j.jom.2007.01.020.

and deaths resulting from traffic accidents, loss of greenfield sites and open space, and damage to infrastructure and (historical) buildings from heavy vehicles (Browne and Allen, 1999; Banister *et al.*, 2000). Currently, these negative effects have the upper hand in residents' and policy makers' perceptions of urban freight transport and form the motivation for policies aimed at reducing it. One of the most popular urban freight transport policy measures aiming at improving social sustainability in urban areas, especially in Europe, is the use of time access windows (OECD 2003).

A time access window forces all distribution activities to be carried out within the time window period at the time window area. The objective of time windows is to improve the quality of the city centres, by reducing (the perceived) negative impacts caused by large vehicles in shopping centres, as well as to separate the freight carriers from the shopping public that uses cars to visit the shopping areas (Allen *et al.*, 2004; Munuzuri *et al.*, 2005). The use of time windows has increased in the Netherlands over recent years. In 1998, 41 per cent of the 278 largest Dutch municipalities used time windows. This increased to 53 per cent in 2002. The larger the municipality, the more likely it is that it uses time windows: of the Dutch top 100 municipalities, 71 per cent used time windows in 2002 and all municipalities in the top 20 did so. In 2002, the average time window length was about 4.5 hours (PSD 2002). Many carriers and large retail chains consider time windows one of their biggest problems in delivering to their shops in urban areas (Crum and Vossen, 2000). Groothedde and Uil (2004) estimate that the current cost caused by time window restrictions for Dutch retail is about €270 million annually.

6.2.2 Theory

6.2.2.1 Object of study

The object of study is the distribution activities by retailers from a retailers' distribution centre to the shops during one week.

6.2.2.2 Concepts

The concepts of interest are:

- *Time access window pressure.* This pressure consists of (a) the *number of windows* (*number of areas* in which time access windows are present) and (b) the *length* of these time windows.

▪ *Distribution costs.* Four dimensions of distribution costs are distinguished: number of roundtrips, number of vehicles, total travel distance, and total time.

6.2.2.3 Proposition

Our theory states that distribution costs increase in *all four dimensions* if time window pressure increases, for the following reasons: first, because shops cannot always be reached in a vehicle roundtrip at times that are convenient for the retailer, the *number of roundtrips* from a distribution centre will increase. Second, because most of this higher number of roundtrips will take place at the same time, *more vehicles* will be needed. Third, we expect that the *total travel distance* and *total time* spent on roundtrips will increase because, due to the time windows, it will not be possible to always make roundtrips, which are the most efficient in terms of distance and time. Based on this theory, we formulated the following deterministic proposition:

> *Proposition*: Each realistic increase in time access window pressure causes an increase in all four dimensions of distribution costs.

The contention of this proposition is that there are no retailers that do not feel the consequences of a higher time window pressure in all four dimensions of distribution costs. With "realistic increase" we mean levels of increase that could be realized in practice (not just an increase in minutes but at least a quarter of an hour) and realistic duration (e.g. maximum a few hours, not up to 24 hours per day). The absence of a qualifier such as "often", or "likely", makes the proposition a deterministic one.

6.2.2.4 Domain

The theory applies to the typical Western European distribution context and within this context to all large retailers that distribute goods from a distribution centre to shops that are (at least partly) located in shopping areas in cities in which time access windows could be installed. Dutch retailers are instances from this domain.

6.2.2.5 Conceptual model

The theory states that higher time access window pressure results in higher distribution costs as specified in the proposition, and as visualized in the following conceptual model.

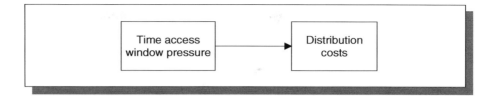

6.2.3 Research objective

The objective of this research is to contribute to the theory about the relationship between time access window pressure and distribution costs for large retailers by testing the following new proposition:

> *Proposition*: Each increase in time window access pressure causes an increase in all four dimensions of distribution costs.

6.2.4 Research strategy

Testing of our proposition requires that we try to find at least one instance of one dimension of one retailer's distribution costs that does not increase if time window pressure is increased. In order to do this we need to study a diverse set of retailers and to assess for each retailer whether increases of time window pressure always cause increases on all four dimensions of distribution costs. This test thus needs to be conducted for each dimension and for each retailer separately (or, in other words, instance-by-instance or case-by-case). The testing of this proposition, therefore, requires a case study design.

Our study requires that time window pressure varies. In the Netherlands, there has been a steady increase in time window pressure due to changes in municipal policies, but this increase is slow. This implies that a test of our theory with actual data would require us to collect data that go back for years. However, it would be difficult to collect accurate historical data on both time window pressure and distribution costs. We solved this problem by formulating 19 scenarios (0–18) with different levels of realistic window pressure, ranging from no pressure (scenario 0) to severe pressure (scenario 18), and then to use the retailers' current distribution data to calculate the distribution costs for each of these scenarios. In this way, we could conduct a *parallel longitudinal case study*.

6.2.5 Candidate cases

The universe of instances of the object of study to which our theory is applicable consists of all distribution activities of all (large) retailers that are (at least partly) located in shopping areas in cities in which time access windows could be installed. In everyday terms, this is the universe of distribution activities undertaken from large retailers' distribution centres. Obviously there is no comprehensive list of such retailers' distribution centres or activities worldwide, but it would be possible to construct such an (almost complete) list of such distribution centres in the Netherlands, particularly in specific branches such as supermarkets, department stores, fashion shops, and specialist shops (including pharmacies), which are most common in shopping areas (measured in gross floor space and number and size of the shipments). We drew up such a tentative list.

6.2.6 Case selection

From this list we selected 14 Dutch retailers that distribute goods from a distribution centre in the Netherlands to shops in the Netherlands. We selected retailers with different competitive strategies: discounters (lower end of the market), retailers that focus on cost (middle segment of the market), and retailers that focus on response or differentiation (higher end of the market). Some retailers distribute goods from their distribution centre in the Netherlands to shops located outside the Netherlands. These shops were excluded, except for three retailers for which it was not possible to separate some foreign shops from Dutch shops in this study, because these shops are interweaved with shops in the Netherlands in one roundtrip or one vehicle during a day. Therefore, we also considered foreign shops in Belgium and Germany for cases 2, 3, and 7. Figure 6.1 shows all considered store locations of the 14 retailers involved in this study.

All retailers use a weekly recurring roundtrip planning, except cases 2 and 4 that use a 4-week or a 2-week recurring scheme. For reasons of comparison, for these cases we use the average for one week. Furthermore, in case 4 we included four distribution centres. In this case all shops were supplied from one national distribution centre, but some shops were also supplied from three regional distribution centres. Table 6.1 shows the main case characteristics of the 14 selected retail chains.

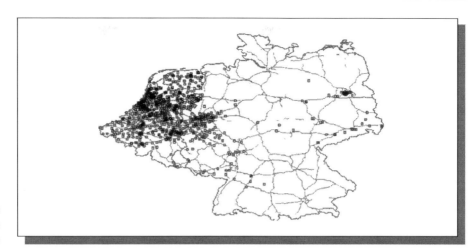

Figure 6.1
Locations of the
stores of the
selected retailers

Table 6.1

Main case characteristics

Case	Retailer type	Competitive strategy	Number of stores considered	Number of warehouses considered	Number of deliveries (per week)
1	Drug	Costs	498	1	515
2	Department store	Costs (discounter)	106	1	132
3	Department store	Costs	275	1	791
4	Department store	Differentiation	93	4	751
5	Department store	Differentiation	13	1	68
6	Fashion	Costs	108	1	510
7	Fashion	Costs (discounter)	475	1	952
8	Fashion	Response	180	1	900
9	Fashion	Response	122	1	244
10	Fashion	Response	133	1	266
11	Food (dry groceries)	Costs (discounter)	77	1	224
12	Food (dry groceries)	Differentiation	134	1	663
13	Food (dry groceries and fresh)	Costs (soft discounter)	38	1	820
14	Food (fresh)	Differentiation	134	1	1,431
Total			2,386	17	8,267

6.2.7 Hypotheses

The independent variable in this study is time window pressure. In scenario 0 there are no time window restrictions. In the other scenarios we

Table 6.2
Scenarios of time access window pressure

Time window length	Number of time window restricted areas					
	Only 5 largest cities in the Netherlands	Only 10 largest cities in the Netherlands	Only 25 largest cities in the Netherlands	Only 50 largest cities in the Netherlands	Only 100 largest cities in the Netherlands	Only 250 largest cities in the Netherlands
6:00am–noon	A1	A2	A3	A4	A5	A6
6:30am–11:00am	B1	B2	B3	B4	B5	B6
7:00am–10:00am	C1	C2	C3	C4	C5	C6

varied both dimensions of *time window pressure* (see Table 6.2). The *time window length* varies from a 6-hour period between 6:00am and noon in subscenarios A_{1-6}, via a 4.5-hour period from 6:30am to 11:00am in subscenarios B_{1-6}, to the third series of subscenarios C_{1-6} with a time window length of only 3 hours, from 7:00am to 10:00am (see rows in Table 6.2). The *number of time window restricted areas* varies from the shopping centres in the five largest Dutch municipalities in scenario 1 to the shopping centres in the 250 largest municipalities in scenario 6 (see the columns in Table 6.2 for the differences in number of time restricted areas).

For each retailer we formulated the following two hypotheses.

Hypothesis 1: For a given time window length (A, B, or C) the values of all four dimensions of distribution costs will be ranked in the perfect order according to the increasing number of time window restricted areas (1–6).

Hypothesis 2: For a given number of time window restricted areas (1–6) the values of all four dimensions of distribution costs will be ranked in the perfect order according to time window length (A–C).

6.2.8 Measurement

We have generated the values for distribution costs by calculating the realistic effects (i.e. based on current distribution activities) of different realistic (but not actual) levels of time window pressure on these 14 Dutch retailers' costs. In order to be able to do that we first collected data on the actual distribution activities of the 14 retailers for a period of one week.

The measurement process followed the same procedure for all cases, and consisted of four steps:

- *open interview with the distribution or logistics manager* to get familiar with each retailer's operations and urban freight transport activities and the current or likely retailer's reaction on time window pressures;
- a *questionnaire* to collect detailed data on each retailer's operational level;
- *company documents* (and additional information) with information on each retailer's entire transport planning for one week;
- e-*mail and/or telephone contact* for additional information needed.

Collected data were put into a mathematical model that generated the distribution costs in all four dimensions, for a given time access window pressure. In this model we needed to solve a number of vehicle routing problems with time windows. The number of extra vehicles was kept to a minimum. To plan the new roundtrips we used the vehicle routing software SHORTREC 7.0, developed by Ortec Consultants. From the new calculated retailers' roundtrip planning, we derived the values for the dimensions of *distribution costs*. (For a detailed description of the collection of actual retailers' distribution data as well as of the model we refer to Quak and De Koster, 2007.)

6.2.9 Data presentation

We filled all 18 cells of Table 6.2 for each retailer and for each of the four dimensions of distribution costs, resulting in 56 (4 × 14) tables. The tables can also be represented in graphs, as is shown in Figure 6.2 for one of the 14 retailers (case 8). The two *time window pressure* dimensions are represented in Figure 6.2 as follows: the *x*-axis represents the *number of time window restricted areas* resulting from each scenario for this retailer. The different values of *time window length* are represented by a line for each scenario (A, B, and C).

6.2.10 Data analysis

Hypothesis 1 states that for each of the 14 retailers and for each of the four dimensions of distribution costs the six values (1–6) in each of the

Figure 6.2
Distribution costs as an effect of time window pressure (Case 8)

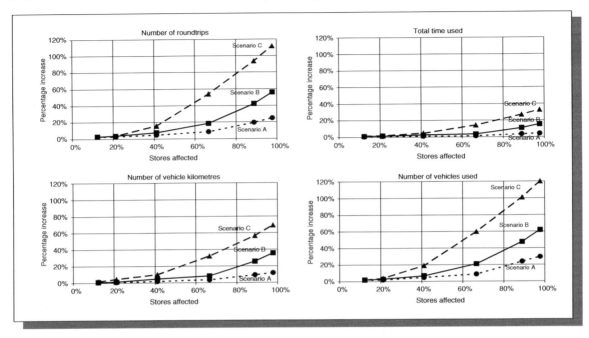

three rows (A, B, or C) in this table are in a perfect order of increasing costs. Hypothesis 2 states that for each of the 14 retailers and for each of the four dimensions of distribution costs the three values (A, B, or C) in each of the six columns (1–6) in this table are in a perfect order of increasing costs.

We tested both hypotheses in each of the 56 tables by looking at the actual numbers, and use Figure 6.2 here only as means of presentation. It shows that the value of all four dimensions of cost, increased with the number of shops affected by a time access window, an effect that is clearly visible as a rise in each of the lines if one goes from left (small number of restricted areas) to right (high number of areas). In each graph the line for scenario C is consistently higher than the line for scenario B, which is consistently higher than the one for A, which represents the fact that the value of all four dimensions of cost increased with the decrease of length of the time access windows.

Because no instance was found in which, for a given value of number of restricted areas, the value of a dimension of cost was higher for scenario A than for scenario B or C, and because the value for B never exceeded the one for C, and because no instance was found in which a value of a dimension of cost decreased with an increase of the number of restricted areas, proposition 1 was considered to be confirmed for this case (case 8). We conducted the same test for all 14 cases and no instance was found in which the hypothesis could not be confirmed.

6.2.11 Implications for the theory

The two hypotheses were confirmed in all cases. This is an indication that the proposition from which these hypotheses were derived is correct.

6.3 Methodological reflection on Case Study 3

6.3.1 Theory

The *object of study* in Case Study 3 is clearly presented. The *concepts* and their operationalization into variables were precisely defined: time access window pressure consisting of (a) the number of windows (number of areas in which time access windows are present) and (b) the length of these time windows, and distribution costs which depend on number of roundtrips, number of vehicles, total travel distance, and total time. This was necessary because otherwise it would not have been possible to generate data for the different scenarios.

The *proposition* states that each realistic increase in time window pressure causes an increase in all four dimensions of distribution costs. It is explicitly formulated as a deterministic relation, although there are some (unrealistic) circumstances in which no increase in costs is expected with any increase of time window pressure. For example, if the time window pressure increased only a few minutes, this would realistically not require a new vehicle.

The *domain* of the theory included all large retailers that distribute goods from a distribution centre to shops that are (at least partly) located in shopping areas in cities in which time access windows could be installed. The universe of instances of the object of study is bounded by the geographical boundary of Western Europe where retailers and local governments are familiar with the concept of time access windows. Implicitly it seems that the theory is applicable in different sectors, as the study was done in the supermarket, department store, fashion shop, and specialist shop sectors.

6.3.2 Research objective

The study's *objective* was to test a new proposition about the relation between time access window pressure and distribution costs for retailers.

6.3.3 Research strategy

The proposition specifies a *deterministic* relation between time window pressure and distribution costs. A deterministic proposition can best be tested in a *serial experiment* in which it is demonstrated in a single experiment that each manipulated change of the independent variable results in a corresponding change in the value of the dependent variable. Such an experiment is not feasible for this study, because it would require that local governments would vary time window pressure for the purpose of this research (which is not possible in practice).

If an experimental research strategy is not feasible, as in this study, a *longitudinal single case study* is commendable. Case Study 3 discusses this possibility and concludes that it is not feasible because it is too difficult to collect accurate historical data on both time window pressure and distribution costs. However, this problem is solved by formulating realistic scenarios with different levels of window pressure and by using the retailers' current distribution data to calculate the distribution costs for each of these scenarios. In this way, Case Study 3 imitates a *longitudinal single case study*. Furthermore, the study was designed as a *parallel* longitudinal case study. As discussed above in 5.3.3, an advantage of the parallel case study approach is that the chance of finding a rejection of the proposition in one round of (parallel) testing is higher than with a test in a single case. A disadvantage of this approach is that more tests will be performed than are necessary. Also, with this large number of parallel cases, the danger that a probabilistic approach will unwittingly creep into the analysis is present.

6.3.4 Candidate cases

The universe of instances of the object of study to which the theory is applicable consists of all distribution activities of all (large) retailers in Western Europe with shops that are (at least partly) located in shopping areas in cities in which time access windows could be installed. It is correctly stated in 6.2.2.4 that Dutch retailers are instances from this domain.

6.3.5 Case selection

Fourteen Dutch retailers were selected from the set of candidate cases. Retailers with different competitive strategies were selected: discounters (lower end of the market), retailers that focus on cost (middle segment of the market), and retailers that focus on response or differentiation (higher end of the market). This attempt to select a "representative" sample of cases also shows that the study was designed as a *parallel* case study. This representativeness was not needed for this study.

6.3.6 Hypotheses

Because the proposition in this study specified a *deterministic* relation, and implicitly a continuously increasing relation, the hypothesis stated that the rank order of measurement points according to the observed values of the dependent variable was exactly the same as the rank order of measurement points according to the observed values of the independent variable. Because the independent variable time access window pressure had two independent dimensions, number of time window restricted areas and time window length, two hypotheses needed to be formulated.

6.3.7 Measurement

In order to generate realistic roundtrip data for all retailers under the conditions defined by the 18 scenarios, actual current roundtrip data needed to be collected. It is described how multiple data sources were used, namely interview data (face-to-face, e-mail, telephone), questionnaire data, and documents. The quality of the collected data cannot be evaluated because no further detail is provided. The four dimensions of distribution costs for all 14 cases in all conditions defined by the 18 scenarios were generated by a mathematical model. A reference is provided to another article in which the model is described and discussed in more detail.

6.3.8 Data presentation

Figure 6.2 presents the data generated for the different scenarios in one case, as an example. The mode of presentation is such that it directly provides the rank orders needed for testing the hypothesis.

6.3.9 Data analysis

A number of 36 rank orders were generated for each retailer (four tables containing three rows and six columns). Each of these 36 rank orders is inspected to see whether their order is perfect. This implies 12 tests of hypothesis 1 (three rows for four dimensions of distribution costs) and 24 tests of hypothesis 2 (six columns for each dimension) for each retailer. Both hypotheses were confirmed.

6.3.10 Implications for the theory

Case Study 3 concludes that the two hypotheses were confirmed in all cases. The implications for the theory were not discussed, apparently considering it obvious that the proposition had been proven to be true, at least for large retailers in the Netherlands. An obvious practical implication of this study's result is that it can be taken as a fact that an increase in the number of time access windows and a decrease in window length both result in higher distribution costs, and that, for instance, organizations of retailers could use this information in discussions with local governments and with the national government regarding the economic costs of social sustainability measures.

6.3.11 Replication strategy

Case Study 3 gives no suggestions for further replications. For the development of theory, it would be important to know to which types of retailers the proposition is applicable and to which types it is not. For instance, would the proposition be true for retailers with a system of multiple, decentralized distribution centres? Or would it be true for retailers in other countries? Hence, a replication in other countries with other types of distribution system would help to develop the theory further.

6.4 References

Allen, J., Browne, M., Tanner, G., Anderson, S., Chrisodoulou, G., and Jones, P. 2004, Analysing the potential impacts of sustainable distribution measures in UK urban areas, pp. 251–262, in: Taniguchi, E. and Thompson, R.G. (eds), *Logistics systems for sustainable cities*. Amsterdam: Elsevier.

Banister, D., Stead, D., Steen, P., Akerman, J., Dreborg, K., Nijkamp, P., and Schleicher-Tappeser, R. 2000, *European transport policy and sustainable mobility.* London: Spon Press.

Browne, M. and Allen, J. 1999, The impact of sustainability policies on urban freight transport and logistics systems, pp. 505–518, in: Meermans, H., Van De Voorde, E., and Winkelmans, W. (eds), *8th World Conference on Transport Research (WCTR).* Antwerp: Elsevier.

Crum, B. and Vossen, M. 2000, Knelpunten in de binnenstadsdistributie, inventarisatie van de beschikbare kennis en ervaringen. Leiden: Research voor Beleid.

Groothedde, B. and Uil, K. 2004, Restrictions in city-distribution and a possible alternative using the citybox, pp. 1–16, in: Bovy, P.H.L. (ed.), *A world of transport, infrastructure and logistics, 8th TRAIL Congress 2004.* Delft: DUP Science.

Munuzuri, J., Larraneta, J., Onieva, L., and Cortes, P. 2005, Solutions applicable by local administrations for urban logistics improvement. *Cities* 22(1): 15–28.

OECD 2003, Delivering the goods – 21st century challenges to urban goods transport. OECD working group on urban freight logistics, Paris.

PSD 2002, *Van B naar A.* Platform Stedelijke Distributie, Den Haag.

Quak, H.J. and De Koster, M.B.M. 2007, Exploring retailers' sensitivity to local sustainability policies. *Journal of Operations Management,* doi:10.1016/j.jom.2007.01.020.

CHAPTER 7

Testing a probabilistic relation with a case study

In the preceding chapters we discussed how to design and conduct a case study that tests a proposition with a *sufficient condition*, a *necessary condition*, or a *deterministic relation*. Many propositions in business research express (explicitly or implicitly) a probabilistic relation between variables. The methodology of testing a probabilistic relation with a case study is different. This chapter discusses how to design and conduct a case study in which a *probabilistic relation* is tested.

As in previous chapters, we present here a "How to do" guide (7.1), an example of an actual case study (7.2), and a "methodological reflection" (7.3). Thus, the contents of this chapter are as follows:

- 7.1 How to test a probabilistic relation;
- 7.2 Case Study 4: The influence of a retailer's distribution strategy on a retailer's sensitivity to urban time access windows (by Hans Quak);
- 7.3 Methodological reflection on Case Study 4.

7.1 How to test a probabilistic relation with a case study

7.1.1 Introduction

This chapter deals with theory-testing case study research for testing a *probabilistic relation*. A probabilistic proposition presumes that if the value of the independent concept changes, it is likely that the value of the dependent concept changes in the predicted way. The proposition is formulated as follows:

"If A is higher, then it is likely that B is higher"

A probabilistic relation can be tested with a *comparative* case study.

7.1.2 Candidate cases

The issues regarding the universe for case selection are the same for all theory-testing case studies. See 5.1.2 for a discussion of this topic.

7.1.3 Case selection

The most common reason for conducting a comparative case study, rather than a survey, is that it is not possible to collect data from a large sample, either because there simply are no more cases or because it is not feasible (in terms of access or in terms of necessary investments in time or other costs) to collect data from a larger sample. If there are no more cases, the obvious case selection procedure is to include all cases that are available. If data can be collected from only a small number of cases (but from more if more money or time would be available), a case selection strategy has to be chosen. The preferred selection strategy is probability sampling such as random sampling, which is in accordance with the fact that this kind of study is a quasi-survey. However, selecting a truly representative sample of a large population with a large variety of types of instances is very difficult, and it is quite likely that replication studies with different samples from the same population would result in different outcomes. For this reason it is recommended to avoid sampling in a large population but instead to identify very small specific populations in which the variation between the instances is much less than in the larger population. Probability sampling in such a small population is much easier and the population could even be so small that all instances of the population could be included in the study (census). Generalizability could be achieved through replications in a series of small populations from different parts of the domain.

It is not possible to give specific advice on the number of cases that must be selected for testing a probabilistic relation with a quasi-survey comparative case study. In general, the more cases that can be used for the analysis the better. However, the number of available cases will be limited, because otherwise a survey would have been chosen as a research strategy. The best advice for the number of instances that should be included in the study, therefore, is to select the maximum number of cases that are available and that can be handled within the resource constraints of the study.

7.1.4 Hypothesis

If the proposition states that it is likely that the value of the dependent variable increases (or decreases) with an increase of the value of the independent variable, then the hypothesis in a *comparative* case study, in which the tested part of the relation is presumed to be continuously increasing or decreasing, is that the rank order of cases according to the observed values of the dependent variable is *like* the rank order of cases according to the observed values of the independent variable. The probabilistic nature of the hypothesis is encapsulated in the word "like". In a deterministic hypothesis the two rank orders are *exactly* the same.

7.1.5 Measurement

The values of the dependent and independent variables in all cases of the sample need to be measured.

7.1.6 Data presentation

If the tested part of the relation between the independent and dependent variables can be considered as continuously increasing or decreasing, the cases are ranked according to the value of the independent variable. Separately, the cases are also ranked according to the value of the dependent variable.

7.1.7 Data analysis

The data analysis consists of comparing the ranking according to the values of the independent variable with the ranking according to the value of the dependent variable. If the two rank orders are exactly the same (same order of cases), the hypothesis is confirmed. If the rank orders differ, it must be determined whether the difference is such that it can be concluded that the two rank orders have no relation to each other, or that the rank orders have the same tendency. In a survey, statistical methods can be used to determine whether there is a relation between the two distributions. However, in a comparative survey, statistics are not possible due to the small number of cases.

A simple way of conducting such a test without statistics is to divide the first rank order (ranked according to the value of the independent variable) in groups (e.g. into quartiles), compute the average rank number of the members of these groups, and inspect whether the rank order of these groups (ranked according to the value of the dependent variable) is perfect. A perfect rank order of group averages is evidence of a probabilistic relation.

7.1.8 Implications for the theory

The issues regarding the implications for the theory are the same for all theory-testing case studies. See 5.1.8 for a discussion of this topic.

7.1.9 Replication strategy

The issues regarding the replication strategy are the same for all theory-testing case studies. See 5.1.9 for a discussion of this topic.

7.2 Case Study 4: Theory-testing research: testing a probabilistic relation

The influence of a retailer's distribution strategy on a retailer's sensitivity to urban time access windows[1]

by Hans Quak

7.2.1 Introduction

In Chapter 6 we presented a case study, which showed that retailers that are confronted with time access windows for entering cities to

---

[1] This chapter is based on: Quak, H.J. and De Koster, M.B.M., Exploring retailers' sensitivity to local sustainability policies, *Journal of Operations Management* (2007), doi:10.1016/j.jom.2007.01.020.

deliver their goods have higher distribution costs. For some retailers this increase in costs might be (relatively) much more than for other retailers, depending on their distribution strategy, such as the number of stops per roundtrip.

7.2.2 Theory

7.2.2.1 Object of study

The object of study is distribution activities by retailers. This is the same object of study as in Case Study 3.

7.2.2.2 Concepts

The concepts of interest are:

- *Distribution strategy.* This includes the following five dimensions: (a) the *number of stops* per roundtrip (which number will correlate with the number of occasions that a time access window could be encountered during one roundtrip), (b) *vehicle capacity* (which influences the possible amount of goods carried in one vehicle roundtrip and with that the drop-size and the number of drops), (c) *stopping time* (which is an indicator for the time that will be used within time window areas), (d) the *distance* of the retailer's shops from the distribution centre, and (e) *self-imposed time windows* (such as a policy to deliver only after or before shopping hours, or a policy to deliver only when staff is available to receive the goods).
- *Time access window pressure.* This pressure consists of (a) the number of windows (number of areas in which time access windows are present), and (b) the lengths of these time windows.
- *Total distribution costs.* In the present chapter we use only one indicator for distribution costs, which is the total costs in terms of money (which results from the four dimensions that were used as indicators of distribution costs in the previous chapter).

7.2.2.3 Propositions

Our theory states that the higher the value of a retailer on a dimension of distribution strategy the more likely it is that the retailer is more "sensitive to time window pressure". In other words, retailers with a higher value on a dimension of strategy (such as a higher number of stops per roundtrip) will often have a relatively higher increase in distribution costs that occur with a given change in time access window pressure than retailers with a lower value on that dimension of distribution strategy.

Based on this theory, we formulated a probabilistic proposition for each of the dimensions of distribution strategy:

> *Proposition 1*: Retailers with a higher number of stops per roundtrip are likely to have a higher increase in total distribution costs that occur with a given change in time access window pressure than retailers with a lower number of stops per roundtrip.

> *Proposition 2*: Retailers with a vehicle fleet with a higher capacity per vehicle are likely to have a higher increase in total distribution costs that occur with a given change in time access window pressure than retailers with a fleet of lower capacity per vehicle.

> *Proposition 3*: Retailers with longer stopping times are likely to have a higher increase in total distribution costs that occur with a given change in time access window pressure than retailers with shorter stopping times.

> *Proposition 4*: Retailers with longer distances from the distribution centre to their shops are likely to have a higher increase in total distribution costs that occur with a given change in time access window pressure than retailers with shorter distances from the distribution centre to their shops.

> *Proposition 5*: Retailers with less strict self-imposed time windows are likely to have a higher increase in total distribution costs that occur with a given change in time access window pressure than retailers with stricter self-imposed time windows.

7.2.2.4 Domain

As with the theory tested in Case Study 3, this theory applies to all large retailers that distribute goods from a distribution centre to shops that are (at least partly) located in shopping areas in cities in which time access windows could be installed.

7.2.2.5 Conceptual model

In the conceptual model we presume that there is a deterministic relation between time access window pressure and total distribution costs – this is the relation that was tested in Case Study 3. We, additionally, presume that the size of the "proportion" (i.e. the relative increase in total distribution costs between different levels of time access window pressure) depends on a retailer's "distribution strategy".

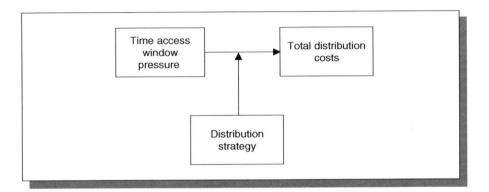

7.2.3 Research objective

The objective of the present study is to contribute to the theory about the relationship between distribution strategy and the retailers' sensitivity to time access windows by testing the propositions 1–5.

7.2.4 Research strategy

A *comparative* case study strategy was chosen for this study.

7.2.5 Candidate cases

For convenience, our candidate cases were the set of cases that we had selected for Case Study 3.

7.2.6 Case selection

All 14 cases from the set of candidate cases were selected for the present study.

▪ 7.2.7 Hypotheses

The propositions state that for a specific change of time access window pressure differences between retailers with different levels on the dimensions of distribution strategy will be observable. For the present test, we decided to keep time window length (scenario A, B, or C) constant and to change only the number of time access windows (levels 1–6). The following hypotheses were formulated, which must be tested separately for each scenario A, B, and C.

> *Hypothesis 1*: Retailers with a higher number of stops per roundtrip have, on average a steeper rise in total distribution costs with an increase in the number of time windows from level 1 to level 6 than retailers with a lower number of stops per roundtrip.
>
> *Hypothesis 2*: Retailers with a vehicle fleet with higher capacity per vehicle have, on average a steeper rise in total distribution costs with an increase in the number of time windows from level 1 to level 6 than retailers with a fleet of lower capacity per vehicle.
>
> *Hypothesis 3*: Retailers with longer stopping times have, on average a steeper rise in total distribution costs with an increase in the number of time windows from level 1 to level 6 than retailers with shorter stopping times.
>
> *Hypothesis 4*: Retailers with longer distances from the distribution centre to their shops have, on average a steeper rise in total distribution costs with an increase in the number of time windows from level 1 to level 6 than retailers with shorter distances from the distribution centre to their shops.
>
> *Hypothesis 5*: Retailers with less strict self-imposed time windows have, on average a relatively higher increase in total distribution costs that occur with an increase in the number of time windows from level 1 to level 6 than retailers with stricter self-imposed time windows.

▪ 7.2.8 Measurement

We could make use of the same data that we used in the study reported in Case Study 3.

Time access window pressure was determined by the number of shops that are affected by time access windows and the time-window length.

Total distribution costs in euros per week were determined by converting our data on the weekly number of vehicle kilometres, the total time used (including the loading and unloading times as well as driving and waiting time), the number and types of vehicles used, and the number of roundtrips, into a monetary value. The variable costs are mainly based on costs per hour and cost per kilometre. We validated the costs with all retailers, and adapted them slightly in case the retailers felt this would give a better representation of the actual costs. The costs for overtime are higher per hour than in the normal situation.

The five dimensions of *distribution strategy* were determined as follows.

■ *Stops per roundtrip.* This was measured by calculating the average number of stops per vehicle roundtrip during a week. This equals the average number of different shop deliveries that are combined in one vehicle. This can vary from full-truckload (FTL) deliveries, in which a vehicle only makes one stop per roundtrip, to less-than-truckload (LTL) deliveries, implying that a vehicle makes more than one delivery per roundtrip (Stock and Lambert, 2001).

■ *Vehicle capacity.* Based on McKinnon *et al.* (2003) we distinguished six different vehicle types. We sorted these types on increasing load factor, starting with the smallest capacity and ending with the largest vehicle capacity (see Table 7.1). We calculated each retailer's average vehicle fleet capacity based on the number of vehicles in each category.

■ *Stopping time per vehicle.* Stopping time can be split into two parts: a fixed stopping time per stop and a variable stopping time per

Table 7.1

Vehicle types sorted on capacity

Value	Type	Characteristics	Example
1	Small rigid	2 axles, <7.5 tons	
2	Medium rigid	2 axles, >7.5 and <18 tons	
3	Large rigid	≥2 axles, >18 tons	
4	City semi-trailer	articulated, 3 axles	
5	Articulated vehicle	articulated, >3 axles	
6	Drawbar combination	combination, >3 axles	

stop. The fixed time is the result of activities, such as looking for a place to park, parking the vehicle, and notifying a shop's staff of the driver's presence. Variable stopping time depends on the amount of product carriers that has to be (un)loaded. For example, one retailer (case 13) uses detachable swap bodies, which can be unloaded in the absence of the vehicle. The vehicle brings a full container and picks up the (empty) container of the previous delivery in less than 10 minutes. Another way to speed up the (un)loading process at the shops is to have shop staff available to assist the driver during the (un)loading of the vehicles.

■ *Distance between shops and distribution centre* (DC). This dimension is measured by the average distance (in kilometres) between the retailer's shops and its distribution centre(s).

■ *Self-imposed time windows.* We use a three-point ordinal scale for this dimension. Self-imposed time windows are strict, normal, or long. A reason for a retailer to impose a strict time window is, for example, to separate the shopping public from the supplying activities, so the shelves are full before the shop opens. Other retailers want to make sure a vehicle leaves a governmental time window restricted area, before the time window ends. Usually this is the case if the area is physically closed, by for example rising posts, outside the time window period. If the vehicle does not leave the area in time it results in a fine and a delay. Retailers that have normal self-imposed time windows supply their shops during the hours that staff is available to receive the goods. The retailers that use long self-implied time windows even deliver their stores at times when no staff is present in the shops. In these cases the driver possesses a key to the shop (or the shop's depot) to deliver the goods.

7.2.9 Data presentation

Table 7.2 shows the values for the initial distribution strategy dimensions for all 14 cases.

In Figure 7.1 we depict, for each of the five dimensions of distribution strategy, how the increase of this dimension increases the average total distribution costs.

The graphs in Figure 7.1 differ from those in the previous chapter in the following way. The lines represent the different values on distribution strategy, not time window length.

Table 7.2

Distribution strategy dimensions per case

Case	Stops per roundtrip	Vehicle capacity	Stopping time per vehicle	Distance between stores and DC	Self-imposed time windows
1	5.4	3.9	64	110	normal
2	1.2	5.6	122	127	normal
3	2.4	3.5	155	103	normal
4	3.4	4.9	83	76	normal
5	1.0	4.9	63	89	strict
6	4.2	5.5	185	116	normal
7	9.1	5.0	181	198	long
8	8.3	1.8	165	103	long
9	7.2	1.0	72	86	normal
10	10.2	2.6	256	102	long
11	1.2	4.9	47	71	normal
12	1.3	4.7	78	42	normal
13	1.1	3.0	17	32	normal
14	6.3	4.9	134	42	normal

7.2.10 Data analysis

Our hypotheses state that it is likely that a retailer's sensitivity to time window pressure in cases with comparatively high values on distribution strategy dimensions is higher than in cases with comparatively low values on these dimensions. We tested them by classifying the cases into four groups for each dimension of distribution strategy separately: number of stops, vehicle capacity, stopping time, and distance to shops. We used the following procedure. First, we sorted the cases by increasing value on that dimension, and then for each dimension we formed Group 1 by taking the three cases with the lowest value, Group 2 consisting of the next four cases, Group 3 consisting of the subsequent four cases, and finally Group 4 with the three cases with the highest value on the dimension. For the dimension self-imposed time windows, we grouped all cases into three groups corresponding to the three values available on our measurement scale for this variable (see Table 7.2). After having formed these groups, we compared the steepness of the rise in distribution costs resulting from the increase in the number of time access windows (from level 1 to 6) between these groups.

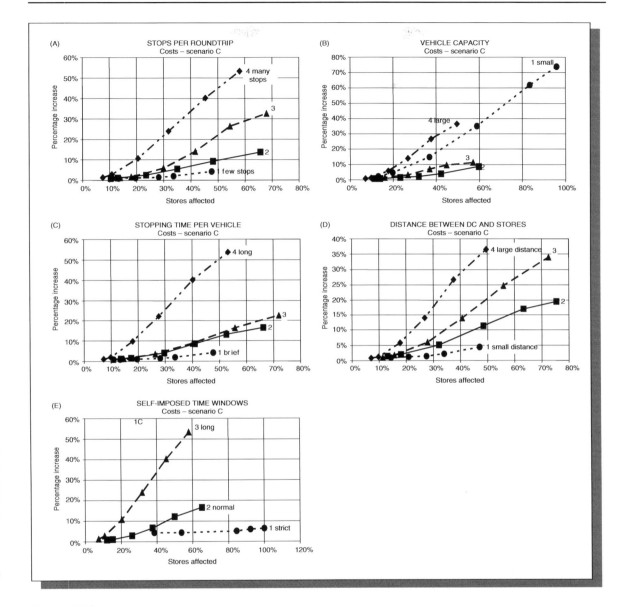

Figure 7.1
Increase of distribution costs due to increase of time window pressure for different values of the dimension of strategy. Each graph (A–E) represents a dimension of strategy and each line within a graph represents a value of the dimension of strategy. All graphs are for stable time window length (scenario C, see Table 6.2).

Our hypotheses predicted the following pattern for each dimension of distribution strategy: Group 1 will have the lowest and the least steep line; Group 2 will have a higher and steeper line than Group 1; Group 3 will have a higher and steeper line than Group 2; and Group 4 will have the highest and steepest line. Figure 7.1 (window length 3 hours, scenario C) shows that the observed pattern is as expected for the dimensions *stops per roundtrip, distance between DC and shops, stopping time,* and *self-imposed time windows.* For one dimension, *vehicle capacity,* the pattern in Group 1 in Figure 7.1B does not correspond with the expected pattern.

The patterns that we observed for time window length scenarios A and B are similar to the pattern for scenario C, with an expected difference; namely that the magnitude of the impacts differs. However, the corresponding data are not shown here.

We concluded that hypotheses 1 and 3–5 were confirmed in this study and that hypothesis 2 was rejected.

7.2.11 Implications for the theory

Four hypotheses were confirmed. This is an indication that the proposition from which these hypotheses were derived is correct. However, the hypothesis on vehicle capacity was rejected.

The proposition on vehicle capacity was based on the idea that, due to time windows, the possibilities of combining deliveries in one vehicle roundtrip would decrease, resulting in an increase in the number of vehicles and a corresponding decrease in the vehicle load factor. We hypothesized that, in particular, retailers using large trucks would have difficulties filling their vehicles and that they would be forced to make roundtrips with only partly filled trucks. As a result they would make trips with more empty than filled capacity, whereas a retailer using small vehicles would still make trips with well-filled (smaller) vehicles.

From the rejection of the hypothesis we conclude that this reasoning was wrong. It appears that vehicle capacity in itself is not a determinant of the sensitivity to time windows. How can this be explained? We think now that there are other, much more important determinants of the (under)use of the capacities of the available vehicles. If we take into account that the length of a vehicle roundtrip can either be determined by the vehicle's capacity actually used in that roundtrip, or by other factors (e.g. the driver's working times, opening hours of shops, etc.), then we would be able to see how those other factors might explain the extent to which underuse of vehicle capacity contributes to total distribution costs. The effect of time window pressure might be that more vehicle roundtrips are getting constrained because of such non-capacity constraints. If such non-capacity constraints apply, this would imply that it is more cost efficient to use smaller vehicles, but it would not imply that retailers starting with smaller vehicles (before time window pressure increases) are less sensitive to time windows. This reasoning can be formulated as a new proposition:

> *Proposition 6*: Retailers with a lower *ability to use their (full) vehicle capacity* are likely to have a higher increase in total distribution costs that occur with a given change in time access window pressure than retailers with a higher *ability to use their (full) vehicle capacity*.

7.2.12 Replication strategy

Since we formulated a new proposition, we need new theory-testing research. For such testing we need to define the concept "ability to use the full vehicle capacity" as well as to determine how its values could be measured.

7.3 Methodological reflection on Case Study 4

7.3.1 Theory

The *object of study* in Case Study 4 is the same as in Case Study 3: distribution activities by retailers from a retailer's distribution centre to the shops during one week.

The *concepts* and their operationalization into variables were precisely defined similar to the definitions in Case Study 3. However, the dependent variable is total distribution costs, which is the result of the separate distribution costs studied in Case Study 3.

There are five *propositions* for each of the dimensions of distribution strategy. Each proposition states that there is a probabilistic relation between this dimension and total distribution costs.

As in Case Study 3, the *domain* of the theory included all large retailers that distribute goods from a distribution centre to shops that are (at least partly) located in shopping areas in cities in which time access windows could be installed. The universe of instances of the object of study is bounded by the geographical boundary of Western Europe where retailers and local governments are familiar with the concept of time access windows. Implicitly it seems that the theory is applicable in different sectors as the study was done in supermarket, department store, fashion shop, and specialist shop sectors.

7.3.2 Research objective

The study's *objective* was to test five new propositions about the effect of five dimensions of distribution strategy on the retailer's sensitivity to time access windows.

7.3.3 Research strategy

Each proposition specifies a *probabilistic* relation between time window pressure and distribution costs. A probabilistic proposition can best be tested in an *experiment*. However, an experiment was not feasible for this study, because it would require that retail chains would vary their distribution strategy for the purpose of this research (which is not possible in practice).

Because an experimental research strategy was not feasible in this study, a *survey* was the second-best strategy. However, for a survey, a large number of instances must be available in order to be able to make the required statistical analyses. In this study the number of instances is too small for a statistical analysis. Therefore the third-best strategy was chosen in the *comparative case study*.

7.3.4 Candidate cases

The universe of instances of the object of study to which the theory was applicable consists of all distribution activities of all (large) retailers in Western Europe that are (at least partly) located in shopping areas in cities in which time access windows could be installed. Dutch retailers are instances from this domain.

7.3.5 Case selection

We recommend selecting a (very) small population in order to avoid problems regarding the representativeness of the sample used for the test (see 7.1.3). In 6.2.6, it was explained how a sample of 14 Dutch retailers with different competitive strategies was selected for this study, which could be considered representative for Dutch distributors in terms of type of retail, including discounters (lower end of the market), retailers that focus on cost (middle segment of the market), and retailers that focus on response or differentiation (higher end of the market). It was mentioned in the methodological reflection with Case Study 3 (in 6.3.5) that such representativeness was not needed for that study. For the current quasi-survey, a probability sample was preferred. However, it is clear (particularly also from the discussion in 6.2) that such sampling was not realistic for the current study.

7.3.6 Hypotheses

Because the propositions in this study specified *probabilistic* relations, the hypothses stated that the rise in total distribution costs is steeper (*"on average"*) for *subgroups* of retailers with higher values on the dimensions of distribution strategy than for *subgroups* of retailers with lower values on these dimensions.

7.3.7 Measurement

Cost data were generated by the same model that was used in Case Study 3, which in its turn used empirical data as input.

7.3.8 Data presentation

Figure 7.1 presents the data generated for one scenario, as an example. The mode of presentation is such that it directly provides for the comparison of the steepness of the increase in average total costs between the subgroups that were constructed for each independent variable.

7.3.9 Data analysis

Averages per subgroup (three or four for each independent variable) should be perfectly rank ordered. Such a perfect rank order is represented in each graph in Figure 7.1 by four lines above each other in the right order (subgroup 1 the lowest, and subgroup 4 the highest line) and without any crossings between these lines. Figure 7.1 allows for a visual inspection in which it can be assessed whether this is actually true. This is the case for the independent variables *stops per roundtrip*, *distance between DC and shops, stopping time,* and *self-imposed time windows.* For one dimension, *vehicle capacity* (Figure 7.1B), the pattern in Group 1 does not correspond with the expected pattern.

7.3.10 Implications for the theory

Four hypotheses were confirmed and one (regarding vehicle capacity) was rejected. The implications of these findings for the theory, particularly the rejection of the hypothesis on vehicle capacity, were discussed. A new proposition was formulated.

7.3.11 Replication strategy

Case Study 4 concluded with a proposal for new theory-testing research aimed at testing the newly formulated proposition. It is also necessary to replicate the tests of the propositions that were supported in new theory-testing research.

7.4 References

McKinnon, A.C., Ge, Y., and Leuchars, D. 2003, Analysis of transport efficiency in the UK food supply chain. Edinburgh: Logistics Research Centre Heriot-Watt University.

Quak, H.J. and De Koster, M.B.M. 2007, Exploring retailers' sensitivity to local sustainability policies. *Journal of Operations Management* (forthcoming).

Stock, J.R. and Lambert, D.M. 2001, *Strategic logistics management.* New York: McGraw-Hill.

Part III

Theory-building research

CHAPTER 8

Theory-building research (general)

The objective of theory-building research is to contribute to the development of theory by formulating new propositions based on the evidence drawn from observation of instances of the object of study. The general format of the research objective of theory-oriented research, of which theory-building research is a part, was formulated as follows (see 3.1.1 "General research objectives of theory-oriented and practice-oriented research"):

> *The general objective of this study is to contribute to the development of theory regarding topic T {specify the research topic}.*

This very general format of a theory-oriented research objective must be further specified as one of two different types: (a) theory-testing research; or (b) theory-building research. We described in 3.2.5 "Exploration for theory-oriented research" how this specification could be achieved through an exploration of theory followed by an exploration of practice (see Flowchart 2). In this Part III, we discuss theory-building research.

In Chapter 3, we claimed that a combination of exploration and theory-testing research (in that order) is a more effective contribution to theory development than spending the same time and resources on theory-building research. We made that claim on the basis of the assumption that usually a whole set of rudimentary theories about the object of study already exists in the minds and talk of practitioners, and that these "theories-in-use" will be discovered quite easily in exploration. Because such an exploration (consisting of identifying and evaluating all kinds of publications, talking to practitioners, visiting real-life situations, and participating in them) can be completed in a relatively short time as a part of the development of a research proposal, we think that exploration is a much more efficient and effective way to find or formulate propositions than "discovering" new propositions through "exploratory" or "theory-building" research.

Even though we claim that, very often, propositions can be formulated on the basis of an exploration, there might be (rare) situations in which this is not successful. We define theory-building research as research that aims to formulate propositions that are "grounded" in research. The general research objective for a theory-building study can be formulated as follows:

> *The objective of this study is to contribute to the development of theory regarding topic T {specify the object of study} by formulating new propositions {specify the phenomenon about which a proposition should be built}.*

This very general format of a theory-building research objective must be further specified as one of four different types of theory-building research. This is shown in Flowchart 2B and will be discussed below.

8.1 Research objectives in theory-building research

In Flowchart 2B a distinction is made between four different starting points for the research.

- Both the independent and dependent concepts are known but the type of relation (deterministic or probabilistic) between the two concepts is not yet known. The research is aimed at specifying the type of relation.
- The independent concept is known but not yet the dependent concept. The research is aimed at identifying and specifying the dependent concept as well as specifying the type of relation between the two concepts.
- The dependent concept is known but not yet the independent concept. The research is aimed at identifying and specifying the independent concept as well as specifying the type of relation between the two concepts.
- Both the independent and dependent concepts are not yet known. The research is aimed at finding concepts and sometimes also at specifying the type of relation between them.

Flowchart 2B
Theory-building research

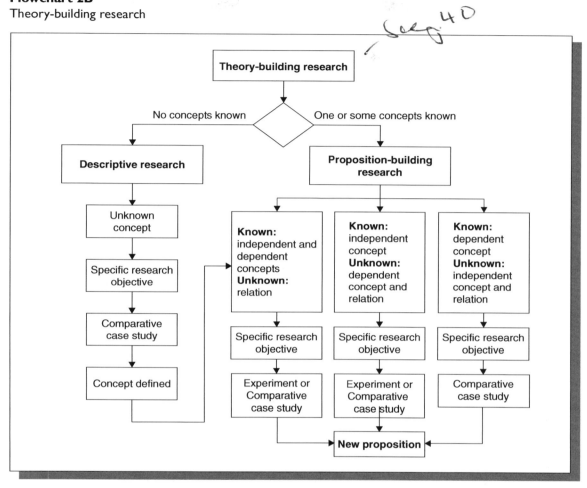

8.1.1 Specifying the relation between known concepts

Figure 8.1 depicts the situation in which the independent and dependent concepts are both known but not yet the type of relation (deterministic or probabilistic) between them.

The research objective of a theory-building study that begins from this situation can be further specified as follows:

The objective of this study is to contribute to the development of theory regarding topic T {specify the object of study} by specifying the relation between concepts A and B {specify the independent and the dependent concept}.

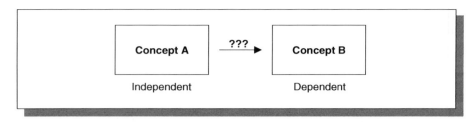

Figure 8.1
Conceptual model
with not yet known
relation

Note that such a theory-building study (rather than further exploration followed by testing) is only necessary and appropriate if no educated guess is possible about the most likely type of relation. In most situations in which we know the independent and dependent variables, we will also have an idea about the most likely relation between them. For instance, often practitioners will implicitly or explicitly talk about some factors as "having an influence" (implying a probabilistic relation), and about others as "critical". If it is said that concept A is quite likely a "critical" success factor for a project, it is implicitly defined as a necessary condition. In other words, it is quite rare that we genuinely do not know what the best formulation would be for a proposition expressing a relation between two already known concepts.

8.1.2 Discovering a not yet known concept

If we need to design and conduct theory-building research, it is more likely that this concerns a situation as represented in Figures 8.2 and 8.3, in which we know either the independent or the dependent concepts but do not yet know the other.

The research objective of a theory-building study that begins from such a situation, with one known and one unknown concept, can be further specified as follows:

> *The objective of this study is to contribute to the development of theory regarding topic T {specify the object of study} by finding an independent*

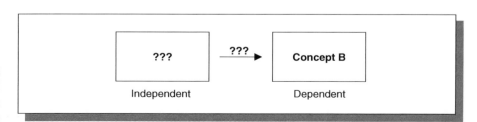

Figure 8.2
Conceptual model
with not yet known
determinants

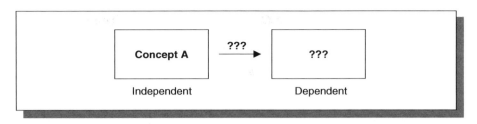

Figure 8.3
Conceptual model
with not yet known
effects

*concept A ("cause") for a known concept B {define the concept} or finding a
dependent concept B ("effect") for a known concept A {define the concept}
and, next, by specifying the relation between concepts A and B.*

We think that most theory-building research takes this form, in which
a cause must be found in order to explain a (desired or undesired) effect
or an effect must be found for a given cause.

8.1.3 Discovering concepts and their relation

A theory-building study might also start from the (probably quite rare)
situation in which there is no known concept (see Figure 8.4).

The research objective of such a theory-building study can be further specified as follows:

> *The objective of this study is to contribute to the development of theory regarding
> topic T {specify the object of study} by discovering and explaining a
> phenomenon of interest {specify the phenomenon}.*

On first sight, this appears to be a nonsensical aim. How could one
begin to conduct an empirical study with the aim of finding something
(concepts and a relation between them) without having any idea of
what one is searching for? But actually this is a quite common situation
in academic research, which is stimulated by the implicit or explicit
aim of "being original", meaning that it is a good thing to discover and
describe a phenomenon that no one has seen before. This is one of the
implicit aims of Grounded Theory (see 9.1.4).

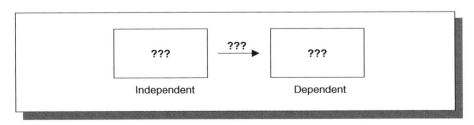

Figure 8.4
Conceptual model
that is entirely
empty

8.1.4 Discovering concepts

Figure 8.5
Not yet known
concept

A theory-building study might start from a strictly descriptive aim of discovering and describing concepts that might later become relevant for a theory (see Figure 8.5).

Often the objective of such a study is to build and describe a typology of a phenomenon of interest in order to get more insight into how the phenomenon looks in different situations, but without an attempt to explain the occurrence of specific types (by finding relations with independent factors) or to find or explain effects (by finding relations with dependent factors). The research objective of such a theory-building study can be specified as follows:

> *The objective of this study is to contribute to the development of theory regarding topic T {specify the object at study} by discovering and describing a phenomenon of interest {specify the phenomenon}.*

8.2 Principles of theory-building research

Propositions can be built by exploration and by theory-building research. Because exploration is *not* research, we think that it is important to define what is distinctive in theory-building *research*.

Research is building and testing statements by analysing evidence *drawn from observation*. Whereas it is perfectly acceptable in exploration to derive propositions from what practitioners (and other people) *say about the phenomenon* (whether or not this is based on evidence that is accessible to the researcher), propositions derived from theory-building research should be grounded in observations that can be justifiably seen as indicators or measurements of the concepts of the proposition that is built.

In theory-testing, the concepts of a proposition are operationalized in procedures that specify how they can be validly and reliably measured (see Appendix 1: "Measurement"). Although it looks as if the criteria of measurement validity and reliability do not apply in theory-building because the concepts emerge from the data, we consider it essential to good theory-building research (in comparison to mere exploration) that the emerging proposition is proven to be true in the instances of the object of study that are selected for the study. This implies that each concept that emerges from the research must be defined precisely (after its "emergence") and that it must be assessed whether the data, on the basis of which the concept was developed, can be considered valid and reliable indicators of the value of that concept in the instances studied. Measurement validity and reliability are, thus, equally important criteria for the quality of theory-building research as they are in any other type of research.

The same kind of reasoning as applied here to the measurement of concepts (which are discovered and described in the study itself) applies to the type of relations between concepts that is discovered in the study. If a proposition is developed in theory-building research, it should be demonstrated that the proposition is true in the instances from which scores were obtained (**internal validity**). This implies that the result of a theory-building study is not only one or more new propositions but also an initial test of them within the study.

8.3 Research strategies in theory-building research

We have described how the type of proposition (either deterministic or probabilistic) determines which research strategy is preferred in theory-testing (Chapter 4). However, the reason why we want to design a theory-building study is precisely because we do not yet have any proposition. How could we make a reasoned choice for one specific research strategy? We think that the most important criteria for this choice are efficiency and convenience. Because the only aim of the study is to generate propositions (that need to be tested in further studies anyway), it makes sense to keep the theory-building study as simple and cheap (in terms of time and costs) as possible, i.e. at the minimum level of investment that is necessary to generate some relevant propositions (or concepts). This is consistent with our preference for exploration in situations in which propositions need to be formulated.

The relative efficiency or convenience of different research strategies will differ for different topics or phenomena. But in general we advise selection of an appropriate research strategy in the following way:

1. decide whether experimental research would be useful and feasible, if not;
2. conduct a theory-building comparative case study.

Regarding point (1), above, theory-building experimental research is useful in principle in two following situations:

■ if an independent concept A is known and an independent concept B must be found; and
■ if both the independent and dependent concepts are known but not yet the type of their relation.

In these two situations an experiment could be designed and conducted in which the value of concept A is manipulated and the effects are observed. If the dependent concept B is known, its value will be measured in the different experimental situations defined by different values of the independent concept A. If the dependent concept B is not yet known, it must be discovered first. The value of the independent concept is experimentally varied and the experimenter attempts to discover interesting differences between the different experimental conditions (as well as with the control condition, if any). As mentioned earlier in the context of theory-testing research (Chapter 4), experimental research is usually not feasible in business research.

If an experiment is not feasible, then the principles of convenience and efficiency point to selecting only a small number of instances for observation (point (2), above). On the other hand, a minimum number of instances is required for several reasons. First, if the researcher does not know what the relevant factors or effects could be and does not know how the concepts in the resulting proposition will be related (e.g. in a deterministic or probabilistic way), it must be discovered whether there is a range of relevant causes or effects and, therefore, a range of diverse instances needs to be compared. But, second, if it is already known from the start that there is some evidence for a deterministic relation, an effect must be found consistently in more than one case (in order to find a candidate sufficient condition) or a cause in more than one case (in order to find a candidate necessary condition). In order to find other types of candidate relations (such as a deterministic relation or a probabilistic relation) even more cases are needed – three is the bare minimum. This means that the **comparative case study** is the preferred research strategy.

8.4 Outcome and implications

The outcome of a successful theory-building study usually consists of one or more new propositions that also have been put to an initial test. As discussed in Chapter 3, theory development consists of building propositions, testing them in an initial test, and enhancing robustness and generalizability through replications. This means that theory-building research always needs to be followed by testing in another instance of the object of study (or in other groups or populations).

8.5 Summary

This chapter can be summarized by the following list of four types of theory-building research:

- specifying a relation between two known concepts – proposition-building by an experiment, or a comparative case study;
- specifying a relation between a known (independent or dependent) concept and an as yet unknown (dependent or independent) concept – proposition-building by an experiment or a comparative case study;
- specifying a relation between as yet unknown independent and dependent concepts – proposition-building by a comparative case study;
- discovering and describing a relevant concept by a comparative case study.

We will discuss in detail how to design and conduct theory-building *case studies* in Chapter 9.

CHAPTER **9**

The theory-building
case study

In this chapter we assume that a theory-building research objective (of one of the four types discussed in Chapter 8) has been formulated and that, after it has been assessed that an experiment is not possible, it has been decided that a theory-building case study needs to be designed and conducted.

This chapter has the same structure as the preceding ones:

- 9.1 How to design and conduct a theory-building case study;
- 9.2 Case Study 5: Building propositions about the kind of company representatives involved in communication with providers of business services (by Wendy Van der Valk and Finn Wynstra);
- 9.3 Methodological reflection on Case Study 5.

9.1 How to design and conduct a theory-building case study

9.1.1 Introduction

This chapter deals with theory-building case study research, which is always a comparative case study. It discusses case selection, the discovery of yet unknown concepts, measurement, data presentation, and the manner in which relationships can be discovered in the obtained scores.

9.1.2 Candidate cases

Obviously, candidate cases should be instances from the object of study. The following two principles guide the identification of a smaller set of candidate cases: convenience, and the maximization of the likelihood that an existing relation between the concepts will be discovered. The latter principle requires that one or more sets of candidate cases be found (or constructed) which are as similar to each other in all respects apart from the independent and dependent concepts from which a proposition should be constructed. A difficulty in achieving this is that in most theory-building research one or both of these concepts are not known. The most efficient way of finding sets of "similar" instances is by identifying small populations in the theoretical domain and selecting cases from such a population.

9.1.3 Case selection

If a small population of similar instances is identified, some instances must be selected from this population in such a way that instances differ as much as possible in terms of the value of the known concept.

The number of cases to be selected depends on the type of the concepts that are known (i.e. concept B in Figure 8.2; concept A in Figure 8.3; concepts A and B in Figure 8.1) and the known variation of the value of these concepts in the list of candidate cases. For instance, if we are interested in discovering as yet unknown success factors for a project (Figure 8.2), it depends on the type of concept B how many cases (and what type of cases) should be selected. If B is dichotomous (presence or absence of success) we could begin with just a couple of instances of each possible value (e.g. success and lack of success). If B is measured as a rational or interval variable (e.g. if success is measured in amounts of money earned), variation in the value of that variable should be maximized. If we are interested in discovering as yet unknown effects of a given condition or intervention A (Figure 8.3), it depends on the type of concept A how many cases (and what type of cases) should be selected. If A is dichotomous, we could begin with just a couple of instances of each possible value (e.g. presence or absence of condition A). If A is measured as a rational or interval variable (e.g. the size of the workforce or the amount of money spent), variation in the value of that variable should be maximized. If both the concepts A and B are known (Figure 8.1), it is recommended to select cases in such a way that the variation in the value of both concepts is maximized.

If no concept is known at the beginning of the study (as depicted in Figures 8.4 and 8.5), cases cannot be selected on the basis of the variation of these concepts and must, therefore, be selected more or less randomly.

Box 12 Michael Porter's case selection

Michael Porter's theory on *The competitive advantage of nations* (1990) is based on case study research. Porter and his team wanted to find conditions for a nation's industries that could explain the success of a nation's global competitiveness. The theory focused on the strategies of firms rather than the strategies of nations, as "firms, not nations, compete in international markets". The team selected, from ten important trading nations, the companies that were internationally successful (the dependent concept). Then they identified the determinants that could explain the nation's success (the independent concepts).

Porter and his team found four determinants (four points of a "diamond") of a nation's success: (1) the nation's position in factors of production such as skilled labour or infrastructure; (2) demand conditions, the home-market demand for the industry's product or services; (3) related and supporting industries, the presence or absence in the nation of supplier industries and other related industries that are internationally competitive; and (4) firm strategy, structure, and rivalry, the conditions in the nation governing how companies are created, organized, and managed, as well as the nature of the domestic rivalry. These four determinants are *necessary* for achieving and sustaining competitive success, or as Porter (1990:73) puts it: "Advantages throughout the 'diamond' are necessary for achieving and sustaining competitive success in the knowledge-intensive industries that form the backbone of advanced economies".

Porter's case selection procedures are problematic for two main reasons. One is that, by not including non-successful companies or nations in his study, Porter is not able to distinguish between necessary and sufficient conditions on the one hand, or between necessary and trivial conditions on the other hand. If, for instance, the factors found could exist in any company or sector in an industrialized country, including non-successful ones, this would make the discovered determinants not less "necessary" but it would make them trivial for policy. Apparently, Porter implicitly relies on his readers' knowledge about conditions in non-successful companies and nations. The second reason is that this form of case selection prohibits finding probabilistic relations. If Porter had found only one single instance without the "necessary" determinants, he would not only have failed to identify the necessary condition but would also not have been able to find another type of relation between determinants and success. Porter's case selection procedures, thus, were appropriate *only* for finding candidate necessary conditions and he was lucky to find them.

9.1.4 Extracting relevant evidence

If the theory-building case study begins with a conceptual model with an unknown concept (as in Figures 8.2–8.5), candidate concepts must be found in the selected cases. If we start with known concepts and only need to find out what type of relation between these concepts should be formulated in the proposition (as in Figure 8.1), this phase can be skipped and the researcher can immediately start measuring the concepts (as described below in 9.1.5).

There is no specific "method" for how candidate concepts should be found in a theory-building case study. In principle "everything goes", just as in other types of exploration (described in Chapter 3). This exploration can take place in only one case, or in more than one case, or in all selected cases at the same time. There is one widely known method of discovering concepts through the comparison of data from multiple cases, Grounded Theory (GT). The GT literature, particularly the widely used textbook of Strauss and Corbin (1998), describes in detail how a concept can be discovered by (a) "coding" data (in a procedure that is called "open coding"), and (b) comparing these codes between different instances.

The result of this stage of the theory-building case study is a candidate concept for the initially unknown concept in the conceptual model with which the study started, as depicted in Figures 9.1 and 9.2.

Although the precise process of discovering concepts (candidate causes and effects) and its quality criteria cannot always be described clearly in exploratory activities, at some point such concepts emerge as

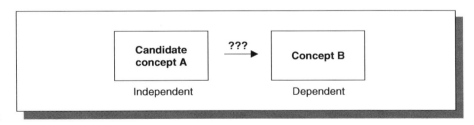

Figure 9.1
Conceptual model with candidate determinant

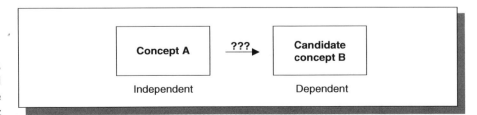

Figure 9.2
Conceptual model with candidate effect

an outcome. In our approach to the theory-building case study, the lack of criteria for the quality in this exploration activity is balanced by an emphasis on quality control after a candidate concept has been "discovered". This is discussed below.

9.1.5 Coding

If theory-building research stopped at the point depicted by Figures 9.1 and 9.2, and if the resulting candidate concepts in a publication were offered to other researchers for testing, the study would hardly qualify as research and could better be called a form of "intensive exploration". As we discussed in Chapter 8, we consider it essential to good theory-building research (in contrast to mere "exploration") that the emerging proposition is proven to be true in the instances studied and that, thus, the candidate concept is measured in a valid and reliable way in these instances. A first necessary step is that the concept is defined precisely after its "emergence". This step is not different in principle from how definitions of concepts are usually developed, i.e. if the researcher wants to define a concept that has not been "discovered" in theory-building research. The usual criteria such as precision and non-ambiguity apply.

Grounded Theory argues that, if a theory is "discovered", the definition of the concept should be "grounded" in the data collected in the study. For instance, Strauss and Corbin (1998) describe how a concept that is discovered in "open coding" can be refined and defined in a next step of coding (which they call "axial coding"). In our view, such a grounding of a definition is not a requirement for good theory-building research. However, an advantage of axial coding is that, when a concept is defined, its value in the different cases is already validly "measured" because the GT result consists of a definition of the concept *with* references to the data in which it was "grounded".

If a definition of a concept is derived in another (not "grounded") way, or if we start with known concepts (as in Figure 8.1), a next necessary step in the research is to develop a valid and reliable measurement instrument. Procedures for measurement are discussed in Appendix 1 "Measurement".

9.1.6 Data presentation

The result of a successful measurement is that the scores of the relevant concepts are known for each case. These scores can be presented in a **data matrix**. The simplest form is a matrix consisting of two columns, one for concept A and one for concept B, and a number of rows (one row for each case). This matrix is the basis for the final analysis of the theory-building case study.

9.1.7 Data analysis

The aim of this analysis is to draw a conclusion about (a) whether there is a relationship between the concepts A and B (or not) and, if so, (b) what type of relation this is.

We advise starting this process of "discovering" relations between concepts by determining whether the stronger types of causal relations (deterministic ones) are discernable in the data matrix and to look for weaker causal relations (probabilistic ones) if such stronger types are not found. The rationale of this procedure is that it is important to find strong causal relations (which, say, explain 100 per cent of variance) if they exist. Or, in other words, this procedure helps the researcher to avoid the error that only a probabilistic relation is discovered even in situations in which the data matrix contains evidence for stronger relations. The exploration of the data matrix is proposed in this order:

1. looking for a sufficient condition;
2. looking for a necessary condition;
3. looking for a deterministic relation;
4. looking for a probabilistic relation.

We will discuss now how this could be done.

9.1.7.1 Sufficient condition

First, assess whether there is evidence for a sufficient condition. A sufficient condition exists if a specific value of concept A *always* results in a specific value of concept B. The existence of a sufficient condition in the selected cases can be assessed by ordering the data matrix in such a way that cases with the same value of concept A are grouped together. If the value of concept B is constant in a subgroup of cases with the same value of A, then this can be taken as evidence that this specific value of A is a sufficient condition for the value of B observed in this subgroup of cases. This procedure is very similar to the way in which a sufficient condition is tested in a theory-testing case study. This relation can then be formulated as follows:

> *Proposition 1*: Value X_A of A is a sufficient condition for value X_B of B.

In this proposition, X_A is the value of A by which the subgroup is defined in which this relation was discovered (e.g. a minimum level of management commitment) and X_B is the value of B observed in that subgroup (e.g. success of a project).

9.1.7.2 Necessary condition

Next assess whether there is evidence for a necessary condition. A necessary condition exists if a specific value of concept B *only* exists if there is a specific value of concept A. The existence of a necessary condition can be assessed by ordering the data matrix in such a way that cases with the same value of concept B are grouped together. If the value of concept A is constant in a subgroup of cases with the same value of B, then this can be taken as evidence that the specific value of A is a necessary condition for the value of B. This relation can then be formulated as follows:

> *Proposition 2*: Value X_A of A is a necessary condition for value X_B of B.

In this proposition, X_B is the value of B by which the subgroup is defined in which this relation was discovered (e.g. success of a project) and X_A is the value of A observed in that subgroup (e.g. minimum level of management commitment).

9.1.7.3 Deterministic relation

Next assess whether there is evidence for a *deterministic relation*, meaning that an increase or decrease in the value of concept A consistently results in a change (in a consistent direction) in the value of concept B. The existence of a deterministic relation can be assessed by rank ordering the cases in the data matrix in accordance with the value of concept A. If, in the resulting rank order, the value of concept B consistently increases or decreases as well, then this can be taken as evidence that A and B have a deterministic relation. This relation can then be formulated as follows:

> *Proposition 3*: Concept A has a deterministic relation with concept B.

9.1.7.4 Probabilistic relation

Finally, assess whether there is evidence for a *probabilistic relation*, meaning that an increase or decrease in the value of concept A results in a higher chance of an increase or decrease in the value of concept B. The existence of a probabilistic relation can, again, be assessed by rank ordering the cases in the data matrix in accordance with the value of concept A. If, in the resulting rank order, the value of concept B seems also to increase or decrease, though not consistently, then this can be taken as evidence that A and B have a probabilistic relation. The same criteria for assessing whether the probabilistic relation actually exists between A and B (in this data set) apply as discussed in Chapter 7 for the testing of a probabilistic relation. This relation can then be formulated as followed:

> *Proposition 4*: Concept A has a probabilistic relation with concept B.

If correctly derived from the data (and, thus, proven to be true in the selected cases), the proposition is an appropriate result of the theory-building case study.

9.1.8 An example of data analysis

The following (invented) example of a data matrix generated in a theory-building study of factors that determine the success of innovation projects, shows ten very diverse cases, five with success and five without success (Table 9.1). The table has ten rows, one row for each case, four independent concepts (or "success" factors) and the dependent concept (absence or presence of success).

9.1.8.1 Sufficient condition

A sufficient condition exists if a specific value of concept A *always* results in a specific value of concept B. In this data matrix, we have four potential success factors and each value of each of these factors could be a sufficient condition for a specific value (Yes or No) of success.

If we look at all four cases with value high on management commitment, we see that they all have been successful, whereas the two cases with low levels of management commitment have been unsuccessful. A high level of management commitment, thus, seems to be a sufficient

Table 9.1

Data matrix regarding "success" factors of innovation projects

	Management commitment	Infrastructure	Investment in money	Team size	Success
Case 1	H	H	H	10	Y
Case 2	H	H	H	7	Y
Case 3	H	H	H	7	Y
Case 4	H	H	L	6	Y
Case 5	M	H	L	4	Y
Case 6	M	L	L	11	N
Case 7	M	H	L	6	N
Case 8	L	H	L	6	N
Case 9	M	L	L	3	N
Case 10	L	L	L	3	N

(H=high; M=medium; L=low; Y=yes; N=no)

condition for success (in this invented example), and a low level of management commitment seems to be a sufficient condition for lack of success. The resulting propositions, thus, are:

Proposition 1a: High management commitment is a sufficient condition for success of innovation projects.

Proposition 1b: Low management commitment is a sufficient condition for lack of success of innovation projects.

If these propositions are true, then it is clear how an innovation project could be made successful. However, these propositions have been *built* in this (invented) theory-building case study, and only initially tested.

If we continue our inspection with other potential success factors, we see that all three cases with a low value on the concept infrastructure have not been successful. This might lead to the formulation of a third proposition:

Proposition 1c: Low infrastructure is a sufficient condition for lack of success of innovation projects.

In the same way we could formulate further propositions about team size *three* being sufficient for lack of success, and team size *seven* being a sufficient condition for success. But these latter propositions seem to make little sense without additional propositions about the effects of other values of team size.

9.1.8.2 Necessary condition

A necessary condition exists if a specific value of concept B *only* exists if there is a specific value of concept A. In this data matrix, we have two values (Yes or No) of success and, therefore, we can see whether one or more of the potential success factors have the same value in each of the successful cases (Table 9.2) and, next, whether one or more of the potential success factors have the same value in each of the unsuccessful cases (Table 9.3).

We can see in Table 9.2 that only infrastructure has the same (high) value in all five successful projects. We can formulate this finding as follows:

> *Proposition 2a*: A high value of infrastructure is a necessary condition for success of innovation projects.

In the same way, we see in Table 9.3 that all five unsuccessful projects have a low level of investment. We can formulate this finding as follows:

> *Proposition 2b*: A low level of investment is a necessary condition for lack of success of innovation projects.

Table 9.2
Data matrix regarding successful innovation projects

	Management commitment	Infrastructure	Investment in money	Team size	Success
Case 1	H	H	H	10	Y
Case 2	H	H	H	7	Y
Case 3	H	H	H	7	Y
Case 4	H	H	L	6	Y
Case 5	M	H	L	4	Y

Table 9.3
Data matrix regarding unsuccessful innovation projects

	Management commitment	Infrastructure	Investment in money	Team size	Success
Case 6	M	L	L	11	N
Case 7	M	H	L	6	N
Case 8	L	H	L	6	N
Case 9	M	L	L	3	N
Case 10	L	L	L	3	N

9.1.8.3 Deterministic relation

A deterministic relation entails that an increase or decrease in the value of concept A consistently results in a change (in a consistent direction) in the value of concept B. This type of relation, thus, assumes that both the independent and the dependent concept have more than two values (and these values have a rank order). There is one independent concept that has more than two values in a rank order (management commitment), but the only dependent concept (success) has only two values. Therefore, we cannot identify a candidate deterministic relation in this data matrix.

9.1.8.4 Probabilistic relation

A probabilistic relation entails that an increase or decrease in the value of concept A results in a higher (or lower) chance of an increase or decrease in the value of concept B. The existence of a probabilistic relation can be assessed by rank ordering the cases in the data matrix in accordance with the value of concept A. If, in the resulting rank order, the value of concept B seems also to increase or decrease, though not consistently, then this can be taken as evidence that A and B have a probabilistic relation. In this data matrix, we can perform this procedure for all four independent concepts.

Table 9.4 supports the existence of a probabilistic relation between team size and success. Only two cases (case 5 and case 6) violate the

Table 9.4
Data matrix regarding team size

	Team size	Success
Case 6	11	N
Case 1	10	Y
Case 2	7	Y
Case 3	7	Y
Case 4	6	Y
Case 7	6	N
Case 8	6	N
Case 5	4	Y
Case 9	3	N
Case 10	3	N

Table 9.5

Data matrix regarding management commitment

	Management commitment	Success
Case 1	H	Y
Case 2	H	Y
Case 3	H	Y
Case 4	H	Y
Case 5	M	Y
Case 6	M	N
Case 7	M	N
Case 9	M	N
Case 8	L	N
Case 10	L	N

assumption that there is a deterministic relation between team size and success (which could be formulated as "Team size seven and up is sufficient for success" and "Team size lower than six is sufficient for lack of success"). The trend in this data matrix can be formulated as follows:

> *Proposition 3a*: The larger the team size, the more likely the success of an innovation project.

Table 9.5 supports the existence of a probabilistic relation between the independent concept management commitment and the dependent concept success. However, such a proposition would not add much to propositions 1a and 1b. Similarly, probabilistic relations between infrastructure and success and between investment and success that could be proposed do not add much to propositions 2a and 2b. These examples demonstrate how statistical tests in surveys, which suggest probabilistic relations, could easily hide factually existing deterministic relations. This is the reason why one always needs to look first for deterministic relations in theory-building research, before looking for probabilistic relations.

9.1.9 Outcome

The likely outcome of the discussed analytic procedures consists of one or more propositions. If the relationship between the concepts A and B in the data matrix is more or less random, the study has failed to generate propositions. If this is the case, another (perhaps more intensive) exploration might be attempted, which might result in other candidate concepts and hence other candidate propositions.

If the analysis has been performed in an appropriate way (i.e. if the procedures as described in the Chapters 5–7 for theory-testing have been applied correctly), then the resulting propositions are proven to be true in the set of selected cases from which these propositions have emerged. This implies that an initial test has been conducted and that replication studies can be designed and conducted.

Box 13 Building a theory on successfully helping city government

Yin (2003: 49) discusses Peter Szanton's (1981) book *Not well advised* as an "excellent example of a multiple-case replication design". This study, as presented by Yin, is not a replication study (in our definition of replication) but a good example of a theory-building comparative case study.

Szanton studied eight cases of attempts by university groups to collaborate with city officials, which all failed. Then he provides five more cases in which non-university groups failed as well. A third group of cases showed how university groups successfully helped businesses, not city government. A final set of three cases was successful in helping city government. The latter three groups "were concerned with implementation and not just with the production of new ideas, leading to the major conclusion that city governments may have peculiar needs in receiving advice". Two conclusions seem to have been formulated:

1. supporting city governments is successful if there is an implementation of the newly generated ideas; and
2. city governments have other needs than businesses. (This conclusion is presented by Yin as "the major one".)

Neither of these two conclusions is the result of replication, because the concept of replication concerns conducting a next test after initial testing. No initial proposition was formulated in this study and no testing was conducted, so there was no instance of replication in this study. Both conclusions are the result of theory-building through a comparative case study.

Proposition 1, stating that "being concerned with implementation" is a necessary condition for successfully helping city governments, might have been based on an inspection of the data matrix of the 16 (8 + 5 + 3) groups that tried to help a city government, provided that there is sufficient evidence for the absence of implementation activities in the 13 non-successful groups. Proposition 2, stating that "city governments have peculiar needs", might have been inferred from an inspection of the data matrix of the six (3 + 3) successful groups, provided that there is sufficient evidence for the absence of implementation activities in the three groups that successfully supported businesses.

Building propositions about the kind of company representatives involved in communication with providers of business services[1]

by Wendy Van der Valk and Finn Wynstra

9.2.1 Introduction

Research in purchasing has traditionally focused on the procurement of (industrial) goods. The purchase of services, however, is substantially different from the purchase of goods (Fitzsimmons *et al.*, 1998; Axelsson and Wynstra, 2002; Smeltzer and Ogden, 2002). The basic characteristics of services (intangibility, heterogeneity, and perishability) affect the purchase process in such a way that some of its aspects become more important, more difficult, or just different in comparison with the purchase process for goods (Axelsson and Wynstra, 2002). The services marketing discipline has continuously emphasized that services are being produced in interactive processes between customers and service providers (Lovelock, 1983; Zeithaml and Bitner, 1996; Grönroos, 2000). Researchers in the field of purchasing seem to have failed to acknowledge this characterizing aspect of continuous interaction.

Our study focuses specifically on the ongoing interaction between the buying and providing companies after the purchase decision (i.e. collaboration during the contract period). An interaction between buyer and provider does not only take place at the moment that products and/or services are sold and purchased (exchanged) but also after the transaction, when the service has become part of the business of the buyer. Then there is an ongoing business relation between buyer and provider. Elements of the buyer–provider interaction during ongoing service exchange that might vary are:

- the frequency of the interaction;
- the intensity of the interaction;

---

[1] This Chapter is based on: Van der Valk, W., F. Wynstra, and B. Axelsson (2006), "Identifying buyer-seller interaction patterns in ongoing service exchange: Results of two explorative case studies," Internal working paper, May 2006.

■ the type of buyer and provider representatives (hierarchical and functional scope of the customer–supplier contacts (Cunningham and Homse, 1986)).

Wynstra *et al.* (2006) propose a classification of business services based on how the buying company uses the service with respect to its own offerings. They claim that this usage dimension is one of the main determinants of how buyer–seller interaction processes should be designed. They distinguish between four types of services.

1. *Consumption services*: these services remain within the buying company and do not affect how the buying company's primary processes are carried out (e.g. office cleaning services for an airline).
2. *Instrumental services*: these services remain within the buying company and affect how the buying company's primary processes are carried out (e.g. information and communication technology services used to support flight operations).
3. *Semi-manufactured services*: these services are used as an input by the buying organization for particular offerings to final customers and are thus passed on to end customers of the buying company (e.g. weather forecasts which are transformed into specific flight schedules).
4. *Component services*: these services are directly passed on to end customers of the buying company (e.g. baggage handling at the airport).

Wynstra *et al.* (2006) suggest that the type of service affects:

■ the key objectives of the interaction;
■ the type of representatives involved on the buying company's and the service provider's side; and
■ the capabilities deemed critical for buyer and service provider.

Van der Valk *et al.* (2006) claim that variation with regard to these effects may be stronger for services that the buying company perceives as having high risk.

In the present study we are, specifically, interested in how experienced buying companies organize their interactions with the service provider with respect to the type of representatives that deal with the interaction. We assume that buying companies have implicit "theories" about which types of representatives are needed for the success of a purchase of a service, and that they differentiate their representation according to the different types of services. Based on previous research and discussions with buyers, we also assume that these companies will estimate the risk involved in purchasing a service and that they take this into account as well in their decisions about who is going to represent the company in the after-purchase ongoing interaction. Based on these assumptions, we decided to build a theory of how buying companies actually organize their interaction in terms of the selection of the kind of representatives that are involved in the buyer–provider interaction for the four types of services and with different levels of perceived risk.

9.2.2 Candidate cases

Because the entities to which our theory applies are instances of the ongoing interaction between buyers and providers of business services after the purchase of such a service, we needed to look into a number of instances ("cases") of ongoing interaction between buyers and providers of business services. Because our ultimate aim is to build a theory of how the type of interaction influences the success of the purchase, we thought that we should limit this theory-building study only to instances in which the buying companies are experienced buyers of services and are generally successful in these purchases.

We selected cases from buyer companies that are service companies themselves (and not manufacturers) for two reasons. First, we presumed that service companies have a more professional approach to buying services than manufacturing companies. Second, we expected that the chances of finding two types of services that are passed on to the end customers of the buying company (the component and semi-manufactured services), were larger at service providers than at manufacturers. We purposefully aimed at selecting large companies with professional purchasing organizations, since we thought it likely that buyer–provider interaction patterns developed by these companies would reflect their tacit knowledge of what works well in terms of the eventual success of the purchase.

We conducted our study at two buying companies as opposed to one company, for two reasons: (1) to have multiple observations for each value of the independent concept (the type of service); and (2) to be able to determine whether the variation observed is consistent/systematic across buying companies, even if these are quite different. We selected two service companies that are very different.

One is a *routine* service provider, i.e. a company that solves relatively simple problems for its customers (Axelsson and Wynstra, 2002). Such routine services usually involve large numbers of similar, rather standardized transactions (e.g. establishing ADSL connections, mobile telephony services). We selected *KPN Royal Dutch Telecom*, market leader in the major segments of the Dutch telecom market, as the routine service provider in this study.

The other is a *professional* service provider (knowledge provider), i.e. a company that solves complex problems (Axelsson and Wynstra, 2002). Transactions are substantial and involve considerable creative moments in direct contact with the supplier (e.g. reintegration trajectories for employees that have been ill or unemployed, conducting medical examinations). We selected *UWV*, a Dutch institution with about 18,000 employees responsible for the administration and implementation of insured benefits for around 1,000,000 employees in the Netherlands, as the professional service provider in this study.

9.2.3 Case selection

KPN and UWV were contacted by means of a formal letter, followed up by a telephone call to set up an introductory meeting. During this first meeting, the case study protocol (in which it was specified how the study would be conducted, how much time would be required from company representatives, etc.) was discussed with the buying company's primary contact person in order to give the company a clear idea of what we expected from them and what they could expect from us. After the companies had agreed to participate, a next meeting with the contact person was set up to identify the services to be studied (one instance of each of the four types of services in each company). KPN offered us the opportunity to study two instrumental services in-depth. Since our informant associated these services with differing degrees of success (one highly successful, one not successful at all), we included them both in our study.

The cases selected at KPN and UWV are listed and briefly described in Tables 9.6A and 9.6B. As the study progressed, the two cases that were originally selected in the semi-manufactured category were found to fit better in the category of component services. Rather than selecting new semi-manufactured cases, we decided to reclassify these cases as component services.

9.2.4 Extracting relevant evidence

We collected data through semi-structured interviews. For each service, two to three interviews were conducted. One interview with the *buyer* involved in sourcing the service focused mainly on the purchasing process, whereas an interview with the *contract owners* and/or a *user*

Table 9.6A

Selected cases, descriptions, and informants KPN

Type	Service	Informants
Component	Call centre	■ Category Manager Marketing and Call Centre Services ■ Human Resources Representative Call Centre
Component	Construction activities at office buildings and homes (e.g. for ADSL connections)	■ Category Manager Construction and Engineering
Instrumental	IT outsourcing	■ Manager Group Category ICT ■ Chief Information Officer Royal KPN ■ Former Chief Information Officer Division Fixed
Instrumental	Marketing (media, promotions, PR agency, market research, and contents)	■ Category Manager Marketing and Call Centre Services ■ Category Purchaser Marketing Communications ■ Category Purchaser
Consumption	Temporary labour (e.g. people that come to help clean out cupboards ("hands"))	■ Manager Procurement Professional, Financial and HR Services ■ Human Resources Representative Call Centre

Table 9.6B

Selected cases, descriptions, and informants UWV

Type	Service	Informants
Component	Pension administration (collecting fees from employers, carrying the administration of these fees, and making payments to pensioners)	■ Senior Buyer Personnel and Organization ■ Secretarial Officer Pension Fund
Component	Payment of social benefits (executing payments on behalf of UWV)	■ Senior Buyer Facilities ■ Manager Cash Management
Instrumental	Office automation (software, hardware, and generic services)	■ Senior Buyer ICT ■ Project Leader European Tender Office Automation
Consumption	Office infrastructure (phone, Internet) including occupancy administration and maintenance of workspaces	■ Senior Buyer ■ Portfolio Manager Work Unit Services ■ Service Manager

focused on what happened after the purchase. Most often, the buyer involved was approached first. Other informants were usually identified by the buyer. The informants for each service are listed in Tables 9.6A and 9.6B.

The interviews lasted about 1.5–2 hours each because we also collected data about a variety of other dependent concepts (capabilities, key objectives, communication and adaptation, and success), as well as about the level of buyer-perceived risk associated with the service to be purchased. The list of interview questions was based on the questionnaires used in similar studies conducted by the Industrial Marketing and Purchasing (IMP) Group (Håkansson, 1982). This allowed for the collection of a large amount and wide variety of information (informants could say whatever they deemed relevant) while at the same time ensuring that information about all relevant topics would be obtained. Extensive summaries were made of each interview, which were sent back to the interviewees for verification. These summaries were merged into descriptions at case level, which were again sent to the interviewees in order to eliminate any inconsistencies and to provide further clarification if necessary.

Specifically to investigate what kind of people interacted with the supplying company after the purchase of the service, the following questions were asked in each interview:

- Which departments/functions are primarily involved in the interactions?
- Which departments/functions are involved in managing the ongoing supply after the purchase of a service? How does this take place?
- Which departments/functions are involved in managing the supplier? How does this take place?
- Who are the counterparts of these functions on the supplier side?

The representatives involved in interaction with the service provider are shown in Table 9.7A.

The answers to the question about the level of buyer-perceived risk associated with the service to be purchased are summarized in Table 9.7B (where H = high, M = medium, L = low).

9.2.5 Coding

In order to facilitate comparison of observations for building propositions, we categorized the different representatives in terms of the

Table 9.7A

Representatives involved in interaction with the service provider

	Representatives involved at KPN	Representatives involved at UWV
Component 1	■ Purchasing (category manager) ■ Business division representatives	■ Representatives board pension fund ■ Representatives employer's pension bureau ■ Purchasing ■ External consultant
Component 2	■ Procurement ■ Business representatives	■ Director financial–economic affairs ■ Cash management department ■ Purchasing ■ Legal representatives ■ External consultant
Instrumental 1	■ IT ■ Procurement ■ Legal ■ Former director IT business divisions ■ Higher management	■ Director ICT ■ Purchasing ■ Contract management ■ Legal ■ Service management ■ Architects
Instrumental 2	■ Purchasing (category manager) ■ Marketing/communications ■ Business stakeholders	
Consumption	■ Level and type of involvement depends on type of temporary labour being purchased	■ Legal ■ Financial control ■ ICT control ■ Service management ■ Facility experts ■ External people

Table 9.7B

Level of perceived risk

	Consumption		Instrumental			Component			
	KPN	UWV	KPN1	KPN2	UWV	KPN1	KPN2	UWV1	UWV2
Risk	L	L	H	M	H	H	L	H	H

different value-creating functions distinguished by Porter (1985: 45–48). In addition to his seven functions, we included an eighth one, "internal customer", in order to avoid confusion between involving a discipline because of its specific functional expertise on the one hand, and involving it because it is the user of the service on the other hand.

Regarding consumption services, at UWV ICT has a dual role being both the internal customer and having a sub-department, which is involved with production of the service. Because the ICT department's main role is that of internal customer, representatives in UWV were categorized as representing the internal customer.

For the instrumental services, in the case of KPN1, IT specialists perform the role of business process engineers, aligning the service provider's operations with KPN's. Various business representatives are involved in the role of internal customer. For UWV, people from service management (operational ICT representatives) are occupied with the daily management of the service provider, and thus with actual service delivery processes. We categorized the participation of higher management in these two service purchases, as well as the participation of accounting representatives and external consultants at UWV as representing infrastructure. For KPN2, the marketing discipline performs the role of process engineers, bringing the activities of marketing agencies in line with KPN's business strategy. At the same time, marketing is the internal customer of the marketing agencies.

Regarding the component services, legal representatives at UWV as well as an external consultant were categorized as representing infrastructure.

9.2.6 Data presentation

Scores obtained through this coding procedure are presented in Table 9.8. The marked cells in this table indicate the presence of involvement of a representative from one of the eight categories (rows) in an instance of service purchase (columns).

9.2.7 Data analysis

An initial inspection of Table 9.8 shows three things:

1. within each service type the cases have a relatively similar set of representatives that are involved in the interaction;
2. between the service types the set of representatives that is involved in the interaction is different;
3. purchasing representatives are involved in all cases for all types of services.

Because no variation occurs with regard to purchasing involvement across the different types of services, purchasing involvement will be excluded from the analysis.

Table 9.8

Type of buying company representatives involved

| | Type of Service | | | | | | | | |
| | Consumption | | Instrumental | | | Component | | | |
	Case 1 KPN	Case 2 UWV	Case 3 KPN1	Case 4 KPN2	Case 5 UWV	Case 6 KPN1	Case 7 KPN2	Case 8 UWV1	Case 9 UWV2
Risk	L	L	H	M	H	H	L	H	H
Marketing/sales						☼		☼	☼
Process engineers			☼	☼	☼				
Production (service delivery)					☼				☼
Infrastructure			☼		☼			☼	☼
Procurement	☼	☼	☼	☼	☼	☼	☼	☼	☼
HRM									
Technology									
Internal customer	☼	☼	☼	☼	☼		☼		

Regarding *consumption services,* we formulate the following proposition with the form of a *sufficient* condition:

> *Proposition 1a (P1a):* In ongoing interaction associated with *consumption services,* representatives of the internal customers are always involved.

This proposition formulates what is common to the two cases (1 and 2) of a purchase of a consumption service in this study. For the *instrumental services* we formulate the following proposition with the form of a *sufficient* condition:

> *Proposition 1b (P1b):* In ongoing interaction associated with *instrumental services,* people representing the primary processes of the buying company are always involved, as well as representatives of internal customers.

This proposition formulates what is common to all three cases of a purchase of an instrumental service in this study. It does, therefore, not include a statement about the representatives of infrastructure or of production because there were contradicting findings in the three cases for this type of service.

Regarding the *component services*, we formulate the following proposition with the form of a *sufficient* condition:

> *Proposition 1c (P1c):* In ongoing interaction associated with *component services with a high level of perceived risk*, representatives of external customers (often the marketing discipline) are always involved.

This proposition formulates what is common to the three cases (6, 8, and 9) of a purchase of a component service with high level of perceived risk, because the instance with low perceived risk (case 7) shows a very different pattern. Here, procurement represents the *internal customer*. The pattern observed in case 7 is similar to the pattern for consumption services, which are also purchases with a low perceived risk. Based on these observations, we develop the following proposition with the form of a *sufficient* condition:

> *Proposition 2 (P2):* Services associated with a *low level of perceived risk* always have a similar pattern of interaction, namely one in which only representatives of the internal customers are always involved. This pattern equally applies to each of the service types, and is different from the pattern associated with a service of that same type characterized by a moderate to high level of perceived risk.

P2 is derived from observations about the three instances in this study of purchases with a low perceived risk. Because we do not have an instance of a purchase of an instrumental service with low risk in our study, we have no indication whether *P2* would apply to the purchase of instrumental services as well. In order to stay closer to the data we have, we reformulate *P1b* as follows:

> *P1b:* In ongoing interaction associated with *instrumental services with moderate to high levels of perceived risk*, people representing the primary processes of the buying company are always involved, as well as representatives of internal customers.

9.2.8 Outcome

In this theory-building case study we found that buying companies distinguish between different types of services and organize their activities accordingly. Our data suggest that for the different types of services different types of representatives from the buying company are involved in after-purchase contact.

The following propositions have been built in this study:

> *P2*: Services associated with a *low level of perceived risk* have a pattern of interaction in which only representatives of the internal customers are always involved.

> *P1a*: In ongoing interaction associated with *consumption services*, representatives of the internal customers are always involved.

> *P1b*: In ongoing interaction associated with *instrumental services with a moderate to high level of perceived risk*, people representing the primary processes of the buying company are always involved, as well as representatives of internal customers.

> *P1c*: In ongoing interaction associated with *component services with a high level of perceived risk*, representatives of external customers (often the marketing discipline) are always involved.

All four propositions represent a sufficient condition.

These results have been presented in a round-table meeting with representatives from KPN and UWV. We regard the feedback obtained during the round-table meeting to support our idea that the propositions we developed are relevant. The nature of the relationship between the type of representatives involved and success needs to be specified and tested in future research projects.

9.3 Methodological reflection on Case Study 5

9.3.1 Justification of a theory-building case study

Case Study 5 starts implicitly with a proposition with an empty space at the position of the dependent concept. This proposition has a form (Figure 9.3), similar to Figure 8.3.

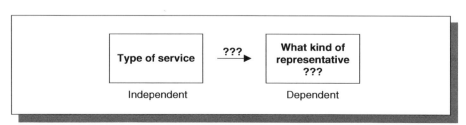

Figure 9.3
Proposition with unknown dependent concept

At the beginning of this study it was known which *kind* of dependent concept was sought, namely the variation in the composition of the teams of representatives of the buying company that interact with representatives of the supplying company. It was, however, not known what the relevant *concept* was by which this variation could be characterized, nor was there a proposition available which linked the variation of the values of this as yet unknown concept to different types of services that were bought.

No information is given about whether any "exploration" (as meant in Chapter 3) was attempted. The results of the round-table meeting with company representatives, mentioned in 9.2.8, suggest that an exploration could have been quite successful. These company representatives might have been able to generate versions of the propositions that have been built in this study.

Because the type of service that is bought by a company cannot be experimentally manipulated, it is clear that an experiment was not feasible.

9.3.2 Candidate cases

Our advice is to find a candidate case for theory-building research in small populations in the theoretical domain. The proposition that had to be built in this study (then still a proposition with an empty space) concerned the domain of communications between buyers and sellers of business services after the purchase of such a service. Because the authors of this study had built contacts with a large network of purchasing managers in the Netherlands, they were able to identify a number of Dutch companies that had been buying services, and they knew that they might be able to collect data on interaction patterns regarding these purchases by getting access through these purchasing managers.

Within this set of Dutch companies, the search for candidate cases was limited to large companies with professional purchasing organizations that are service companies themselves. This choice of large companies with professional purchasing organizations made sense indeed, if the aim of the study was not just to find relations between type of service and type of interaction in the broad spectrum of all instances of a purchase of a service, but rather was more specifically aimed at finding such relations in companies with much experience in purchasing services.

9.3.3 Case selection

The criterion of maximum variation of the value of the known concept required that at least two instances of a purchase per type of service should be selected. It would have been acceptable for this theory-building study to select cases (i.e. instances of a service purchase) from the small population of all such purchases in one company. This would enhance the chance of finding specific relations between type of service and kind of representative, but the resulting propositions would next need to be tested in other groups or populations (i.e. other companies and types of companies). It could be possible that the propositions built in the study would only hold in the one company in which they were found. In order to avoid this scenario, cases were selected from two different companies. By doing this, the chance of finding an effect of the type of purchased service on the kind of representative involved in the communication was reduced (which could be overshadowed by the effects of differences in policy between the companies in the way they select representatives) but at the same time it increased the likelihood that found propositions would be robust in replication tests.

9.3.4 Extracting relevant evidence

Data were collected by asking informants which departments/functions were involved in managing the ongoing supply after the purchase of a service. The answers that were obtained are listed in Table 9.7. In order to translate these various answers into values of one concept, the seven value-creating functions described by Porter (1985: 45–48) were applied. An eighth value of this concept was added based on the data that had been collected, namely the value "internal customer" (i.e. a representative of the users of the service) as distinct from persons with a functional expertise. The result of the study thus far is depicted in Figure 9.4.

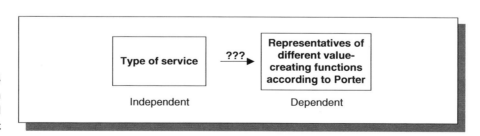

Figure 9.4
Proposition
with discovered
dependent concept

9.3.5 Coding

Although Porter's functions are not defined in this text, there is no reason to doubt the valid and reliable coding of the collected data (represented in Table 9.7A) in terms of these functions (as represented in Table 9.8). No information is given about how the level of perceived risk was coded. Probably the company informants were asked to rate the level of risk for each purchased service as either high, or medium, or low. The reclassification of some services that originally had been considered semi-manufactured services as component services suggests that the independent concept had been measured validly and reliably.

9.3.6 Data presentation

The obtained scores are presented in the format of a data matrix (Table 9.8).

9.3.7 Data analysis

In 9.1 "How to design and conduct a theory-building case study", we advise to assess first whether there is evidence for a *sufficient* condition. A sufficient condition exists if a specific value of the independent concept *always* results in a specific value of the dependent concept. This means that it must be assessed for every value of the independent concept whether a specific dependent concept is always present. In this study, inspection was needed of the three different types of service that were left after the semi-manufactured services were reclassified as component services *and* at the level of buyer-perceived risk of each project.

It appears that a representative of procurement is always present. Because this appears to be a constant, not a concept, it can be left out of the analysis.

Table 9.9, which is identical to Table 9.8, clearly shows in the first two columns (case 1 and case 2) that a representative of the internal customer was always present in consumption services (CNS). Based on these findings it can be argued that purchasing a consumption service is a sufficient condition for having a representative of the

Table 9.9

Type of buying company representatives involved

	Consumption		Instrumental			Component			
	Case 1 KPN	Case 2 UWV	Case 3 KPN1	Case 4 KPN2	Case 5 UWV	Case 6 KPN1	Case 7 KPN2	Case 8 UWV1	Case 9 UWV2
Risk	L	L	H	M	H	H	L	H	H
Marketing/ sales						☼		☼	☼
Process engineers			☼	☼	☼				
Production (service delivery)				☼					☼
Infrastructure			☼		☼			☼	☼
Procurement	☼	☼	☼	☼	☼	☼	☼	☼	☼
HRM									
Technology									
Internal customer	☼	☼	☼	☼	☼		☼		

internal customer function involved in the interaction (*P1a*). In the same way it is argued from columns case 3, case 4, and case 5 that purchasing an instrumental service is a sufficient condition for having a representative of the internal customer function, as well as one from the process engineers function, involved in the interaction (*P1b*). Regarding component services (CMP), the only commonality between the four instances is the representation of procurement. However, there is a clear common pattern for the three instances with a high perceived risk, namely involvement of marketing/sales, which was interpreted as representing the external customer. It is argued that purchasing a component service with a high perceived risk is a sufficient condition for having a representative of the external customer function involved in the interaction (*P1c*). This leaves component service KPN2 to be interpreted. If purchases with low perceived risk are grouped together, a common pattern is discernable, namely representation of the internal customer. It is argued that a purchase of a service with a low perceived risk is a sufficient condition for having a representative of (only) the internal customer function involved in the interaction (*P2*).

9.3.8 Outcome

Each of the four propositions that have been formulated in this study would have been proven to be true if this had been a theory-testing study in which these four propositions were tested. They now, however, need to be tested in further studies. Alternatively, as proposed in Case Study 5, they could be used as building blocks of other propositions, e.g. on factors that influence or determine the success of a purchase of a service.

Box 14 Other propositions that can be derived from Table 9.9

In Case Study 5, evidence was found for *sufficient* conditions in which the type of service determines the representation.

Table 9.9 also gives evidence for certain *necessary* conditions. A necessary condition exists if a specific value of the independent concept *cannot exist without* a specific value of the independent concept. This means that every value of the dependent concept must be assessed to see whether a specific independent concept is always present. When looking at the eight functions that might be represented in the ongoing interaction after the purchase, four propositions, each representing that the type of service is a necessary condition, can be formulated:

P3a: Marketing/sales (representing the external customer) is only involved in ongoing interaction if the type of service is a component service.

P3b: Process engineers only are involved in ongoing interaction if the type of service is an instrumental service.

P3c: Infrastructure is only involved in ongoing interaction if the type of service is an instrumental service or a component service.

P3d: Production is only involved in ongoing interaction associated with component services.

However, for the goal of the present study, these types of necessary conditions are less relevant.

Based on the dataset of Table 9.9, P3c could also have been formulated as a probabilistic proposition, stating that the chance of involvement of infrastructure in ongoing interaction is higher with instrumental services than with component services, and is higher with component services than with consumption services. We advise first to develop and test propositions on deterministic conditions and, only later, if test results show that such deterministic propositions cannot hold, to reformulate them as probabilistic ones.

9.4 References

Axelsson, B. and Wynstra, F. 2002, *Buying business services*. Chichester: Wiley.

Cunningham, M.T. and Homse, E. 1986, Controlling the marketing–purchasing interface: resource development and organisational implications. *Industrial Marketing and Purchasing*, 1: 3–27.

Fitzsimmons, J.A., Noh, J., and Thies, E. 1998, Purchasing business services. *Journal of Business and Industrial Marketing*, 13(4/5): 370–380.

Grönroos, C. 2000, *Service management and marketing: a customer relation management approach* (2nd edn). Chichester: John Wiley & Sons Ltd.

Håkansson, H. (ed.) 1982, *International marketing and purchasing of industrial goods: an interaction approach*. London: Wiley.

Lovelock, C.H. 1983, Classifying services to gain strategic marketing insights. *Journal of Marketing*, 47: 9–20.

Porter, M.E. 1990, The competitive advantage of nations. *Harvard Business Review*, March–April: 73–93.

Porter, M.E. 1985, *Competitive advantage: creating and sustaining superior performance*. New York: The Free Press.

Smeltzer, L.R. and Ogden, J.A. 2002, Purchasing professionals' perceived differences between purchasing materials and purchasing services. *Journal of Supply Chain Management*, 38(1): 54.

Strauss, A.L. and Corbin, J. 1998, *Basics of qualitative research: techniques and procedures for developing grounded theory*. Thousand Oaks (CA): Sage.

Szanton, P. 1981, *Not well advised*. New York: Russell Sage Foundation and The Ford Foundation.

Van der Valk, W., Wynstra, F., and Axelsson, B. 2006, Identifying buyer–seller interaction patterns in ongoing service exchange: results of two explorative case studies. Internal working paper, May 2006.

Wynstra, F., Axelsson, B., and Van der Valk, W. 2006, An application-based classification to understand buyer–supplier interaction in business services. *International Journal of Service Industry Management*, 17: 474–496.

Yin, R.K. 2003, *Case study research: design and methods* (3rd, revised edn). Thousand Oaks (CA): Sage.

Zeithaml, V.A. and Bitner, M.J. 1996, *Services marketing*. Singapore: McGraw-Hill Companies, Inc.

Part IV

Practice-oriented research

CHAPTER **10**

Practice-oriented research (general)

The objective of practice-oriented research is to contribute to the knowledge of a specific practitioner (not practitioners in general). A practitioner is a person or group of persons with either a formal or an informal responsibility for a real life situation in which he acts or must act. A practitioner can be a person (a manager, an entrepreneur, a policy maker, a staff member, etc.) or a group of persons (a team, a company, a business sector, a nation, etc.). A practitioner needs knowledge to solve or clarify a "problem" in an identified practice.

We define a practice as the real life situation for which a practitioner has either a formal or an informal responsibility and in which he acts or must act. For practice-oriented research, the general objective of the research can be formulated as follows (see 3.1.1):

> *The general objective of this study is to contribute to the knowledge of practitioner P {specify the practitioner by mentioning a name and by referring to the real life context in which this practitioner acts or must act}.*

This very general format of a practice-oriented research objective must be further specified as one of three different types; (a) **hypothesis-testing research**, (b) **hypothesis-building research**, or (c) **descriptive research**. We described in 3.3.3 how this specification could be achieved through an exploration of practice followed by an exploration of theory (see Flowchart 3).

Flowchart 3
Deciding on the type of practice-oriented research

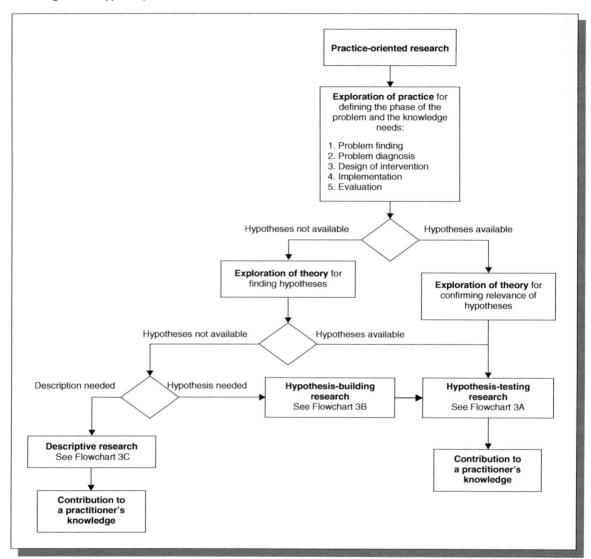

10.1 Hypothesis-testing research

The exploration of practice and of theory might have resulted in the formulation of a knowledge need that includes one or more hypotheses. An example is a practitioner's need to know whether it is true that "some projects are not successful because they lack top management commitment". Next it might have been decided that it is useful to test one or more of these hypotheses in order to get the knowledge that is relevant for making decisions in the current phase of the problem.

In order to check whether hypothesis-testing is appropriate, the following questions could be raised.

- Do relevant parties agree on the phase of the problem in the intervention cycle?
- Do relevant parties agree that the research question that is formulated is the most relevant in the current circumstances?
- Is it agreed that the hypotheses as formulated must be tested in order to get satisfactory and useful knowledge?

If the answers to such questions are conclusive, hypothesis-testing research needs to be designed and conducted.

10.1.1 Research objective in hypothesis-testing research

If it is decided after a successful exploration that *hypothesis-testing research* is needed, the general research objective for such research can be formulated as follows:

The objective of this study is to contribute to the knowledge regarding problem P {specify here the problem and its phase in the intervention cycle} by testing the following hypotheses H:

- {specify hypothesis H1}
- {specify hypothesis H2}
- {… etc.}.

The format of this research objective is similar to the format of theory-testing research. The obvious differences regard (a) the overall orientation to either a contribution to the development of a theory or to the development of a practitioner's knowledge, and (b) the terminology (proposition or hypothesis). In the context of practice-oriented research we use the word hypothesis rather than proposition because this research does not aim at contributing to theory (see Box 7 in 3.3.3).

Similar to the propositions in theory-testing research, hypotheses must be specified before an appropriate research strategy can be chosen. As with propositions, we distinguish four types of hypotheses:

- hypotheses that express that variable A is a *sufficient condition* for variable B;

■ hypotheses that express that variable A is a *necessary condition* for variable B;

■ hypotheses that express a *deterministic relation* between variable A and variable B.

Within the category of probabilistic hypotheses we have one type:

■ hypotheses that express a probabilistic relation between variable A and variable B.

10.1.2 Research strategy in hypothesis-testing research

Table 10.1 depicts the preferred research strategies for testing the different types of *hypotheses*. This table is the same as Table 4.2, which depicts the preferred research strategies for testing the different types of *propositions*. After it is specified whether the hypothesis expresses a deterministic condition, a deterministic relation, or a probabilistic relation, the appropriate research strategy can be chosen.

The *experiment* is the preferred research strategy for testing all types of hypothesis. If the experiment is not feasible, the *survey* is the second-best research strategy for testing a probabilistic relation. The *single case study* is the second-best research strategy for testing hypotheses that express a sufficient condition or a necessary condition. The case study (either the *longitudinal single case study* or the *comparative case study*) is the second-best strategy for testing a deterministic relation and the comparative case study is the third-best strategy for testing a probabilistic relation.

The one important difference between hypothesis-testing research and theory-testing research is the domain from which instances are selected for the test. Instances of the object of study (or groups of instances or populations) in theory-oriented research must be selected from the theoretical domain to which the theory is assumed to apply. The aim of practice-oriented hypothesis-testing research is not to prove or to test

Table 10.1

Preferred research strategies for testing different types of hypotheses

Hypothesis	Experiment	Case study	Survey
Sufficient condition	Preferred	Second-best (single case study)	Third-best
Necessary condition	Preferred	Second-best (single case study)	Third-best
Deterministic relation	Preferred	Second-best (longitudinal single case study or comparative case study)	Third-best
Probabilistic relation	Preferred	Third-best (comparative case study)	Second-best

whether a theoretical relation (which is generalizable to a theoretical domain) exists, but whether a hypothesis is correct for the practice for which the study wants to be locally relevant. We call this the **practice domain**, which is the universe of instances of the object of study in practice-oriented research. Therefore, instances must be selected from the practice to which the research is oriented or from other practices that are similar. Apart from this difference regarding the domain (practice-related or local, versus theoretical or global), principles of selection of instances are the same in practice-oriented research and in theory-oriented research.

Because the design of the experiments and single case studies for testing a hypothesis that expresses a *sufficient* condition is almost identical to the design of the research for testing a hypothesis that expresses a *necessary* condition (as discussed in Chapter 5), we group these two forms together in one type of hypothesis-testing research. Summarizing,

Flowchart 3A
Hypothesis-testing practice-oriented research

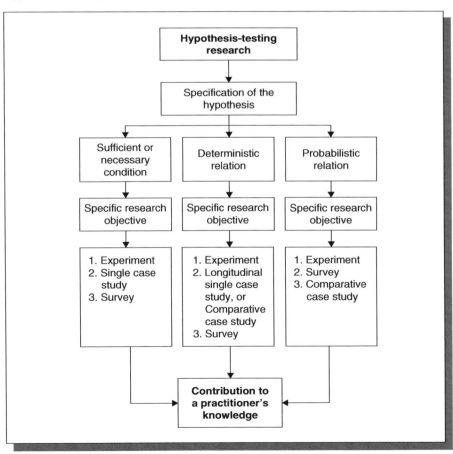

there are three main types of hypothesis-testing research, depicted in Flowchart 3A. The outcome of the research contributes to the practitioner's knowledge.

10.2 Hypothesis-building research

The exploration of practice and of theory might not have resulted in knowledge needs that contain one or more hypotheses. An example is a practitioner's need to know the reason why some projects are not successful, but without specification of one or more candidate causes. Then it might be found *useful* or *necessary* to build and test hypotheses in order to get the knowledge that is relevant for making decisions in the current phase of the problem. In order to check whether such a situation exists, the following questions could be raised.

- Do relevant parties agree on the phase of the problem in the intervention cycle?
- Do relevant parties agree that the knowledge needs that are formulated are the most relevant in the current circumstances?
- Is it agreed that hypotheses need to be formulated (and tested) in order to get satisfactory and useful knowledge?
- *How could research help to build relevant hypotheses?*

If the answers to such questions are conclusive, hypothesis-building research needs to be designed and conducted.

10.2.1 Research objective in hypothesis-building research

If the researcher has decided after a successful exploration that *hypothesis-building research* is needed, the general research objective for such research can be formulated as follows:

> *The objective of this study is to contribute to the knowledge regarding problem P {specify here the problem and its phase in the intervention cycle} by formulating hypotheses on the relation between variables V {specify the variables between which a relation will be formulated in the hypothesis}.*

The format of this research objective is similar to the format of theory-building research. The differences, similar to the differences between theory-testing and hypothesis-testing research, regard (a) the overall orientation to either a contribution to the development of a theory or

Flowchart 3B
Hypothesis-building practice-oriented research

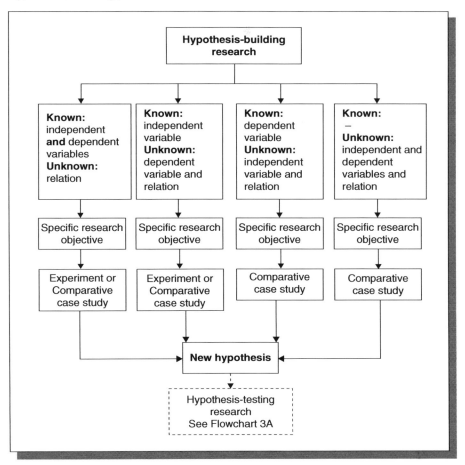

to the development of a practitioner's knowledge, and (b) the terminology (proposition or hypothesis, and concepts and variables).

The known and unknown variables of the hypothesis to be built must be further specified before an appropriate research strategy can be chosen. This results in four different types of hypothesis-building research, depicted in Flowchart 3B.

The four types of hypothesis-building research are the same as the four types of theory-building research:

1. research that starts with known **independent** and **dependent variables** and is aimed at specifying the relation between them;
2. research that starts with a known independent variable and is aimed at, first, identifying and specifying a relevant dependent variable and, next, specifying the relation between the independent and dependent variable;

3. research that starts with a known dependent variable and is aimed at, first, identifying and specifying a relevant independent variable and, next, specifying the relation between the independent and dependent variable;

4. research that starts with an unknown independent variable and an unknown dependent variable and is aimed at, first, identifying and specifying relevant independent and dependent variables and, next, specifying the relation between them.

10.2.2 Research strategy in hypothesis-building research

The choice of a research strategy in hypothesis-building research is governed by the same rules and principles as in theory-building research. First, it must be determined whether experimental research would be useful and feasible. If experimental research is not feasible, a hypothesis-building comparative case study must be designed and conducted.

The one important difference between hypothesis-building research and theory-building research concerns, as with hypothesis-testing research, the domain from which instances are selected. In hypothesis-building research, instances are selected from the practice domain to which the research is oriented or from other practices that are similar.

If a hypothesis has been built, usually it will be tested in the same study according to the principles discussed in 10.1 above. Only after such a test can the research contribute to the practitioner's knowledge.

10.3 Descriptive research

The exploration of practice and of theory might have resulted in a specification of the knowledge needs that does not contain one or more hypotheses, and it might have been decided that it *is not necessary* to build and test hypotheses in order to get the knowledge that is relevant for making decisions in the current phase of the problem. An example is a practitioner's need to know what his employees on the shop floor think about current working conditions. In order to check whether such a situation exists, the following questions could be raised.

■ Do relevant parties agree on the phase of the problem in the intervention cycle?

- ■ Do relevant parties agree that the knowledge needs that are formulated are the most relevant in the current circumstances?
- ■ Is it agreed that it is not necessary that hypotheses are formulated in order to get satisfactory and useful knowledge, but that rather it is necessary that one or more variables are discovered and described?
- ■ *How could research help to satisfy this knowledge need?*

If the answers to such questions are conclusive, descriptive research needs to be designed and conducted.

10.3.1 Research objective of descriptive practice-oriented research

If the researcher has decided after a successful exploration that *descriptive research* is needed, the general research objective for such research can be formulated as follows:

> *The objective of this study is to contribute to the knowledge regarding problem P {specify here the problem and its phase in the intervention cycle} by identifying and describing the following variable(s):*
>
> ■ *{specify variable V1}*
> ■ *{specify variable V2}*
> ■ *{… etc.}.*

The format of this research objective is similar to the format of theory-building research aimed at the discovery of concepts (discussed in 8.1.4), with an interesting difference. The aim of descriptive theory-oriented research is to discover and describe concepts of theoretical interest, whereas the aim of descriptive practice-oriented research is to discover and describe variables of a type that is already indicated in the knowledge needs (such as "what employees on the shop floor think about current working conditions").

The aim of descriptive practice-oriented research is to discover and describe variables within a broader category, which is already indicated in the research question. Examples of such research questions that specify categories are:

- ■ an overview of the kinds of things about which our workers complain;

Flowchart 3C
Descriptive practice-oriented research

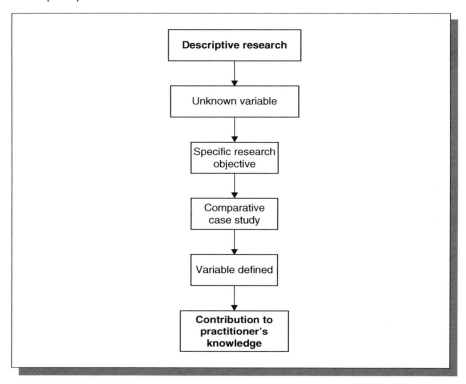

- the possible implementation strategies available for this type of design; and
- the best practice for a specified procedure or process.

This process of conducting practice-oriented descriptive research is shown in Flowchart 3C.

10.3.2 Research strategy of practice-oriented descriptive research

If the relevant variable is not known at the start of the study, it is not possible to specify indicators that can be observed or measured. It is, therefore, not possible to make use of research strategies (and their inherent methods of data analysis) such as experiments or surveys that assume that at least one relevant variable (such as an independent variable in an experiment) is known. The researcher needs rather to explore a range of situations in which it can be expected that the variable that must be identified and described can be found. For instance, in order to find knowledge regarding "the kinds of things about which our workers complain" the researcher needs (a) to identify different situations with different kinds of worker, (b) to identify and to describe different types of complaint, and (c) to compare the findings from the different situations in order to develop a typology of complaints.

Taking another example, in order to find knowledge regarding "the possible implementation strategies available for this type of design" the researcher needs (a) to identify different situations in which similar designs have been implemented, (b) to identify and to describe the different types of implementation strategy, and (c) to compare the findings from the different situations in order to develop a typology of implementation strategies. The selected situations are *cases*, because they are instances from the domain of relevant situations (such as the domain of situations in this practice in which complaints exist, or the domain of similar practices in which a similar design has been implemented) that are selected for study. The analysis is comparative. Therefore, the usual research strategy in descriptive practice-oriented research can be characterized as a *comparative case study*. The outcome of the research contributes to the practitioner's knowledge. An example of such a study will be discussed in Chapter 11 (in 11.4 and 11.5).

10.4 Summary

This chapter can be summarized by the following list of possible types of practice-oriented research:

- testing of a hypothesis that expresses a necessary or sufficient condition – hypothesis-testing by an experiment or a single case study;
- testing of a hypothesis that expresses a deterministic relation – hypothesis-testing by an experiment or a comparative case study;
- testing of a hypothesis that expresses a probabilistic relation – hypothesis-testing by an experiment, a survey or a comparative case study;
- specifying a relation between two known variables – hypothesis-building by an experiment, or a comparative case study;
- specifying a relation between a known (independent or dependent) variable and an as yet unknown (dependent or independent) variable – hypothesis-building by an experiment, or a comparative case study;

■ specifying a relation between as yet unknown independent and dependent variables – hypothesis-building by a comparative case study;

■ discovering and describing a relevant variable by a comparative case study.

We will discuss in detail how to design and conduct practice-oriented *case studies* in Chapter 11. We refer to other textbooks that discuss experimental research and survey research for advice about how to design and conduct hypothesis-testing and hypothesis-building experiments and surveys.

CHAPTER 11

The practice-oriented case study

In this chapter we assume that a practice-oriented research objective (hypothesis-testing, hypothesis-building, or descriptive) has been formulated and subsequently it has been decided that a practice-oriented case study will be designed and conducted.

The structure of this chapter is as follows:

- ■ 11.1 How to design and conduct a practice-oriented case study;
- ■ 11.2 Case Study 6: Assessing whether a company has sufficient flexibility to develop successfully a new product (by Murthy Halemane and Felix Janszen);
- ■ 11.3 Methodological reflection on Case Study 6;
- ■ 11.4 Case Study 7: Building a model of best practice of company standardization (by Henk De Vries and Florens Slob);
- ■ 11.5 Methodological reflection on Case Study 7.

11.1 How to design and conduct a practice-oriented case study

11.1.1 Introduction

There is a strong parallel between the seven types of practice-oriented research formulated in 10.4, and the corresponding seven types of theory-oriented research that were discussed in Part II (Chapters 5, 6, and 7) and Part III (Chapter 8). Many steps in designing and conducting a practice-oriented case study are exactly the same as in the theory-oriented case study, and therefore will not be repeated here. There are two main differences between practice-oriented and theory-oriented case study research, which both follow from their different aims. These differences concern case selection and the implications of a study's outcome. In this chapter we will only discuss these two issues.

11.1.2 Case selection

When a proposition is tested in a *theory-testing study*, the "most likely" or "least likely" case (or cases, or population) is selected from the domain *on theoretical grounds*, but the researcher in hypothesis-testing research is not interested in knowing whether the cases in this practice are "most likely" or "least likely" in terms of a theory. For instance, when the researcher wants to test a hypothesis regarding the success factors of the innovation projects of a specific company, a project or several projects from within that company are selected for the test.

Similarly, case selection in hypothesis-building research is confined to the boundaries of the practice to which the research is oriented or to the domain of similar practices. The most important criterion for case selection in hypothesis-building research, just as in case selection in theory-building case study research, is that the range of values of the known variables is maximized. For instance, if there is an unknown cause for a known effect (e.g. an undesirable effect), cases must be selected in such a way as to have maximum variation of the value of the dependent variable. Similarly, if there is an as yet unknown effect of a given cause, cases must be selected in such a way as to have maximum variation of the value of the independent variable.

Case selection in descriptive practice-oriented research is also confined either to the practice to which the research is oriented or to the domain of similar practices from which something could be learned.

11.1.3 Implications of the research results

In theory-oriented research, a confirmation or a rejection of a hypothesis (representing a proposition) in a theory-testing study has implications for the theory. The researcher might want to reformulate the tested proposition or to replicate the test in other instances. One test does not tell us whether the proposition is correct for all instances or populations to which the theory is assumed to apply. However, a confirmation or a rejection of a hypothesis in a practice-oriented study definitely tells us whether the hypothesis is true for this practice (if the test is conducted in a case or cases from within that practice) or for very similar situations (if the test is conducted in a case or cases that are very similar to the practice situation to which the study is oriented). Test results, therefore, have direct implications for the practitioner's options for action.

The result of a successful hypothesis-building study is a hypothesis, or a set of hypotheses, of which it is known (by means of the practice of initial testing) that they are true in the set of selected cases from which these hypotheses have emerged. Before the generated hypothesis can be considered true for the practice to which the study is oriented, it must first be tested in a (next) hypothesis-testing study. The exception to this rule is the situation in which the hypothesis was built by studying the entire practice to which the research is oriented (e.g. if a hypothesis was built about a relation between a department's management team's style and the department's performance in all departments of a company). In the latter case a fact regarding this practice has been discovered and no further testing is needed.

The result of (good) descriptive practice-oriented research is a true or valid description of types of variables (complaints, practices, strategies) that definitely exist (in the described range of values or types) in the instances in which they were identified. This result is "true" for the practice if the entire practice to which the research is oriented was studied.

Box 15 A practice-oriented "flash case study"

Refer to Flowchart 1.

Preparation phase

1. Define research topic
    - ■ In this book we define the terms "proposition" and "hypothesis" as having distinct meanings. We define a proposition as a part of a theory and a hypothesis as a part of a study. We noticed that some of our colleagues used these terms as synonyms. This alerted us to the possibility that we used these words in an idiosyncratic way.
2. Define general research objective (see Flowchart 3)
    - ■ We wanted to do a quick practice-oriented case study to find out if the distinction that we make between the terms hypothesis and proposition is accepted in the field of business research.

■ Exploration of practice. Problem finding, hypothesis available. We formulated the following hypothesis: "In high quality business research journals published by the American Academy of Management, the term proposition is used in the context of theory and the term hypothesis in the context of an empirical study."

■ Exploration of theory for confirming relevance. In the methodological literature it is common to define and use the words hypothesis and proposition separately, as suggested by us.

3.   Determine the specific research objective (see Flowchart 3A)

■ The objective of this study is to contribute to our knowledge about the use of the words proposition and hypothesis in business research by testing the hypothesis (hypothesis-testing practice-oriented research).

Research phase

4.   Choose the research strategy

■ Specification of the hypothesis: (a) in research papers in the *Academy of Management Review (AMR)*, the word proposition is used (sufficient condition); (b) in research papers in the *Academy of Management Journal (AMJ)*, the word hypothesis is used (sufficient condition).

■ Research objective: to test the two hypotheses.

■ Research strategy: a parallel single case study for each hypothesis.

5.   Select instances

■ Candidate cases: issues of both journals of the last 4 years.

■ Case selection: arbitrary selection of two issues per journal and five research papers per issue.

6.   Conduct measurement

■ Measurement: visual scanning of the papers for the words hypothesis or proposition; counting the number of times the word proposition is used in an *AMJ* paper, and counting the number of times the word hypothesis is used in an *AMR* paper.

7.   Conduct data analysis

■ Analysis: rejection of the hypothesis if the number of times that the unexpected word is used (proposition in *AMR*; hypothesis in *AMJ*) >0.

■ Results: number of times of unpredicted words is $0 \rightarrow$ hypotheses confirmed.

Implications and report phase

8.   Discuss results

■ Test results (20 confirmations and 0 rejections) give sufficient support for the correctness of the statement "In high quality business research journals published by the *American Academy of Management*, the term proposition is used in the context of theory and the term hypothesis in the context of an empirical study."

- ■ Practical decision: there is no need to describe the difference between hypothesis and proposition as a new idea for business research.

9. Report results

- ■ While doing this 10 minute case study research, we realized that the results can be presented as a "flash case study" to illustrate the basic ideas of practice-oriented case study research (this box). Each reader will have similar practical problems that could be addressed with a "flash case study".

Conclusion drawn by the practitioner

- ■ The practitioner (i.e. we as authors of this book) concluded that there is no need to fear that our readers will not accept our definitions of the terms hypothesis and proposition.

11.2 Case Study 6: Hypothesis-testing practice-oriented research

Assessing whether a company has sufficient flexibility to develop successfully a new product[1]

by Murthy Halemane and Felix Janszen

11.2.1 Introduction

In a world where everything changes, doing the same thing as yesterday is the surest way for firms to fail and to lose market position. In a dynamic market, products undergo shorter product life cycles; thus old products need to be replaced frequently. Old products are modified, improved, or completely renewed by new designs. Manufacturing firms need to be able to introduce new products in the market at the right moment and in the right form in order to create competitive advantage.

---

[1] This chapter is based on: Halemane, D.M. and Janszen, F.H.A. (2004) Flexibility in Operations and Businesses Innovation, *Global Journal of Flexible Systems Management*, 5 (2), pp. 23–41.

A firm can successfully develop, manufacture, and market new products if the firm's resource-based capabilities are properly used.

With our research we wanted to contribute to the strategy of a leading European firm that develops, produces, and markets high-technology electronic products of relatively short product life cycle. This firm needed to be able to develop new products and launch them on the market successfully. It was interested in an assessment of whether its current resource-based capabilities were sufficient to allow it to do so. The objective of our research, therefore, was to assess whether there was a problem with this firm concerning its capabilities to design and launch new products (problem finding) and, if so, to specify the problem(s).

11.2.2 Hypothesis

In order to achieve this objective we were keen to make use of a theory that we had developed that states that a firm's *strategic flexibility* is determined by its *operations flexibility*. The concept of strategic flexibility relates to how flexibly the firm can react to demands of the market. We define this type of flexibility as a firm's capability to introduce new products on the market *at the right moment*. We assumed that the earlier a new product with a desired level of attractiveness, quality, and price is introduced, the higher is the resulting market share. We define operations flexibility as a firm's capability to *develop* new products in a *short time*. We assumed that the degree to which standard designs are reused for components in a new product has a direct inverse relation to the time required for the development of the new product.

Based on these theoretical notions we formulated the following hypothesis:

> *Hypothesis*: The degree to which standard designs are reused for components in a new product in this firm has a direct positive relation to the market share of that new product.

Our hypothesis formulates a relation between the degree to which standard designs are reused in the process of product development in this firm and the resulting market share. If this hypothesis is proven to be true, the firm is able to draw a conclusion from it regarding its current resource-based capabilities to design and launch new products.

We could only test this hypothesis by using the firm's expertise and experience regarding the development process of new products as well as regarding the market on which new products are introduced.

We wanted to represent this expertise in a computer model of this firm's product development process and of the market in such a way that we would be able to:

1. generate scenarios with different percentages of components of new products, for which standard designs were reused, in order to estimate the degree to which a shortening of the development process would occur, and
2. generate scenarios with different timings of the introduction of new products, as well as the attractiveness and price of these products, in order to estimate the resulting market share.

We would then determine what level of reuse of standard designs would be required in this firm to produce new products of sufficiently high attractiveness, and at sufficiently low cost, for introducing them at a sufficiently low price to the market, at the right moment. Finally, we would deduce from our model of the development process of new products whether the required level of operations flexibility was present in this firm.

11.2.3 Measurement

We first explored the firm's situation by arranging a "focus group" consisting of two senior managers from the functional area of product development. Although these two managers belonged to a single functional area, their background was different. The expertise of one was in marketing, whereas the expertise of the other was in technology development. Because they also knew other functional areas of the organization very well, they were able to represent those areas with an integrative view. We had meetings with this small group in a relaxed and informal setting in which we could optimally tap their knowledge and expertise. In the group sessions, we explored the nature of the market as well as the kind of competencies required from different functional areas. It was discussed whether the new product strategy of the firm was technology driven or market driven. An inventory was made of the activities in this company that are involved in creating, producing, and marketing new products.

In a second stage of exploration, information was collected from various team leaders of product development projects, and from managers in marketing and technology development. We also reviewed relevant documents and publications concerning production attributes, technology, product portfolio, and market position of competitors, as well as their competencies. Subsequently, in group discussions with team leaders a description of the development process of new products (for one of the firm's product groups) was generated, in which it was specified how much time this firm usually spends in different stages of the development process and what are the determinants of the duration of each phase. This information about the current situation regarding this type of product was modelled in a computer simulation model (Janszen, 2000).

In a next step, the input from the interactive sessions with the focus group and the information collected from team leaders of different product development projects, from managers of functional areas, and from the firm's documents, were used to estimate the effects of increased levels of reuse of standard designs on the duration of the development of new products in this product group. These estimates were discussed with team leaders and evaluated as realistic.

In a similar way we developed, with the firm's experts, a model of how the market share in this group of products is influenced by time of introduction, price, and attractiveness. Similarly, we developed scenarios with different times of market launch, different levels of attractiveness, and different price levels in order to estimate resulting market share in a manner deemed realistic by the firm's experts.

11.2.4 Data analysis

We developed seven scenarios with different degrees of reuse of standard designs in new products, varying from 0 per cent to 30 per cent of the components of the new product. Figure 11.1 shows the annual sales volume in each of these seven scenarios. These results show that the annual sales volume could be increased by *circa* 50 per cent by reusing standard designs for up to 30 per cent of the components.

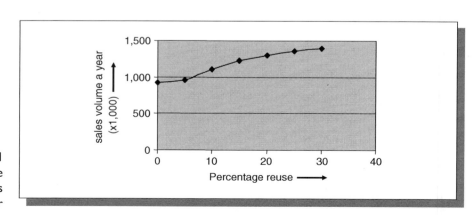

Figure 11.1
Effect of percentage reuse on sales volume a year

11.2.5 Results and implications

Our hypothesis was confirmed. The degree to which standard designs are reused in a new product in this firm has a direct positive relation to the annual sales volume and, we assume, to market share. An increase of 50 per cent of sales can be achieved by reusing standard designs for 30 per cent of the components of the new product.

Because the firm considered all six scenarios as realistic (including the one with 30 per cent reuse of standard designs), it is concluded from the positive test result that this firm had sufficient operational flexibility to realize a sufficient level of strategic flexibility.

11.3 Methodological reflection on Case Study 6

11.3.1 Practice

Case Study 6 is oriented to a leading European firm's practice of new product development. This firm, which develops, produces, and markets high-technology electronic products of a relatively short product life cycle, was interested in an assessment of whether its current resource-based capabilities were sufficient to develop new products and launch them on the market successfully.

11.3.2 Research objective

The result of exploration of practice for this study was the identification of a problem-finding knowledge need regarding the firm's ability to launch successfully new products on the market. In the exploration of theory, some propositions were identified, on the basis of which the following hypothesis was formulated:

> Hypothesis: The degree to which standard designs are reused for components in a new product in this firm has a direct positive relation to the market share of that new product.

This hypothesis represents a deterministic relation.

The research objective of this *hypothesis-testing* study, thus, was *to contribute to the new product development strategy of this firm by testing whether this hypothesis is true.* A confirmation of the hypothesis would inform the firm about for how many components of new products standard designs should be reused in order to achieve a specific level of market share. A rejection of the hypothesis would inform the firm that market share cannot be increased by increasing the number of components for which standard designs are used, but will not be informative about alternative ways of increasing market share.

11.3.3 Research strategy

The experiment was the preferred strategy for testing a hypothesis that represents a deterministic relation. The firm could use standard designs to different degrees in a number of new product developments and then discover how market share varied. However, such an experiment, which would involve assigning different levels of reuse to different new product developments, would require considerable cost and risk that could not be justified by the objective of this research, i.e. (merely) problem finding. The next preferred strategy for testing the deterministic hypotheses would be a case study. A longitudinal case study of new product development in this firm in which the independent variable varies in time in the real life context, did not seem realistic. The use of a computer simulation model, which allows for the generation of (virtual) outcomes for analysis, was a solution for all mentioned problems, (a) the lack of sufficient variance in the independent variable in the practice of this firm, (b) the cost of collecting data about new product development projects, and (c) the costs and risks of experiments. As in Case Studies 3 and 4 (see Chapters 6 and 7), the computer simulation model generated data on multiple cases (scenarios) for comparison.

11.3.4 Candidate cases

The domain of instances relevant for this practice (new product development projects in this firm) consisted of all possible ways in which new products could be developed by this firm. Obviously, this domain was limited to the range of new products that were realistic new products for this firm.

11.3.5 Case selection

A product group was chosen in discussions with the "focus group" consisting of two senior managers. In the simulation, a range of new products within this product group was developed, each with another level of reuse of standard designs. Figure 11.1 shows that data were generated on seven scenarios with different realistic degrees of reuse of components.

11.3.6 Measurement

In order to generate realistic outcomes in terms of market share (dependent on the timing of the market launch of the product), current knowledge of the market and of the process of new product development needed to be collected and, next, to be modelled in the computer program. Two models were built, one of the effect of the timing of the market launch of a new product on market share, and the other of the effect of the extent of reuse of standard designs on the throughput time. The output of the latter model (a date following from a potentially shorter throughput time for development) could be used as input for the first mentioned model.

11.3.7 Data presentation

Figure 11.1 shows the data on annual sales volume for seven cases with different levels of reuse of standard designs. Annual sales volume was chosen as a proxy for market share.

11.3.8 Data analysis

Testing the hypothesis, which represented a deterministic relation, consisted of, first, ranking the seven cases according to the independent variable (extent of reuse of standard designs) as well as ranking them according to the dependent variable (annual sales volume) and, next, ascertaining that both rank orders were exactly the same (see Chapter 6). Figure 11.1 shows that this was indeed the case. Therefore, the hypothesis was confirmed.

11.3.9 Implications for practice

Case Study 6 correctly made a distinction between (a) the results of the study and (b) what practitioners could do with these results. The outcome of the study was a confirmation of the hypothesis, implying that the degree to which standard designs are reused in a new product in this firm, had a direct positive relation to the annual sales volume and, it is assumed, to market share. An increase of 50 per cent of sales could be achieved by reusing standard designs for 30 per cent of the components of the new product. The firm concluded from this positive test result that it had sufficient operational flexibility to realize a sufficient level of strategic flexibility.

It is important to note that the results of this study were based on data generated by the two simulation models and that, therefore, the credibility of the results is dependent on the quality of the input for these models as well as of the models themselves. The input to the models was provided by experts from the firm. This implies that the validity of the conclusions of this study depends on the quality of this input. Therefore, it is of great importance for this study that these experts confirmed in meetings that the simulation models and their results were realistic, in their opinion.

11.4 Case Study 7: Descriptive practice-oriented research

Building a model of best practice of company standardization[2]

by Henk J. De Vries and Florens Slob

11.4.1 Introduction

Companies make use of many different kinds of standards in order to improve their business performance in terms of efficiency and quality. In the process industry (chemical and petrochemical industries), benefits such as reduction of design and construction costs, procurement costs, training costs, and minimization of design errors and rework, have been reported (Simpkins, 2001). Companies in the process industry prefer external standards, for example from the ISO (International Organization for Standardization) and API (American Petroleum Institute) (Barthet, 2000; Qin, 2004; Thomas, 2004). However, these

---

[2] This chapter is based on: Oly, M. P. and Slob, F. J. C. (1999). *Benchmarking Bedrijfsnormalisatie – Een best practice voor de procesindustrie.* Rotterdam: Erasmus Universiteit Rotterdam, Faculteit Bedrijfskunde, and De Vries, H.J. (2006) Best Practice in Company Standardization. *International Journal for IT Standards and Standardization Research*, 4(1), pp. 62–85.

standards do not meet all their needs and, therefore, they complement these with their own standards, "company standards".

In this research project, five big Dutch chemical and petrochemical companies (Akzo Nobel, DSM, Gasunie, NAM, and Shell), later joined by Dow Chemical, agreed with our suggestion that research could help them to improve their own standardization performance by describing, evaluating, and comparing the standardization activities in each of these companies. The main objectives of this research project were (1) to design a "best practice" for company standardization that could be implemented in the six companies participating in the project, and by doing this (2) to contribute to the general body of knowledge of (company) standardization. Case Study 7 will focus on the first practice-oriented objective.

This research was conducted by a research team, supported by a steering group consisting of the standardization managers of the companies, a senior standardization consultant of the Dutch national standards body NEN, and the president of the NKN, the organization of Dutch standards users.

11.4.2 Absence of guidelines or criteria

A "best practice" is a practice that is in actual use at a place and that is deemed better than all other practices that are used or known elsewhere. If a practice is acknowledged as "best", it should be fit for being transferred to those other places as well. Assessing which of the practices in use is the best requires that appropriate criteria be used to evaluate current practices. Which criteria should be used to assess which shaping of standardization is the best?

Although the number of company standards outweighs the number of other standards to a large extent, this relative importance is not reflected in the literature on standardization. The few studies of company standards (Susanto, 1988; Schacht, 1991; Adolphi, 1997; Hesser and Inklaar, 1997 Section 5; De Vries, 1999 Chapter 14; Rada and Craparo, 2001) are descriptive rather than prescriptive, and do not address the question of how to maximize the benefits of company standardization. Therefore, we could not apply an extant theoretical framework.

The companies themselves had no criteria for good standardization practice either. Types of standards and their goals differed widely, both within and between companies. The two main types of standardization in these companies concerned their products (approximately 10 per cent of the amount of standards) and their installations (90 per cent).

Standards for chemical *products* include mainly standards that specify requirements for these products and standards that describe methods to test them. Standards for *installations* primarily concern engineering solutions that define how to design, construct, and maintain manufacturing facilities (Simpkins, 2001). Regarding aims of standards, the main aim of a safety standard might be zero accidents, whereas the main aim of a standard that specifies a preference range for pipes might be cost savings. Because each of these standards should be evaluated on its own terms, it is not possible to use one general criterion for ascertaining the quality of standards in a company. For this reason, we decided that the best practice that should be developed in this study would not be based on criteria for the quality of the *products* of the standardization process (the company standards themselves) but rather on *process* criteria.

A study of the available scientific and professional literature on the process of designing company standards confirmed the expectation that criteria for a good quality process were not available. Such criteria, therefore, as well as the "best" practices related to them, should be "discovered" in this study.

Each of the companies was visited in order personally to meet the company's standardization officer and get a first overview of the company's standardization practices. How was standardization defined in that company? What did the company do in this area, and how and why? The character of this first meeting was more like a chat than an interview. It was unstructured in order to be able to explore the company's situation without any preconceived ideas. It can also be seen as a "quick scan" of company standardization in that company. Partially based on this initial information about the standardization processes in our companies and partially based on the process model of innovation as developed by Chiesa *et al.* (1996), we developed a process model of company standardization. This model made a distinction between four core processes and four supporting processes (see Figure 11.2).

Core processes

1. *Prioritizing.* Which company standard will be developed and which will not? Who decide(s), based on which criteria (if any)?
2. *Company standard development.* This process consists of the composition of draft versions of the standard, commentary rounds, the writing of the final version, and its approval.
3. *Company standard introduction.* The approved standard must be introduced to its users. In this introduction process, the benefits of the standard and the reasons for certain choices in the

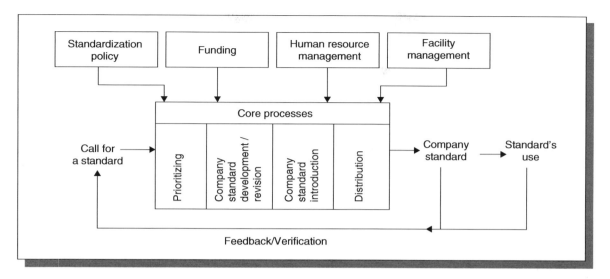

Figure 11.2
Company
standardization model

standard can be explained. The more and the better the standard is known to its potential direct users, the higher the chance that they will actually use it and do so in the way intended by the standard's developers. The "promotion" of the standard can also continue after the introduction period.

4. *Distribution.* The purpose of this process is to ensure that the standards reach the direct user in a fast and easy way. This can be done by, for instance, subscription, ordering on demand, or in the form of "publishing on demand" using an Intranet.

Facilitating processes

1. *Standardization policy* is needed to steer the core processes – a global policy on a company level, more detailed on department level.

2. *Funding* is needed to *finance* the core processes – standardization activities ask for investments. Costs precede benefits. The break-even point may be after, for instance, 3 years.

3. *Human resource management* is a necessary supporting process. Competent *personnel* must enact the established policy.

4. *Facility* management. The core processes are also *facilitated* by IT (e.g. electronic publishing of standards on the Intranet) and other tools.

Figure 11.2 also contains some other relevant concepts. On the right hand side of this model, the required end situation is represented by the concept "standard's use". Company standardization can only be a success when the standard is used in practice, and in the right way. A standard that is of a high quality but that is not used in practice has no value. Potential direct users must be willing to use the standard and be capable of understanding and using it. On the left hand side of the model, the beginning of the process is represented by the concept "call for a standard", which represents the requirement for any standard that it is seen as responding to a perceived problem "on the floor".

Finally, at the bottom of the model, a feedback loop is represented. Evaluation of the standard's use may form the basis for withdrawing, maintaining, or changing the standard. The developed standard should be an answer to the question for which it was produced – are the (potential) users of the standard satisfied? Therefore, user *feedback* to those who have decided to make the standard, as well as to the people who have developed it, is essential. The figure shows only one overall feedback loop, but in actual (best) practice a feedback loop is required in each of the four steps of the standardization process.

The model was presented to the project's steering group, which confirmed that it is a useful representation of the different processes that contribute to good standardization practice. Note that this model is not a representation of a best practice but of a series of processes only. The "best" practice for each of these processes is still to be determined.

11.4.3 Measurement

Our next step was to collect data from actual instances of standardization in the six companies with the aim:

1. to assess in each case whether the core and supporting processes as specified in the model could be identified; and
2. to describe for each case in detail how these processes were conducted, including if possible a description of evaluation procedures and of the criteria-in-use for assessing the quality of the standardization activities.

Using a questionnaire that covered the eight processes of the model as an interview guide, semi-structured interviews with standardization managers were conducted in each of the six companies to investigate how the processes were shaped. The standardization managers introduced us also to other people who were involved in one or more company standardization processes, such as (technical) managers, technical experts who wrote standards, standards users, and standards officers (staff at the standardization department). We spent at least 1 week in each company, conducting a number of 15–20 interviews (of 1–2 hours each) in each company. Additional data were also generated by means of observation, informal conversations, and reading documents (e.g. written descriptions of company standardization processes).

11.4.4 Data presentation

Each company's standardization processes were described in detail, using flowcharts. Our model appeared to be a useful framework for this description. Each of the eight processes of our model was a relevant (sub)process of standardization in each of the companies. Within these processes, practices of the different companies appeared to differ quite a lot, for example:

- In one of the companies, the corporate policy included standardization, in the other companies it did not.
- Three of the six companies had a steering group for standardization, which consisted of line managers. In all cases, the standardization manager was member of this group as well.
- Two companies attached a "why document" to some of their company standards. This document provided the underpinning of the most important choices/decisions that were made during standards development. Often, the authors of the standard were mentioned as well in this document.

11.4.5 Concept definition

Starting from the observed practices in the six companies, in a brainstorming session we formulated statements that expressed criteria that could be applied to each of these practices. Company standardization literature, scientific or professional, played a minor role in this brainstorm because, in general, this literature did not provide any guidance regarding best practice in company standardization. Examples of such statements that we generated are:

- a best practice regarding standardization policy is that there is a clearly stated strategic policy on company standardization;

- a best practice regarding company standards development is that there is a clear organizational framework for standards development and that top management participates in this framework (e.g. in a steering group);
- a best practice regarding company standard distribution is that a "why document" is attached to each company standard to provide the underpinning of the most important choices/ decisions that were made during standards development.

In order to give an idea of how we developed such statements, we describe here how we arrived at the last mentioned best practice statement. One of the interviewees mentioned the example of a standard for durability of piping materials related to corrosion. Because a pipeline in a desert may be less susceptible to corrosion, applying the standard for such a pipeline may lead to an unnecessarily costly design. If there is a "why document" attached to the standard, in which it is explained that a specific treatment is standard and has to be applied in order to prevent corrosion, this might enable the standard user to decide not to follow the standard in specific conditions (such as producing pipes for use in a desert). After having formulated this element of best practice, we were able to also find some support for it in the literature (see Brown and Duguid, 1991: 45).

We applied the criteria we had developed in this way to the practices that we had found in the six companies and chose from these practices those that met these criteria. The result of this procedure was a comprehensive description of a best practice consisting of different elements from each of the six companies. Here we cannot present the entire best practice, as it is a detailed document of 42 pages (Oly and Slob, 1999; summarized in De Vries, 2006). For some criteria, we did not find the best practice in any of the companies but only in the literature, or it was the result of our own brainstorm only. An example of the latter, a criterion that was our own invention, is a best practice for publishing of company standards. Each of the six companies published standards on paper, some of them also on microfilm, and one of the companies on CD-ROM. We, however, considered publishing on the Intranet to be a best practice. At the time of our research (1999), the publication of company procedures (in general) on an Intranet, which is now very common, was not a standard practice in these six companies.

After we had generated our proposal for a best practice for company standard development, we then wanted to assess for each part of this best practice the extent to which it was acceptable to practitioners. This was done by presenting the findings to the companies and asking them for feedback. Following the example of Chiesa *et al.* (1996), we made a scorecard per process for each company on which each element of our proposed best practice could be scored on a scale from 1 (currently not at all) to 5 (currently very much so). If we take the example of our proposal to consider the "why document" as a best practice, the score for a company that currently attaches a "why document" to each of its standards is 5. The score for a company that never does it is 0. In case the "why document" is attached only to a limited number of important standards, the score might be 2. We asked each standardization manager to make scores for his company and the researchers themselves also made scores per company. The score per characteristic per company was the average of these two scores. In case of a difference of more than one point between our and the company's scores, we contacted the standardization manager. Did he disagree with the best practice itself or was the difference in scores due to a difference in perceived quality of the company's current practice? It turned out that there were no significant differences in opinion concerning the best practice, which was a first confirmation for us that our proposal was a good one.

Next, we compiled the resulting scores from the different companies (though anonymously) in tables and a mean score was computed. These figures were presented in tables, the most interesting ones also in graphs. This was done per process. For every process the companies were ordered differently, so the companies could not recognize which score belonged to which other company (see Figure 11.3 for an example). Figure 11.3 shows seven sets of three bars. The first six sets represent the scores of the six different companies on the three criteria for the standard development process as formulated by us in our proposal for a best practice. The seventh set represents the mean scores on these criteria.

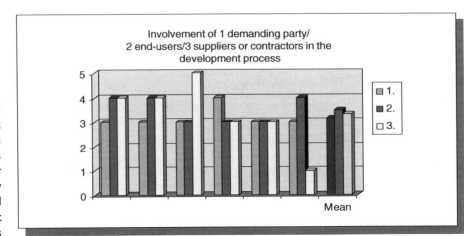

Figure 11.3
Example of a scorecard graph representing scores for three criteria for the company standard development process

By comparing their own score with the best practice and with the other companies, it was possible for the participating companies to identify the gaps between their current practice and our proposal for a best practice, to think about reasons for this gap, and to decide on focus and improvement points for their future policy on company standardization. Moreover, besides an overall research report for all companies, a small report per company was made with a description of their actual company standardization and the focus points for them to work towards best practice. No company scored high or low on most of the characteristics. There was quite a diversity per characteristic but in each company low scores in some characteristics could be balanced against high scores in other points, and each of them had average scores on some characteristics as well, so there was no distinction between "good" and "bad" companies.

In five of the six companies, we organized a focus group. This group consisted of 15–20 people: the standardization manager, one or more technical managers, technical experts, and, in most cases, some other people involved in one or more of the processes: standards officers and standards users. The focus group meeting took 2–3 hours. In the first hour, the project and the main findings were presented. Then we discussed how the relative scores of the company as compared with the best practice and with the other companies should be interpreted. Such interpretations could either involve challenging the best practice or diagnosing reasons for less-than-best practices in the own company or both. Some comments on details of the best practice were made. For instance, the above-mentioned "why document" was recognized to be best practice in all companies, including the ones that did not include one in their current procedures, but still some companies doubted whether the costs of writing it in all cases would outweigh the benefits. However, in general, all best practice characteristics were assessed by each of the five focus groups as real best practice, so the best practice model passed the test with flying colours.

In addition to the focus group meetings, the results were presented to the Steering group and to the Dutch Academic Network of Researchers in Standardization and Certification. Both practitioners and scientists confirmed the main findings without having the time (in a 2 hour meeting) to discuss all best practice details.

11.4.6 Implications

The objective of this research project was to contribute to an improvement of the standardization procedures in six companies by describing, evaluating, and comparing the standardization activities in each of these companies and, next, to design a "best practice" for company standardization to be implemented in the six companies participating in the project. The result of this study consisted of a description of the standardization processes in each company and an evaluation against criteria that were developed in this study. A compilation of these criteria resulted in a proposal for a best practice for standardization procedures.

The resulting best practice has also been published in professional journals in France, Germany, India, and the Netherlands. It also proved to be of interest for an academic audience that was interested in our descriptive data on how companies carry out company standardization (see De Vries, 2006). These descriptions can form a starting point for further research in which propositions might be tested that are based on the assumptions that we used when we formulated the criteria that form the basis of the best practice that we developed.

11.5 Methodological reflection on Case Study 7

11.5.1 Practice

Case Study 7 is oriented to the practice of company standardization in six big Dutch chemical and petrochemical companies. After being contacted by the researchers, these companies expressed the wish that research be conducted in order to help them to improve their own standardization performance by describing, evaluating, and comparing the standardization activities in each of these companies. In this practice-oriented research, the problem was positioned in the "design of intervention" phase of the intervention cycle, and descriptive knowledge was needed about the companies' standardization processes.

11.5.2 Research objective

The objective of this descriptive research was *to contribute to the improvement of the company standardization processes of six companies by designing a best practice.* Because the elements of which this best practice should consist were not yet known and, therefore, must be discovered in this research, and also because finding and describing a design does not involve the discovery and testing of causal relations between variables, a descriptive case study was appropriate.

11.5.3 Research strategy

Because the six companies requesting the development of a best practice also wanted the study to generate an evaluation of their own practices, and because each of these companies had given access to their practices, it was an appropriate decision to include all six companies in this study. The design of this study, thus, became a comparative descriptive case study of the standardization procedures in the six companies that had requested it.

11.5.4 Candidate cases

Because the best practice that should be designed was explicitly meant to be a best practice for the process industry only, candidate cases for the description of elements of current practices from which a best practice could be built should be instances of standardization procedures in the process industry. The six companies were all part of the process industry.

11.5.5 Case selection

In a descriptive case study, case selection should be governed by convenience, feasibility, and likely effectiveness. All six companies were included in the study.

11.5.6 Measurement

The researchers in this study needed to use a framework that helped them to decide which kinds of processes should be looked for in the six companies. Partially based on some initial exploratory measurement about the standardization processes in the six companies, and partially based on a model found in the literature, the researchers developed a process model of company standardization. This model defined four "core" and four "facilitating" processes that had to be "filled" with descriptions of how these processes were actually shaped in the six companies. Using a questionnaire that covered the eight processes of the model as an interview guide, semi-structured interviews with standardization managers and other informants were conducted in each of the six companies to investigate how the processes in these companies were shaped.

11.5.7 Data presentation

The result of this first part of the measurement was a description of each of the six standardization practices in the format of the process model. Each of the elements in these descriptions was a candidate element of a best practice.

11.5.8 Data analysis

Criteria for choosing the best practices, from the description of the separate practices, were developed in a researchers' brainstorming session. These criteria were applied and this resulted in a proposal for a best practice based on a reasoned choice of elements from the six described standardization practices. Next, this proposal was presented to the standardization managers in the six companies and each of them was asked to rate their own practice against the proposal. It appeared that, in this rating procedure, each of the six managers accepted the proposal as a description of the best practice. Finally, in five of the six companies, a focus group discussion was arranged in which the relative scores of the company, as compared with the best practice and with the other companies, were evaluated. It appeared that all elements of the proposal for a best practice were seen by each of the five focus groups as definitely representing the best practice. This best practice was described within the framework of Figure 11.2.

11.5.9 Implications for practice

The practice-oriented objective of this research was to contribute to the improvement of the company standardization procedures of six companies by designing a best practice that was acceptable to each of them. A proposal for a best practice was developed from elements of the current practices of these six companies and practitioners evaluated the result as an improvement upon their current practices. This meant that the objective of this study was achieved.

11.6 References

Adolphi, H. 1997, *Strategische Konzepte zur Organisation der Betrieblichen Standardisierung*. DIN Normungskunde, Band 38. Berlin/Vienna/Zürich: Beuth Verlag.

Barthet, M.-C. 2000, Equipements pétroliers: la pompe normative est bien amorcée. *Enjeux*, 208: 13–15.

Brown, J. and Duguid, P. 1991, Organizational learning and communities of practice: toward a unified view of working, learning and innovation. *Organization Science*, 2(1): 40–57.

Chiesa, V., Coughlan, P., and Voss, C.A. 1996, Development of a technical innovation audit. *Journal of Production Innovation Management*. 13(2): 105–136.

De Vries, H.J. 1999, *Standardization – a business approach to the role of national standardization organizations*. Boston/Dordrecht/London: Kluwer Academic Publishers.

De Vries, H.J. 2006, Best practice in company standardization. *International Journal for IT Standards and Standardization Research*, 4(1): 62–85.

Halemane, D.M. and Janszen, F.H.A. 2004, Flexibility in operations and businesses innovation. *Global Journal of Flexible Systems Management*, 5(2): 23–41.

Hesser, W. and Inklaar, A. (eds) 1997, *An introduction to standards and standardization*. DIN Normungskunde, Band 36, Berlin/Vienna/Zürich: Beuth Verlag.

Janszen, F.H.A. 2000, *The age of innovation: making business creativity a competence, not a coincidence*. London: Pearson Education Limited.

Oly, M.P. and Slob, F.J.C. 1999, *Benchmarking Bedrijfsnormalisatie – Een best practice voor de procesindustrie*. Rotterdam: Erasmus Universiteit Rotterdam, Faculteit Bedrijfskunde.

Qin, C. 2004, China builds its new petroleum industry round International Standards. *ISO Focus*, 1(4): 23–24.

Rada, R. and Craparo, J.S. 2001, Standardizing management of software engineering projects. *Knowledge Technology and Policy*, 14(2): 67–77.

Schacht, M. 1991, *Methodische Neugestaltung von Normen als Grundlage für eine Integration in den rechnerunterstützten Konstruktionsprozess*. DIN Normungskunde, Band 28. DIN Deutsches Institut für Normung e.V. Berlin/Cologne: Beuth Verlag GmbH.

Simpkins, C.R. 2001, Reengineering standards for the process industries: process industry practices, in: Spivak, S.M. and Brenner, F.C. (eds). *Standardization essentials – principles and practice*. New York/Basel: Marcel Dekker Inc.

Susanto, A. 1988, *Methodik zur Entwicklung von Normen*. DIN Normungskunde, Band 23. DIN Deutsches Institut für Normung e.V. Berlin/Cologne: Beuth Verlag GmbH.

Thomas, G.A.N. 2004, Standards as a strategic business asset. *ISO Focus*, 1(4): 11–15.

Appendices

Appendix 1: Measurement

Our definition of the case study (see 1.1) does not include statements on **measurement** or measurement techniques. In our view, research strategies are not defined by their methods of measurement. The measurement methods that are usually associated with case studies (such as the "qualitative" interview and the use of "multiple sources of evidence") could also be used in other research strategies. Similarly, measurement methods that are usually associated with other research strategies, such as standardized questionnaires in surveys and quantitative measurements in experiments, could also be used in case studies. For this reason we have not discussed measurement as an issue deserving special treatment in our chapters on how to design and conduct the different forms of case study research. Obviously, this does not imply that it is not important that concepts are measured validly and reliably. To the contrary, in the case study strategy it is as important that concepts are measured validly and reliably as it is in other research strategies.

We discuss here a stepwise procedure for the development of valid and reliable procedures for the measurement of the value of a concept in an instance of the object of study:

1. formulate a precise definition of the concept;
2. determine the object of measurement;
3. identify the location of the object of measurement;
4. specify how evidence of the value of the variable will be extracted from the object of measurement;
5. specify how sources of evidence will be identified, selected, and accessed;
6. specify how evidence will be recorded;
7. specify how data will be categorized;
8. write a measurement protocol.

We will use the article on measurement validity by Adcock and Collier (2001) as our main methodological reference, and will use the concept of "success" (of a project) as an example of a concept that should be measured.

Step 1: formulate a precise definition of the concept

Potential meanings of the concept of "success" (a "background concept" in the terminology of Adcock and Collier 2001) range from success in terms of financial results, to timely delivery of the results, satisfaction with the results, etc. In the examples of case studies in this book, success has been defined, for instance, as "product launch in the market" (Case Study 1) or "satisfaction with project performance" (Case Study 2). In this appendix we use the following three different definitions of success (or "systematized concepts" in terms of Adcock and Collier 2001).

1. Degree of success of a project in terms of *financial* success can be defined as "the amount of monetary gain for the company resulting from the project".
2. Degree of success of a project in terms of *timely delivery* can be defined as "whether the project has delivered its results before a specified deadline".
3. Degree of success of a project in terms of *satisfaction* can be defined as "the extent to which a project is perceived as successful by the company".

These different meanings of the concept of success might be equally valid for a theory and it might be necessary to measure these three different aspects of "success" in one study. Normally, however, a theory clearly specifies one of these different meanings as the one to which the theory refers, i.e. as the type of success that is explained by the theory or proposition. We will discuss the stepwise development of a procedure for measuring a concept by illustrating it with these three different versions of the concept of "success".

Step 2: determine the object of measurement

In order to measure the actual value of the variable (e.g. the degree of success) in one instance, or in a number of instances of the object of study (e.g. projects), the **object of measurement** must be defined. The object of measurement is usually *not the same* as the object of study (which is projects in this example) but rather an element belonging to the object of study or something to which it is connected. Each of the three indicators of "success" defined above (in Step 1) specifies a different object of measurement.

Financial success. It may be assumed that the company that is involved in the project has arranged its bookkeeping and accounting practices in such a way that it is possible to compute the costs incurred for the project as well as the revenues of it. The financial success of the project (if it can be measured at all) is an attribute of the difference between the project's *costs* and *revenues*. It is an amount in a country's currency that appears on a line or in a cell of a financial record (e.g. in a spreadsheet).

Timely delivery. This is success in terms of the end date of the project (e.g. "early", "late", "on time", or number of days before/after the planned deadline) that can be assigned to a *date*.

Satisfaction. This type of success refers to a value attributed to a project by the company. It is a characteristic of a *company's opinions* and the value of this variable can range, e.g. from "not satisfied at all" to "very satisfied".

These examples show that different specifications of the *concept* of "success" result in different *variables*, i.e. different types of attributes of different types of objects of measurement. Although, in our example, the concept (success) is an element of one object of study (projects), the three variables are elements of different objects of measurement (financial statements, dates, opinions).

Step 3: identify the location of the object of measurement

Measuring the value of a variable involves either bringing a measurement instrument to an instance of the object of measurement or bringing an object of measurement to the instrument. In both situations the researcher needs to know where to go in order to be able to conduct the measurement.

Financial success. In order to measure the presence (or the degree) of financial success, records, accounts, or reports in which the costs and revenues of projects are documented must be identified. The usual place to find such records or reports is in the computers or the network of a finance department of a company.

Timely delivery. In order to assess the end date of the project, a document (e.g. a press release in which the end of the project was announced) containing information on the end date must be identified. In this example, the usual place to find such information is a document in which a decision by management is recorded, an announcement on the company's Intranet, or a similar text.

Satisfaction. The object of measurement of this attribute is not a concrete object that can be located. Assuming that there is not, or not primarily, an interest in an individual's satisfaction with a project but rather in a collective judgement of a team or a board, the object of measurement is the evaluation of a project as formulated in a meeting, or a memo, or an evaluation report. It depends on the degree of formalization of project evaluations in a company whether there are obvious places to find them (such as in formal reports or in written conclusions of meetings). If project evaluations are not formalized, they might only exist in the recollection of individual persons.

Up to now, three aspects of measurement have been specified; (a) different *variables* that are possible indicators of success of projects, (b) different *objects of measurement* of which these variables are attributes, and (c) different *locations* (such as financial and other records, or people's memories) where such objects of measurement can be found. Next it must be determined how to extract the value of the variable from that object of measurement. We distinguish three steps in this process:

1.   extracting "evidence" of the variable's value from the object of measurement (Step 4);
2.   recording this evidence – the recorded evidence is called "data" (Step 5);
3.   coding the data – the coded data is called a "score" (Step 6).

Step 4: specify how evidence of the value of the variable will be extracted from the object of measurement

An instrument must be able to extract **evidence** from the object of measurement that "corresponds" with the value of the variable, not other evidence. Different variables require very different instruments, some of which are very complicated (such as extracting evidence of a person's intelligence by means of a battery of tests) to very simple (such as extracting evidence of a project's costs by means of reading the appropriate lines in a financial report).

Financial success. After identification of the relevant financial records or reports, the relevant financial numbers need to be identified and read. If these records or reports do not provide a number for the total costs and revenues of a project, numbers for subcategories of costs and revenues need to be identified and read in different lines, columns, pages, or files. The set of different numbers that are identified in this way form the "evidence" that is extracted. The required "instrument" for extracting evidence of the value of the variable financial success, thus, is "reading the right numbers".

Timely delivery. After identification of a relevant press release or other document, information about the relevant date must be found in the document and read.

Satisfaction. After an evaluation report that contains evidence of how the company evaluates the project is identified, the report must be read to retrieve the required evidence. If such a report does not exist, one or more persons who are able to report their own evaluation of the project may be approached. Then there must be access to these persons to ask them for their judgements. "Interrogation" is the general term for asking information (such as judgements, opinions, and recollections) from an individual.

Interrogation basically has two forms; (a) interviewing (either face-to-face or by telephone) and (b) through a questionnaire (either paper or electronic).

Step 5: specify how sources of evidence will be identified, selected, and accessed

When it has been determined how evidence will be extracted from objects of measurement, the next step consists of specifying how the relevant sources of evidence will be identified and selecting the instances that will be studied, and then specifying how these will be accessed.

Financial success. The researcher needs to have the cooperation of company staff, usually staff of a finance department, in order to get access to the relevant records or reports. No further "selection" of such sources is needed.

Timely delivery. The researcher needs to find the relevant documents in which the end date of the project can be found. If such documents are public, one just needs to find and read them. If the relevant documents are confidential, company staff will need to cooperate in order to get access to them. Here again, no further "selection" of sources (documents) is needed. However, in order to identify which documents are likely to contain the required information (or in order to get relevant verbal reports if such documents do not exist), the help of informants in the company is needed. This implies that knowledgeable persons need to be found.

Satisfaction. After it has been specified how the success of a project as perceived by the company will be extracted from reports or other documents, the researcher needs to find these texts and "read" them. If the relevant documents are confidential, cooperation of company staff is needed in order to get access to them. In order to identify which documents are likely to contain the required information, help from informants in the company will be necessary. This implies that knowledgeable persons must be found.

Step 6: specify how evidence will be recorded

If evidence is extracted from the object of measurement, the evidence must be taken away from it and stored somewhere where the researcher has access to it when he wants to analyse the obtained information. The method of transporting and storing evidence is not obvious, and needs planning. For instance, if a researcher conducts an interview, the evidence that is extracted is in the words spoken by the respondent. This evidence is gone at the moment it is spoken. There are different ways of recording interview evidence:

- remembering it until data analysis;
- remembering it until one has returned to the office and written it down;

■ writing it down immediately after the interview;

■ making notes during the interview of what the researcher thinks the respondent wants to say;

■ making notes during the interview of what the respondent actually says, as verbatim as possible;

■ making a voice recording.

It is clear that the "evidence extracted from the object of measurement" is already changed considerably before it can be further processed and analysed by all these methods of recording except the last one (voice recording).

The same kind of reasoning applies to other kinds of evidence that is extracted from other kinds of objects of measurement. This can be illustrated with the example of different indicators of success of a project.

Financial success. After the financial records or reports have been identified and the appropriate entries have been read, the retrieved evidence can be remembered and written down later. Evidence can also be recorded by copying by hand on paper, reading into a voice recorder, copying (from paper) with a copying machine, printing (from a digital record), or copying from a digital record to a memory stick.

Timely delivery. Different forms of copying apply here as well.

Satisfaction. After identifying an evaluation report that contains evidence of how the company evaluates the project, that evidence must be copied. If respondents must be interviewed, the discussion above about recording interview evidence applies. If interrogation by means of a questionnaire is preferred, evidence will be automatically stored in a paper or electronic form.

Evidence that is recorded and is stored in the researcher's office is called "data".

Step 7: specify how data will be categorized

Data are stored evidence. They are not yet a "**score**", meaning a representation of a value of a variable that can be used for analysis after measurement. Data must be categorized or **coded** before they count as a score of a value of a variable. One example is measurement of psychological traits through sets of items (scales) in a questionnaire. After the respondent has marked his answers to the items (evidence) and the researcher has stored these answers in a database (data), the respondent's score on the measured trait is generated by some form of computation (score). Another example is measurement of a person's experiences through semi-structured interviews. The interview evidence (i.e. what a respondent has said) is recorded in some form (i.e. through a voice recorder) and transformed into data by transcription. The interview data are these transcripts (together with the voice recording as a backup and as a source of information about tone of voice, etc.). Some form of coding of the data in the transcripts is necessary in order to describe the opinions in them.

Although the researcher must have known all the time what kind of evidence is needed for scoring the value of a specific variable, it is again important in this phase of generating scores from data that the variable to be measured is clearly known, and what its relevant values are, and how these values must be defined. This can be illustrated with the examples.

Financial success. If numbers are copied from financial records (evidence) and these numbers are stored in the researcher's database (data), the researcher must now decide whether these numbers indicate financial success or not. This means that he must apply a procedure by which these numbers can be evaluated as indicating a success (presence/absence) and by which, if needed, the success can be rated in terms of intensity (moderate/huge, etc.). This requires (a) that the numbers must be computed in such a way that one final financial figure appears that indicates the overall financial gain or loss, (b) that a criterion for rating this figure is available, and (c) that there is a procedure for applying that criterion.

Timely delivery. A criterion for identifying the correct date (if more than one candidate date emerges from the data) is needed and that date must be compared to a deadline in order to attribute the value (early, too late, etc.) to the date.

Satisfaction. "Text analysis", "document analysis", and "content analysis" are the terms used for generating scores from texts. Coding is simple if an evaluation report that has been retrieved has a clear conclusion in which the project is unequivocally judged as a success or not. But coding is more complicated if such a judgement must be generated from different, ambiguous, and sometimes contradictory, statements in the report. Then the researcher must have a procedure for generating the evaluation from the text. For generating a score from interview data, if voice recorded, the data must first be transcribed or summarized in written form. The process of generating a score from interview or questionnaire data takes less effort if only standardized answer categories are allowed.

If the procedures as described here are successfully completed, the researcher has scores that indicate a value of a variable (here "success") for each instance of the object of study (here "a project").

Step 8: write a measurement protocol

After completion of steps 1 to 7, the procedures as generated in these steps need to be specified in a protocol. A protocol is a set of instructions for identifying, selecting, and accessing sources of evidence and for generating a valid and reliable score for each of the variables specified at the outset of the study.

After completion of steps 1 to 7 the researcher can specify, for each variable:

- the precise definition of the variable (as resulting from step 1 above);
- precise specifications of procedures for identification of instances of the object of measurement, for selecting them (if needed), and for

getting access to the source of evidence regarding the value of the variable for that object of measurement (as resulting from steps 2–5 above);

- precise specifications of procedures for generating scores regarding the value of the variable for that object of measurement (as resulting from steps 6 and 7 above).

The set of procedures specified in the protocol is the measurement instrument. At this point it can be asked how the quality of the measurement procedures as specified in the protocol can be evaluated. Below we discuss the two main quality criteria that apply to such procedures, measurement validity and reliability.

Measurement validity

Adcock and Collier (2001: 530) report that they have found 37 different adjectives that have been attached to the noun "**validity**" by scholars wrestling with issues of conceptualization and measurement. Examples are "**convergent**", "**construct**", "**content**", "**criterion**", and "**face**" (validity). Adcock and Collier observe that most of these adjectives do not designate different *types of validity* but rather different *types of evidence for validity*. With them, we prefer to use the term **measurement validity** for the overall concept. Valid measurement is achieved when scores can be considered to capture meaningfully the ideas contained in the corresponding concept. The degree to which this has been achieved cannot be assessed "objectively" but is an outcome of argumentation and discussion. We illustrate this with the three indicators of success of a project.

Financial success. After deciding that there is a need to "read" financial records in order to retrieve financial data indicating the degree of success of a project, directly or indirectly (after some computation), the type of financial data that are needed must be precisely specified. It is not possible just to copy any financial number from records but only those numbers whose "meaning" are precisely defined. The "meaning" of a specific number (most often an amount in a country's currency) is known if it is known how it was produced. For instance, if there is a need to retrieve the costs involved in a project (in order to assess whether a financial gain occurred), it must be known how the company assigns costs to projects. When relevant costs are not included in the costs documented in the records or reports, or when revenues are attributed to the project that actually were generated in ways that are not connected to the project, it is possible that the financial success of the project is overestimated. And, conversely, when costs are attributed to the project that actually are not related to the project, or when not all revenue from the project is included in the revenue as documented in the records or reports, underestimation of the project's success is possible. If necessary, financial data must be recalculated in such a way that they exactly represent *the researcher's definition of the variable*. If the records or reports do not contain sufficient information on how the various numbers or amounts have been calculated, it may be necessary to retrieve such information from (financial) staff in order to judge the validity of those data. If these are not valid in terms of the researcher's definition, staff could be asked to identify and retrieve other, more valid evidence.

In sum, a valid way of extracting evidence of the financial success of a project consists of:

- precisely defining what the researcher considers to be the financial success of a project;
- translating or "operationalizing" that definition in terms of precisely described operational procedures;
- evaluating the firm's procedures for computing the financial success of a project, if any, against these procedures;
- if necessary, identifying or computing other, more valid evidence.

A good instrument for financial success, thus, consists of a set of precisely defined procedures for:

1. retrieving and computing financial evidence; and
2. rating the success indicated by these data.

The criterion for measurement validity of this instrument is whether every detail of its procedures can be justified in terms of the researcher's definition of financial success.

Delivery time. There might be different types of delivery time of project results (the publication of the written report, the oral presentation of the results to the management, the final financial record, etc.), of which some might not count as a "real" delivery time according to the researcher's definition. Therefore, the researcher must define in a quite detailed way what is considered a "real" delivery time and what not. Next, the researcher's definition needs to be translated in precise procedures that are then applied to candidate occasions of delivery time, which are identified in "reading" the relevant documents or in the verbal reports from company staff who were involved in the end phase of the project. The criterion for measurement validity of these procedures is whether they can be justified in terms of the researcher's definition of delivery time.

Satisfaction. This indicator of success refers to success as defined by the company, not by the researchers. This is an important distinction, which implies that it is not necessary to apply the procedures outlined in the two previous examples. There is no need to evaluate the "correctness" of the company's judgement. The outcome of the company's evaluation can be accepted, irrespective of how it has been generated (although the researcher might be interested in the company's procedures and might want to try to collect evidence on these procedures as well). Measurement validity in this example regards the validity by which the researcher identifies, retrieves, and codes the company's evaluation, irrespective of how the company has generated its evaluation. If this evaluation has not been recorded in a document by the company, the researcher must (re)construct a company's satisfaction with a project through interviews. There are more and less valid ways of retrieving judgements (such as evaluations of project success) from respondents in interviews and/or through questionnaires, which we will not discuss in this book. We refer to many publications in this field, including Mason's book *Qualitative researching* (Chapter 4) for guidelines on how to develop valid questions for qualitative interviews, and Rossiter's (2002) C-OAR-SE procedure as a guide for developing valid items in standardized questionnaires.

Measurement validity, thus, concerns the quality of the six steps discussed above between the definition of the variable (step 1) and the writing of the protocol (step 8):

- determining the appropriate object of measurement;
- locating the object of measurement;
- extracting evidence from such objects;
- identifying, selecting, and accessing sources of evidence;
- recording the evidence that is extracted;
- coding the recorded data.

The procedures applied in each of these steps can be evaluated against the requirements that can be deduced from the (precise) definition of the variable that is measured.

Reliability

In accordance with the reasoning of Rossiter (2002) and Borsboom *et al.* (2004), we see measurement validity as an issue that precedes reliability. This is because **reliability** is an estimate of the precision of the *score* obtained by a measurement. The score must be assessed for reliability, not the procedures by which it is generated, although the procedure determines the precision. Measurement validity must be convincingly established before precise scores can be taken to mean what they are supposed to mean (Rossiter, 2002: 328).

Reliability, as defined here (i.e. the precision of a score), can itself be measured by generating more than one score of the value of the same variable in the same object of measurement and, next, assessing whether these scores are identical. The level of achieved reliability of the scores can be obtained by calculating the degree of similarity of scores for the same object of measurement and express it as an inter-observer, inter-rater, or test–retest reliability rate. We will discuss here how such procedures could be used to assess the reliability of scores obtained for the three different success variables.

Financial success. If a valid procedure for measuring the financial success of a project is developed, the reliability of this procedure can be tested by arranging that two or more persons, either company staff, or researchers, or their assistants, (a) retrieve the required information using these guidelines and (b) rate the degree of success as indicated by these data. If the reliability of the generated scores is insufficient (in terms of a criterion that was formulated beforehand) the procedures should be further specified until a sufficient level of reliability is achieved.

Delivery time. If a valid procedure for measuring the exact date of delivery *time* and for determining its timeliness is developed, the reliability of the score can be assessed by arranging that two or more persons identify the date the project was ended and then rate it for its timeliness. Scores are reliable if different raters identify the same end date for the project and assign the same timeliness score to it.

Satisfaction. If a valid procedure for the measurement of the value of satisfaction is developed, reliability of the scores obtained through this procedure can be assessed by using the same procedures described above for assessing the reliability of financial success or timeliness of delivery time. If the evidence is extracted through qualitative interviews with persons, structuring the interview can enhance reliability: the more structured a qualitative interview is (e.g. instructions regarding the interview as well as the questions specified in the interview guide), the more reliable will be the data generated in the interview. Different interviewers who interview the same person should obtain the same evidence. If the data are generated through a standardized questionnaire, consisting of questions in a fixed wording and with a fixed set of response categories, reliability is usually considered good, although different measurement conditions (e.g. how the questionnaire was introduced to the respondent, the absence or presence of other people such as supervisors, whether scores are obtained in an interview or by self-completion) can threaten the reliability of the scores that are obtained. Reliability can be assessed by repeated measurement, resulting in a "test–retest" reliability rate.

Measurement in a large number of instances

The procedures described in this appendix apply to all measurement. If the number of instances is large and if it, therefore, is considered costly in terms of time and effort to measure success in accordance with the procedures specified in the protocol in all instances, a researcher might be tempted to short-cut the measurement process. One common way to achieve efficiency is not to access the source of evidence itself but to use *informants* who have *information* about the value of the variable that must be measured. An informant extracts and reports evidence for a researcher but without being instructed as a researcher and, therefore, without knowing the researcher's definition of the variable. Scores obtained in this way should be treated with caution.

References

Adcock, R. and Collier, D. 2001, Measurement validity: a shared standard for qualitative and quantitative research. *American Political Science Review*, 95(3): 529–546.

Borsboom, D., Mellenberg, G.J., and Van Heerden, J. 2004, The concept of validity. *Psychological Review*, 111(4): 1061–1071.

Mason, J. 2002, *Qualitative researching* (2nd edn). London: Sage.

Rossiter, J.R. 2002, The C-OAR-SE procedure for scale development in marketing. *International Journal for Research in Marketing*, 19: 305–335.

Appendix 2: Business journals that publish case studies

Table A.2.1 is a list of scholarly business journals that have published five or more case studies from 2002–2005.

Table A.2.1

Scholarly business journals that have published five or more case studies from 2002–2005

Journal	Strategy	Finance	Marketing	HRM	Operations	Total
International Journal of Operations & Production Management	19			8	35	62
International Journal of Production Research					31	31
International Journal of Technology Management	16				8	24
Industrial Marketing Management	10		7	6		23
European Journal of Operational Research					21	21
Interfaces					21	21
Production Planning & Control					19	19
Journal of Management Studies	9			7		16
Long Range Planning	16					16
Human Relations				15		15
Organization Studies	6			8		14
Journal of Operations Management					13	13
Industrial Management & Data Systems					11	11
California Management Review	10					10
Technovation	10					10
Human Resource Management`				10		10
Journal of Business Research	9					9
Journal of Business Ethics				9		9
Industrial Robot					9	9
						(Continued)

Table A.2.1
(Continued)

Journal	Strategy	Finance	Marketing	HRM	Operations	Total
Journal of the Operational Research Society					8	8
Harvard Business Review	8					8
MIT Sloan Management Review	8					8
Strategic Management Journal	8					8
Academy of Management Executive	6				.	6
International Journal of Technology Management				6		6
Organizational Dynamics				6		6
Organization Science				6		6
Accounting, Organizations & Society		6				6
IIE Transactions					6	6
R&D Management	5					5
Information & Management				5		5
Journal of Manufacturing Systems					5	5
Production and Operations Management					5	5
Transportation Research. Part E, Logistics & Transportation Review					5	5
Total	*140*	*6*	*7*	*86*	*197*	*436*

Note: The total number might contain some overlapping articles. A case study that deals with a strategic issue in operations management might appear in both the fields of Strategy and Operations.

Appendix 3: Flowcharts

1.   A stepwise approach to research
2.   Deciding on the type of theory-oriented research
     a. Theory-testing research (initial theory-testing and replication)
     b. Theory-building research
3.   Deciding on the type of practice-oriented research
     a. Hypothesis-testing practice-oriented research
     b. Hypothesis-building practice-oriented research
     c. Descriptive practice-oriented research

Flowchart 1

A stepwise approach to research

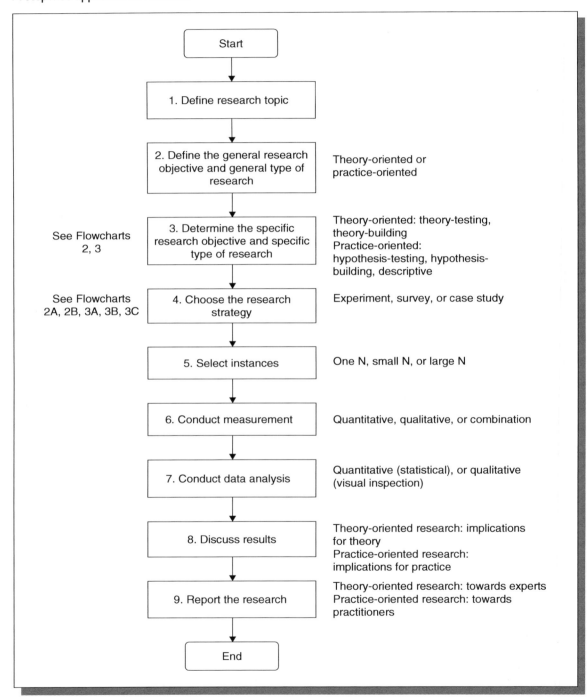

Flowchart 2
Deciding on the type of theory-oriented research

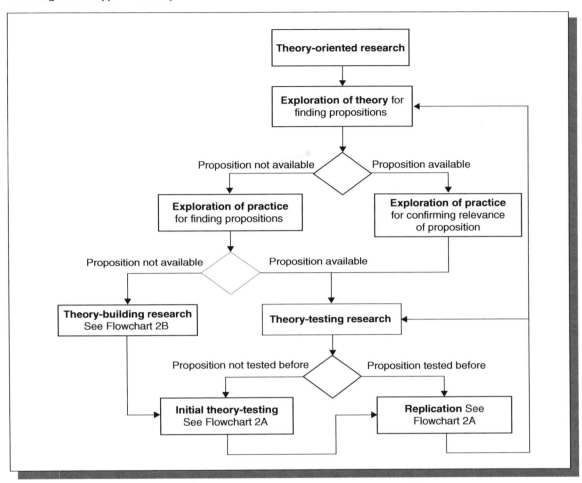

Flowchart 2A
Theory-testing research (initial theory-testing or replication)

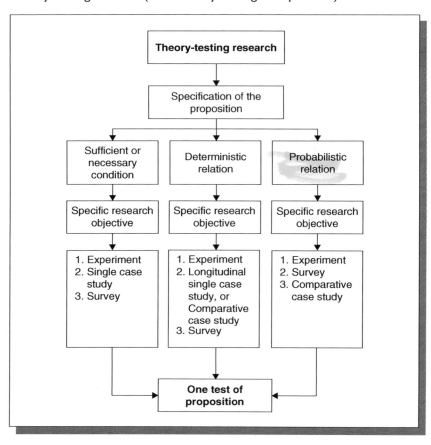

Flowchart 2B
Theory-building research

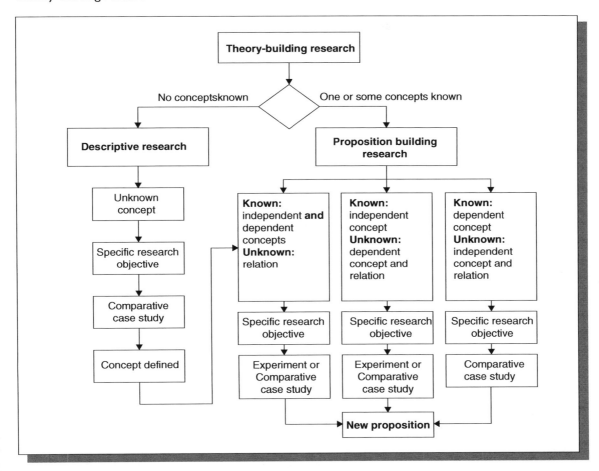

Flowchart 3
Deciding on the type of practice-oriented research

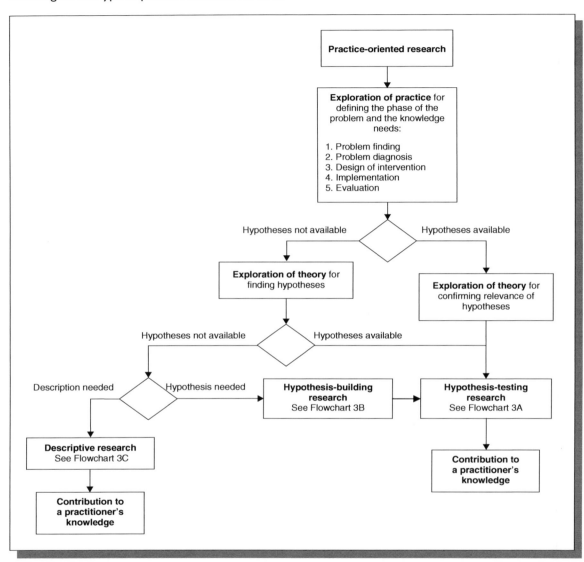

Flowchart 3A
Hypothesis-testing practice-oriented research

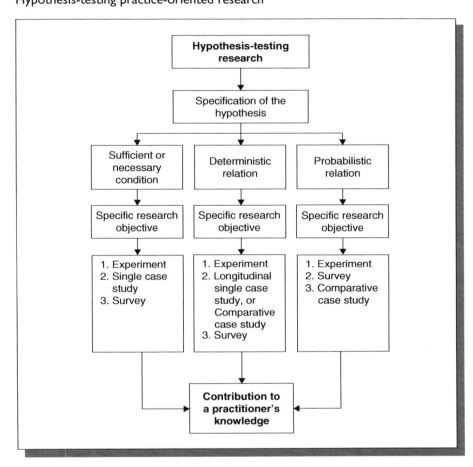

Flowchart 3B
Hypothesis-building practice-oriented research

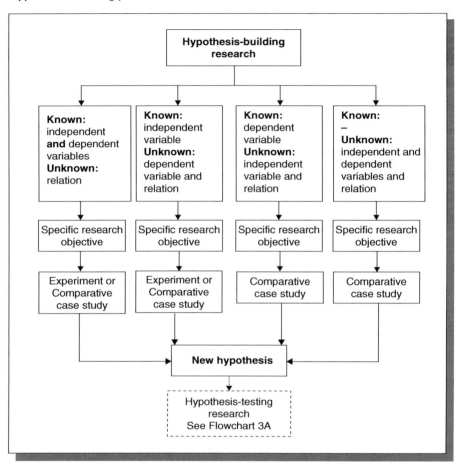

Flowchart 3C
Descriptive practice-oriented research

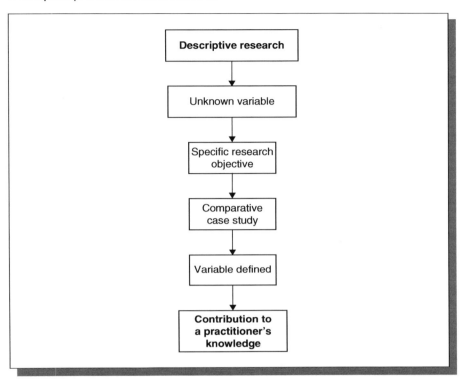

Appendix 4: Writing a case study research report

This appendix provides suggestions for the structure and topics of a case study research report.

Title

The title is the shortest summary of the research. It is read many times more than the report itself. It:

■ is a description of the research topic and the research objective; and
■ can also express the research strategy (for example by inclusion of a phrase such as "using a single case study").

Introduction

In the introduction the results of the preparation phase of the research are summarized. It contains:

■ the research topic;
■ the general research objective (results of the orientation);
■ the body of knowledge regarding the topic of the research (results of the exploration);
■ the specific research objective.

Methods

The methods section (written in past tense) describes how the research itself was done and which methodological choices were made:

■ research strategy – description and justification of the research strategy related to the specific research objective;
■ candidate cases – description and justification of candidate cases from which case(s) were selected;
■ case selection – description and justification of the selection of cases from the candidate cases;
■ measurement – description of how the variables were defined, of how objects of measurement were specified, how sources of evidence were identified, selected, and accessed, how evidence was extracted from these sources, how evidence was recorded, and how data were coded (see Appendix 1: "Measurement" for a discussion of these points);
■ data analysis – description and justification of qualitative analysis techniques.

Results

The results section (written in present tense) describes the results of the research without further interpretation and discussion:

- summary of results of the measurement;
- outcome of the data analysis regarding the specific research objective.

Discussion

In the discussion section, implications of the outcome of the research are discussed:

- limitations of the research (e.g. related to the choices as described in the Methods section) and its possible effects on the study's outcome;
- implications of outcome for theory (for theory-oriented research) or for practice (for practice-oriented research);
- future research needs based on the outcome of the research (for theory-oriented research, also the replication strategy);
- if desired, speculation about the possible contribution to practice (for theory-oriented research) or to theory (for practice-oriented research).

Appendix 5: Glossary

Note for the reader:
This glossary contains definitions of the technical terms used in this book. The definitions below often differ considerably from other definitions of the same term in the literature. Sometimes this is an attempt to improve upon current definitions, such as for case study research and survey research. We also sometimes do not mention meanings of a concept that are not relevant to this book. An example is the definition of research that might include a range of types of research (such as theoretical research and philosophical research) but in this glossary is limited to empirical research only because we do not discuss the other existent types of research in this book.

Candidate case (Page 92)
A candidate case is a member of a set of cases from which the researcher will select one case or a small number of cases for a case study.

Candidate population (Page 46)
A candidate population is a member of a set of populations from which the researcher will select a population for a survey or a quasi survey.

Case (Page 4)
A case is an instance of an object of study.

Case selection (Page 92)
Case selection is selecting one case or a small number of cases from a set of candidate cases for a case study.

Case study (Page 4)
A case study is a study in which (a) one case (single case study) or a small number of cases (comparative case study) in their real life context are selected, and (b) scores obtained from these cases are analysed in a qualitative manner.
    See Qualitative analysis.

Case study research (Page 3)
Case study research (or "the case study") is research in which (a) one case (single case study) or a small number of cases (comparative case study) in their real life context are selected, and (b) scores obtained from these cases are analysed in a qualitative manner.
    See Qualitative analysis.

Causal relation (Page 35)
A causal relation is a relation between two variable characteristics A and B of an object of study in which a value of A (or its change) permits, or results, in a value of B (or in its change).
    See Cause, Dependent concept, Effect, and Independent concept.

Cause (Pages 36–37)
A cause is a variable characteristic A of an object of study of which the value (or its change) permits, or results, in a value (or its change) of another variable characteristic B (which is called the effect).

See Causal relation, Dependent concept, Effect, and Independent concept.

Coding (Page 258)
Coding is categorizing data in order to generate scores.

Comparative case study (Page 45)
A comparative case study is a study in which (a) a small number of cases in their real life context are selected, and (b) scores obtained from these cases are analysed in a qualitative manner.

See Theory-testing comparative case study (or quasi survey), Hypothesis-testing practice-oriented comparative case study, Theory-building comparative case study, and Hypothesis-building practice-oriented comparative case study.

Concept (Page 35)
A concept is a variable aspect of an object of study as defined in a theory.

See Dependent concept and variable, Independent concept and variable, Mediating concept and variable, Moderating concept and variable, and Variable.

Conceptual model (Page 36)
A conceptual model is a visual representation of a proposition in which the concepts are presented by blocks and the relation between them by an arrow. The arrow originates in the independent concept and points to the dependent concept.

Confirmation of a hypothesis (Page 87)
A hypothesis is said to be confirmed if the observed pattern of scores is the same as the pattern predicted by the hypothesis.

See Expected pattern, Generalizability, Observed pattern, Pattern matching, Rejection of a hypothesis, and Support for a proposition.

Construct validity (Page 260)
Construct validity is a type of evidence of measurement validity.
See Measurement validity.

Content validity (Page 260)
Content validity is a type of evidence of measurement validity.
See Measurement validity.

Convergent validity (Page 260)
Convergent validity is a type of evidence of measurement validity.
See Measurement validity.

Criterion validity (Page 260)
Criterion validity is a type of evidence of measurement validity.
    See Measurement validity.

Data (Page 258)
Data are the recordings of evidence generated in the process of data collection.

Data analysis (Page 5)
Data analysis is the interpretation of scores obtained in a study in order to generate the outcome of the study. There are two main approaches to analysis: qualitative and quantitative.
    See Qualitative analysis and Quantitative analysis.

Data collection (Page 5)
Data collection is the process of (a) identifying and selecting one or more objects of measurement, (b) extracting evidence of the value of the relevant variable characteristics from these objects, and (c) recording this evidence.
    See Object of measurement

Data matrix (Page 189)
A data matrix is a visual representation of scores obtained in a theory-building comparative case study. Propositions are built by analysing the patterns of scores in this matrix.

Dependent concept (Page 36)
A dependent concept is a variable characteristic B of an object of study of which the value (or its change) is the result of, or is permitted by a value (or its change) of another variable characteristic A (which is called the independent concept).

Dependent variable (Page 223)
A dependent variable is a variable B which, according to a hypothesis, is an effect of an independent variable A.

Descriptive research (Page 224)
Descriptive research is a type of practice-oriented research of which the objective is to contribute to a practitioner's knowledge by identifying and describing not yet known variable characteristics of the object of study.

Deterministic proposition (Page 66)
A deterministic proposition is a proposition that either expresses a sufficient condition, or a necessary condition, or a deterministic relation.
    See Deterministic relation, Necessary condition, and Sufficient condition.

Deterministic relation (Page 66)
A deterministic relation is a relation between an independent concept and a dependent concept in which their values always increase or decrease at the

same time (positive relation) or in which the value of one always increases as the other decreases (negative relation).

Domain (Page 36)
A domain is the universe of instances to which statements apply.
    See Object of study, Practice domain, and Theoretical domain.

Domain representativeness (Page 45)
Domain representativeness is the degree of similarity between the distribution of the values of the variables in an instance of an object of study (or a group of instances or a population) and their distribution in the theoretical domain, as well as the degree of similarity between the causal relations in these instances and in the domain.
    See Representativeness.

Ecological validity (Page 47)
Ecological validity is the extent to which the outcome of a laboratory experiment applies to instances of the object of study in its real life context.

Effect (Page 36)
An effect is a variable characteristic B of an object of study of which the value (or its change) is the result of, or is permitted by a value (or its change) of another variable characteristic A (which is called the cause).
    See Causal relation, Dependent concept, Effect, and Independent concept.

Empirical cycle (Page 38)
The empirical cycle is the process of formulating propositions, testing them, reformulating them (or not) on the basis of test results, testing them, and so on, until a final formulation of the proposition is considered robust and generalizable to the specified domain.

Evidence (Page 256)
Evidence is the information extracted from an object of measurement.

Expected pattern (Page 95)
An expected pattern is a score or a combination of scores that is predicted by a hypothesis for a case or a small number of cases.
    See Observed pattern and Pattern matching.

Experiment (Page 5)
An experiment is a study in which one or more variable characteristics of an object of study are manipulated in one or multiple ("experimental") instances of an object of study and in which scores obtained in the experimental instance or instances are analysed.

Experimental research (Page 5)

Experimental research (or "the experiment") is a research strategy in which (a) one or more variable characteristics of an object of study are manipulated in one or multiple ("experimental") instances of an object of study, and (b) scores obtained in the experimental instance or instances are analysed in a quantitative or in a qualitative manner.

Expert (Page 33)

An expert is a person with specialized knowledge about a theory and its object of study.

Exploration (Page 38)

Exploration is collecting and evaluating relevant information about theory or about a practice in order to assess exactly how research could best contribute to either the development of theory or a practitioner's knowledge.

See Exploration of practice and Exploration of theory.

Exploration of practice (Page 49)

Exploration of practice is collecting and evaluating relevant information for theory (in theory-oriented research) or for practice (in practice-oriented research) by identifying and evaluating relevant practice literature, communicating with practitioners, and visiting as well as participating in real life situations in which an object of study occurs.

Exploration of theory (Page 48)

Exploration of theory is collecting and evaluating relevant information for theory (in theory-oriented research) or for practice (in practice-oriented research) by conducting a literature review and communicating with experts.

External validity (Page 47)

External validity is the extent to which the outcome of a study in one instance or in a group of instances applies (or can be generalized) to instances other than those in the study. Two important forms of external validity are ecological validity and statistical generalizability.

See Ecological validity and Statistical generalizability.

Face validity (Page 260)

Face validity is a type of evidence of measurement validity.

See Measurement validity.

Generalizability (Page 47)

The generalizability of a proposition is the degree of confidence that it is correct and applies to the entire theoretical domain. Generalizability can (only) be enhanced by replications of tests of propositions.

See Replication and Replication strategy.

Group of instances (Page 46)
A group of instances is a small set of instances of an object of study for comparative case study research.
See Population.

Hypothesis (Page 63)
A hypothesis is a statement about a relation between variables.
See Confirmation and Rejection.

Hypothesis-building practice-oriented comparative case study (Page 222)
A hypothesis-building practice-oriented comparative case study is a case study in which one or more hypotheses are built on the basis of a comparison between scores obtained from a small number of instances.

Hypothesis-testing practice-oriented comparative case study (Page 218)
A hypothesis-testing practice-oriented comparative case study is a case study in which a deterministic or probabilistic hypothesis is tested in a small population or in a sample from a population in a practice.

Independent concept (Page 36)
An independent concept is a variable characteristic A of an object of study of which the value (or its change) permits, or results, in a value (or its change) of another variable characteristic B (which is called the dependent concept).

Independent variable (Page 223)
An independent variable is a variable A which, according to a hypothesis, is a cause of a dependent variable B.

Instance of an object of study (Page 4)
An instance of an object of study is one occurrence of the object of study.

Internal validity (Page 181)
Internal validity is the extent to which the outcome of an analysis is justified by the scores obtained in the study.

Intervention cycle (Page 54)
The intervention cycle is a model of problem solving in which it is depicted as a process of five successive phases.

Longitudinal case study (Page 139)
A longitudinal case study is a single case study in which scores are obtained at two or more points in time.

Measurement (Page 253)
Measurement is a process in which a score or scores are generated for analysis. Measurement consists of (a) data collection and (b) coding. Measurement procedures must be valid and the resulting scores must be reliable.
See Coding, Data collection, Measurement validity, Reliability, and Score.

Measurement validity (Page 260)
Measurement validity is the extent to which procedures of data collection and of coding can be considered to capture meaningfully the ideas contained in the concept of which the value is measured.

Mediating concept (Page 85)
A mediating concept is a concept that links the independent and the dependent concept in a proposition and which is necessary for the causal relation between the independent and the dependent concept to exist.

Mediating variable (Page 85)
A mediating variable is a variable that mediates the relation between the independent and the dependent variables in a hypothesis.

Moderating concept (Page 85)
A moderating concept is a concept that qualifies the relation between the independent and the dependent concepts in a proposition.

Moderating variable (Page 85)
A moderating variable is a variable that qualifies the relation between the independent and the dependent variables in a hypothesis.

Multiple case study (Page 45)
A multiple case study is a case study with more than one case.
    See Comparative case study, Serial single case study, and Parallel single case study.

Necessary condition (Page 66)
A necessary condition is a cause A that must exist in order for effect B to exist. This condition can be formulated as "B only if A". A necessary condition always implies an equivalent sufficient condition formulated as "If non-A then non-B".
    See Sufficient condition.

Object of measurement (Page 254)
An object of measurement is an object that must be accessed in order to extract evidence of the value of a variable. An object of measurement is not the same as the object of study.
    See Data collection and Measurement.

Object of study (Page 35)
An object of study is the stable characteristic of a theory or practice.

Observed pattern (Page 95)
An observed pattern is the score or the combination of scores obtained in a study. In data analysis, an observed pattern is compared ("matched") with an expected pattern.
    See Expected pattern, Pattern matching, Qualitative analysis, and Visual inspection.

Orientation (Page 33)

Orientation is an initial exploration of a topic of interest aimed at identifying and formulating a provisional global research objective. Orientation consists of both orientation of practice and orientation of theory.

See Orientation of practice and Orientation of theory.

Orientation of practice (Page 33)

Orientation of practice is an initial exploration of a topic of interest by identifying and evaluating relevant practice literature, communicating with practitioners, and visiting as well as participating in real life situations.

Orientation of theory (Page 33)

Orientation of theory is an initial exploration of a topic of interest by identifying and evaluating the relevant scientific literature and communicating with experts.

Outcome (Page 87)

The outcome of a study is the outcome of its data analysis, which is a confirmation or a rejection of a hypothesis, a new hypothesis or proposition, or a description of a variable or concept.

Parallel replication strategy (Page 44)

A parallel replication strategy is a strategy in which a number of single cases or single populations are selected at the same time, and the same proposition is tested in each of them without taking into account the outcome of any of the separate tests.

See Serial replication strategy.

Parallel single case study (Page 45)

A parallel single case study is case study research that is designed according to a parallel replication strategy.

See Serial single case study.

Pattern (Page 95)

A pattern is a score or a combination of scores.

See Expected pattern, Observed pattern, and Pattern matching.

Pattern matching (Page 95)

Pattern matching is comparing two or more patterns by visual inspection in order to determine whether patterns match (i.e. that they are the same) or do not match (i.e. that they differ). Pattern matching in qualitative analysis is comparing an observed pattern with an expected pattern.

See Expected pattern, Observed pattern, Qualitative analysis, and Visual inspection.

Population (Page 46)

A population is a set of instances of an object of study defined by one or a small number of criteria.

Population representativeness (Page 47)

Population representativeness is the degree of similarity between the distribution of the values of the variables in a sample and their distribution in the population from which the sample is drawn, as well as the degree of similarity between the causal relations in the sample and in the population.

See Probabilistic sample and Representativeness.

Population selection (Page 46)

Population selection is selecting a population from a set of candidate populations for a survey or a quasi survey.

Practice (Pages 30–31)

A practice is the real life situation for which a practitioner has either a formal or an informal responsibility and in which he acts or must act.

Practice domain (Page 221)

A practice domain is the universe of instances of the object of study in practice-oriented research.

Practice-oriented research (Page 30)

Practice-oriented research is research of which the objective is to contribute to the knowledge of one or more specified practitioners.

Practitioner (Page 52)

A practitioner is a person or group of persons with either a formal or an informal responsibility for a real life situation in which he acts or must act.

Practitioner's knowledge need (Page 56)

A practitioner's knowledge need is knowledge that a practitioner needs in order to act effectively in a practice and that the practitioner currently does not have.

Pragmatic determinism (Page 75)

Pragmatic determinism is the view that it is sometimes preferable to act as if a complete determinism exists, although it is acknowledged that there might be some exceptions to the assumed determinism.

Probabilistic proposition (Page 66)

A probabilistic proposition is a proposition that expresses a probabilistic relation.

Probabilistic relation (Page 66)

A probabilistic relation is a relation between an independent concept or variable and a dependent concept or variable in which their values, on average, increase or decrease at the same time (positive relation) or in which the value of one, on average, increases as the other decreases (negative relation).

Probability sample (Page 47)
A probability sample is a sample that is selected through a procedure of probability sampling.
　　See Probability sampling.

Probability sampling (Page 46)
Probability sampling is a sampling procedure in which each member of the population has a fixed probabilistic chance of being selected.
　　See Random sampling.

Proposition (Page 35)
A proposition is a statement about the relation between concepts. The two main types of proposition are deterministic and probabilistic.
　　See Deterministic proposition and Probabilistic proposition.

Qualitative analysis (Page 5)
Qualitative analysis is identifying and evaluating a pattern in the scores obtained in a study.
　　See Pattern, Pattern matching, and Visual inspection.

Quantitative analysis (Page 5)
Quantitative analysis is generating and evaluating the output of statistical procedures applied to the scores obtained in a study.

Quasi survey (Page 83)
A quasi survey is a comparative case study in which a probabilistic proposition is tested.
　　See Comparative case study.

Random sample (Page 83)
A random sample is a sample that is selected through a procedure of random sampling.
　　See Random sampling.

Random sampling (Page 83)
Random sampling is a sampling procedure in which each member of the population has an equal chance of being selected.
　　See Probability sampling.

Real life context (Page 4)
Real life context is the object of study as it occurs (or has occurred) in reality, without manipulation.

Rejection of a hypothesis (Page 87)
A hypothesis is said to be rejected if the observed pattern of scores is not the same as the pattern predicted by the hypothesis.

See Confirmation of a hypothesis, Expected pattern, Observed pattern, Pattern matching, and Support for a proposition.

Reliability (Page 262)
Reliability is the degree of precision of a score.

Replication (Page 41)
Replication is conducting a test of a proposition in another instance of the object of study (or in another group of instances or population).

Replication strategy (Page 88)
A replication strategy is a plan for the identification and selection of an instance of an object of study (or in a group of instances or population) for a next test of a proposition.

Representativeness (Page 45)
The representativeness of a group of instances of an object of study is the degree of similarity between the distribution of the values of the variables in the instances in this group and their distribution in a larger group of instances (which is usually a domain or a population), as well as the degree of similarity between the causal relations in this group and in the larger group.

See Domain representativeness and Population representativeness.

Research (Page 30)
Research is building and testing statements about an object of study or practice by analysing evidence drawn from observation.

Research objective (Page 30)
A research objective is a specification of the aim of a study.

Research strategy (Page 6)
A research strategy is a category of procedures for selecting one or more instances of an object of study and for data analysis. In this book we distinguish three broad categories of research strategy: experimental research ("the experiment"), survey research ("the survey"), and case study research ("the case study").

See Case study research, Experimental research, and Survey research.

Robustness (Page 44)
Robustness is the degree of support for a proposition.

See Support for a proposition.

Sample (Page 46)
A sample is a set of instances selected from a population.

Sampling (Page 46)

Sampling is the selection of instances from a population.

Sampling frame (Page 83)

A sampling frame is a complete list of the members of a population. A sampling frame is needed for probability sampling.

See Probability sampling.

Score (Page 258)

A score is a value assigned to a variable by coding data.

Serial replication strategy (Page 44)

A serial replication strategy is a strategy in which each test takes into account the outcome of previous tests.

See Parallel replication strategy.

Serial single case study (Page 45)

A serial single case study is case study research that is designed according to a serial replication strategy.

See Parallel single case study.

Single case study (Page 4)

A single case study is a case study with one case.

Statistical generalizability (Page 47)

Statistical generalizability is the likelihood that research results obtained in a sample of a population are also true for the population.

See Generalizability, Probabilistic sampling, and Representativeness.

Study (Page 30)

A study is a research project in which a research objective is formulated and achieved.

Sufficient condition (Page 66)

A sufficient condition is a cause A that always results in effect B. This condition can be expressed in the formulation "If A then B". A sufficient condition always implies a logically equivalent necessary condition, which can be formulated as "Non-B only if non-A".

See Necessary condition.

Support for a proposition (Page 90)

A proposition is said to be supported in a test if the hypothesis is confirmed.

Survey (Page 5)

A survey is a study in which (a) a single population in the real life context is selected, and (b) scores obtained from this population are analysed in a quantitative manner.

See Population, Sampling, and Quantitative analysis.

Survey research (Page 5)
Survey research (or "the survey") is research in which (a) a single population in the real life context is selected, and (b) scores obtained from this population are analysed in a quantitative manner.
See Population, Sampling, and Quantitative analysis.

Test (Page 90)
A test of a proposition (in theory-testing research) is determining whether a hypothesis that is deduced from the proposition is confirmed or rejected in an instance of an object of study (or in a group of instances or population).
A test of a hypothesis (in hypothesis-testing practice-oriented research) is determining whether a hypothesis is confirmed or rejected in an instance of an object of study (or in a group of instances or population).
See Confirmation and Rejection.

Theoretical domain (Page 36)
A theoretical domain is the universe of instances of an object of study of a theory.

Theory (Page 34)
A theory is a set of propositions regarding the relations between the variable characteristics (concepts) of an object of study in a theoretical domain.

Theory-building (Page 38)
Theory-building is the formulation of new propositions.

Theory-building comparative case study (Page 182)
A theory-building comparative case study is a case study in which one or more propositions are built on the basis of a comparison between scores obtained from a small number of cases in a theoretical domain.

Theory-building research (Page 38)
Theory-building research is research with the objective of formulating new propositions based on the evidence drawn from observation of instances of the object of study.

Theory development (Page 38)
Theory development is the process of improving a theory by (a) formulating new propositions (through exploration or theory-building research), (b) enhancing their robustness (through initial theory-testing research or replication research), (c) reformulating them (through initial theory-testing research or replication research), and (d) enhancing their generalizability (through replication research).

Theory-in-use (Page 50)
A theory-in-use is a practitioner's knowledge of "what works" in practice, expressed in terms of an object of study, variables, hypotheses, and a practice domain.

Theory-oriented research (Page 30)

Theory-oriented research is research of which the objective is to contribute to theory development.

See Theory development.

Theory-testing (Page 38)

Theory-testing is selecting one or more propositions for a test and conducting the test.

Theory-testing comparative case study (Page 43)

A theory-testing comparative case study is a case study in which a probabilistic proposition is tested in a small population or in a sample from a population.

See Quasi survey.

Theory-testing research (Page 38)

Theory-testing research is research with the objective to test propositions.

Validity (Page 260)

Validity is the extent to which a research procedure can be considered to capture meaningfully its aims.

See External validity, Internal validity, and Measurement validity.

Variable (Page 35)

A variable is a measurable indicator of a concept in research.

See Concept and Hypothesis.

Visual inspection (Page 5)

Visual inspection is the procedure by which patterns are discovered or compared by looking at the scores.

See Pattern, Pattern matching, and Qualitative analysis.

Index

Accounting/finance case studies, 22, 265–6
Akzo Nobel, 241–51
Alliances, collaborations, 98–119
Appendices, 253–91
Architectural innovations, 120–36
Archival records, uses, 26

Bennett, Andrew, 41
Best practice, company standardization, 229, 240–51
Brainstorming sessions, 245–6, 251
Business process redesigns, 97–8
Business relevance, propositions, 71–6, 88
Business services, 184, 197–213, 243–51
Buyers, business-services providers, 184, 197–213

C-OAR-SE procedure, 262
Call centres, 201–4
Candidate case
  definition, 92, 278
Candidate population, 46, 278
Case
  definition, 4, 278
Case selection, 84, 92–3, 115–16, 132, 139, 157–8, 209, 230, 278
Case study
  definition, 3–6, 19, 40–1, 278
  designs, 10–16, 17, 25–7, 89–172, 184–96, 229–33, 253–64

evaluations, 24, 26–7, 31–2, 77–89, 134–6
fields of business research, 19–29, 88, 265–6
'flash case study', 231–3
guidelines, 24, 25–6
multiple case study, 3–4, 43–5
quality criteria, 26–7
reports, 11–16, 17, 25–6, 233, 276–7
types, 4–5, 6–7, 8–9, 23–4, 30–59, 63
  see also Comparative…; Single…
Case study research
  definition, 3–4, 19, 40–1, 278
  guidelines, 24, 25–6
  how-to-do guides, 10, 90–8, 138–42, 184–96, 229–33
Causal relation
  complex conceptual model, 84–9
  concepts, 35–6, 65–6, 72–89, 176–83, 185–91, 278
  definition, 35–6, 278
Cause, 36–7, 279
Coding
  definition, 87, 279
  Grounded Theory, 179, 187–8
  open coding, 187–8
  see also Score
Collaboration characteristics, innovation projects, 91, 98–119
Company representatives, business-services providers, 184, 197–213

Company standardization, best practice, 229, 240–51

Comparative case study
    definition, 4–5, 40–1, 45, 279
    practice-oriented research, 220–4, 227

Competitive advantage, 37, 186, 203–4, 233–4

The Competitive Advantages of Nations (Porter), 186

Complex conceptual model, 84–9
    see also Conceptual model

Component services, business services, 198–213

Concept
    causal relation, 35–6, 65–6, 72–89, 176–83, 185–91, 278
    definition, 34–7, 65–6, 245–9, 279
    Grounded Theory, 179, 187–8
    measurement, 93, 181, 185–8, 253–4
    mediating concept, 85–6, 284
    moderating concept, 85–6, 284
    open coding, 187–8
    see also Dependent...; Independent...;
        Proposition; Variable

Conceptual model
    complex model, 84–9
    definition, 279

Confirmation of a hypothesis
    definition, 40, 42, 87, 90, 279

Construct validity, 260, 279

Constructivism, 41

Consumption services, business services, 198–213

Content validity, 260, 279

Continuous variable, necessary condition, 72–3

Convergent validity, 260, 279

Coordination integration, organizational configurations, 121–36

Criterion validity, 260, 280

Critical success factors, 35–7, 50–1, 66–7

Data, 153, 209, 256, 258–9

Data analysis
    definition, 5, 280
    see also Qualitative...; Quantitative...

Data collection
    definition, 280
    see also Measurement

Data matrix, 189, 192, 193, 194, 195

Davidsson, Per, 44

Dependent concept, 36–7, 280
    definition
        complex conceptual model, 84–9
        conceptual model, 36–7, 76–82, 84–9, 93, 96–7, 101–2, 123, 130–1, 140–2, 145, 157, 158–9, 160–2, 171–2, 176–83, 185–8, 191–6, 207–10

Dependent variable, 140, 158, 223, 280

Descriptive research
    definition, 225, 280
    objectives, 225–6, 241–4, 248–9, 251
    see also Practice-oriented research

Deterministic proposition
    definition, 66, 280
    see also Necessary...; Sufficient...

Deterministic relation
    complex conceptual model, 85
    definition, 69–70, 138–9, 280–1
    how-to-do guide, 138–42, 190–1, 194
    practice-oriented research, 220–2, 237–8
    proposition, 138–9, 190–1, 194, 212
    research strategiy, 77, 81–2, 88–9, 138–9, 145–6, 152–3, 238
    theory-building research, 177–83, 190–1, 194, 212
    theory-testing research, 77, 81–2, 88–9, 138–55

Domain
    definition, 36, 46, 281
    practice, 221–2

Domain representativeness
    definition, 45–7, 281
    see also Representativeness

Dow Chemical, 241–51

DSM, 241–51

Ecological validity
    definition, 47
    see also Validity

Effect, 36, 281

Empirical cycle, definition, 53

Ethnography, 19

Evidence
    definition, 256, 281

Expected pattern, 95, 281
Experiment
    definition, 5, 281–2
    practice-oriented research, 220–2, 224,
        226–7, 238, 270, 281–2
    replication, 42–4, 77–89
    theory-testing research, 76–89, 170
    see also Research strategy
Experimental research, 5, 282
Expert, theory, 49, 58–9, 64–5, 92, 133
Exploration
    definition, 38, 282
    practice, 49–51, 56–8, 63–4, 92, 175–6,
        217–28, 232
    practice-oriented research, 56–9, 217–28,
        232–51
    theory, 48–51, 53, 56–9, 63–4, 92, 175–83,
        187–9, 217–18, 232
    types, 48–51, 217
    see also Orientation; Theory-building…
External validity
    definition, 47, 282
    see also Validity

Face validity, 260, 282
Finance case studies, 19–29, 265–6
    journals, 20–9, 265–6
'Flash case study', practice-oriented research,
    231–3
Focus groups, 235–40, 248–51

Gasunie, 241–51
General research objective, 30–4, 52, 63–7,
    77–89, 102, 113, 123, 131, 145, 152, 162,
    170, 175–7, 217–20, 222–6, 231–3, 237–8
Generalizability, 3, 6–8, 32, 45, 47–8, 57, 64–5,
    83–4, 88, 93, 95–6, 157–8, 183, 221–2, 282
    definition, 47–8, 282
    see also Statistical…
George, Alexander L., 41
Goertz, Gary, 72
Grounded Theory (GT), 179, 187–8
Group of instances, 46, 283

How-to-do guides
    case study research, 10, 90–8, 138–42,
        184–96, 229–33

    practice-oriented research, 229–33
    theory-building research, 184–96
    theory-testing research, 10, 90–8, 138–42
HRM case studies, 19–29, 243–51, 265–6
    journals, 20–9, 265–6
Hubbard, Raymond, 42, 44
Hypothesis, 6–8, 32, 41–2, 55–9, 63–6, 76–7,
    87–94, 104–5, 110–19, 123–5, 129–36,
    140–1, 147–9, 153–5, 158, 163, 168–9,
    171–2, 217–28, 230–51, 283
    confirmation, 87–8, 90–1, 95–8, 111–12,
        114–15, 117–18, 133, 135–6, 154–5, 168,
        171–2, 212, 230–1, 237–40, 279
    definition, 57, 65–6, 93–4, 231–3, 283
    exploration of theory, 57–8, 217–18, 232
    proposition, 57, 93–4, 231–3
    rejection, 42, 78–9, 87–8, 90–1, 95–8, 111–12,
        114, 117–18, 123, 129–30, 133–6, 150–3,
        168, 171–2, 230–1, 238
Hypothesis-building practice-oriented
    comparative case study, 224, 283
Hypothesis-building research, 17, 55–6, 59,
    217–18, 222–4, 227–8, 230–1, 272, 274, 283
    definition, 56, 222, 283
    known/unknown variables, 223–4, 227, 230
    objectives, 222–4
    research strategies, 224–5
    see also Practice-oriented research
Hypothesis-testing practice-oriented
    comparative case study, 220, 283
Hypothesis-testing research, 17, 55–6, 59,
    217–22, 227–8, 230–1, 232, 272–3, 274, 283
    definition, 56, 218–19, 283
    objectives, 219–20
    research strategies, 220–2, 238
    theory-testing research, 220–1, 230–1
    see also Practice-oriented research

Independent concept
    complex conceptual model, 84–9
    conceptual model, 36–7, 76–82, 84–9, 93,
        96–7, 101–2, 123, 130–1, 140–2, 145, 157,
        158–9, 160–2, 171–2, 176–83, 185–8,
        191–6, 207–10
Independent variable, 223, 283
Informant, measurement, 263

Initial theory-testing, 39–41, 53, 64–5, 77–89, 93, 131
    definition, 39
    see also Theory-testing research
Innovation project
    collaboration characteristics, 91, 98–119
    critical success factors, 35–7, 50–1, 66–7, 99–119, 191–6
    organizational configurations, 91, 119–36, 233–40
    radical/incremental innovations, 99, 120–36
Instance of an object of study, 5–6, 12–15, 46, 220–2, 224–5, 230–1, 232, 283
Intensive exploration, 188
    see also Exploration
Internal validity, 181, 283
Interrogation, 256–8
    see also Interview; Questionnaire
Intervention cycle, 53–5, 57–9, 218–28, 249
    definition, 53
Interview, 5–6, 15, 126–7, 149–51, 154, 200–4, 209–10, 242–5, 250–1, 253, 256–8
    see also Interrogation; Qualitative measurement

Journals, case studies, 20–9, 43, 265–6

Knowledge, 9, 30–4, 52–9, 71–6, 121–36, 200–13, 217–51, 273–5, 286
Knowledge need, practitioners, 53–6, 286
Known/unknown concept, theory-building research, 176–83, 184–213, 223–4
Known/unknown variable, hypothesis-building research, 223–4, 227, 230
KPN Royal Dutch Telecom, 199–212

'Least likely' case, 93, 95–6, 230
Lee, Allen S., 26, 72, 97
Literature review, 48–9, 59, 130, 131–2, 135
Longitudinal case study, 77, 81–2, 89, 139–55, 220–2, 238

Management knowledge, problem-solving, 71–6
Management practice, management theory, 31–2

Management theory, management practice, 31–2
Marketing case studies, 19–29, 265–6
    journals, 20–9, 265–6
Measurement, 5–6, 12–15, 26–7, 35–6, 40–1, 64, 87–9, 93–6, 105–11, 116–17, 125–8, 132–3, 141–2, 149–51, 153–8, 163–6, 181, 185–8, 200–4, 209–11, 232–40, 244–5, 250–64, 276–7
    definition, 93, 181, 185–8, 245–9, 253–4
    evidence, 94–6, 105–11, 116–17, 125–8, 132–3, 149–51, 153–4, 163–6, 181, 187–8, 200–4, 209–10, 235–7, 239–40, 244–5, 250–1, 256–8, 261–2
    informant, 263
    object of measurement, 4, 6–7, 12–15, 253–7, 261–2
    protocol, 259–60
    recording methods, 257–8, 261–2
    stepwise procedure, 253–64
    see also Coding; Data collection; Reliability; Score; Validity
Measurement validity, 260–2, 284
Mediating concept, 85–6, 284
Mediating variable, 85, 284
Moderating concept, 85–6, 284
Moderating variable, 85–6, 284
Modular innovation, 120–36
'Most likely' case, 93, 97, 230
Multiple case study, 3–4, 43–5

NAM, 241–51
Necessary condition, 9–10, 35–7, 66–7, 68–9, 72–5, 77, 80–1, 90–137, 178–83, 186, 190, 193, 212, 220–2, 270, 273, 284
    case study research, 77, 80–1, 90–137, 186, 190, 193, 212, 220–2
    continuous variable, 72–3
    definition, 68–9, 91, 284
    how-to-do guide, 10, 90–8, 190, 193
    hypotheses, 104, 110–11, 116–19, 124–5, 129–30, 132–6, 220–2, 273
    practice-oriented research, 220–2
    research strategy, 77, 80–1, 90–1, 102–3, 113–15, 123, 131

theory-building research, 178–83, 186, 190, 193, 212
theory-testing research, 77, 80–1, 90–137
trivial condition, 96–7, 186
NEN, 241
Nokia, 103–19
Non-statistical methods *see* Qualitative...

Object of measurement, 4, 6–7, 12–15, 94–6, 253–7, 261–2
Object of study, 5–6, 12–15, 30–59, 63–4, 87–8, 92–3, 99, 112–13, 119–20, 130–1, 143–4, 151–2, 160, 169, 176–7, 181, 185, 197–9, 220–2, 284
    definition, 35, 284
    theory, 34–7, 63–4, 87–8, 92–3, 99, 112–13, 130–1, 143–4, 151–2, 160, 169, 176–7, 181, 185
Observation, 15, 30–59, 87–9, 95, 127–8, 133, 180–3, 245–6, 284
Observed pattern, 90, 95, 284
One-shot study, 41–5, 47–8, 88
Open coding, concepts, 187–8
Operations case studies, 19–29, 265–6
    journals, 20–9, 265–6
Operations flexibility, 234–40
Organizational behaviour case studies, 19–29, 265–6
    see also HRM...
Organizational configurations for successful product innovations, case study, 91, 119–36
Orientation, 33–4, 285
    see also Exploration
Orientation of practice, 33–4, 285
Orientation of theory, 33, 285
Outcome of a study, 87–8, 285
    see also Results
Ownership integration, organizational configurations, 121–36

Parallel replication strategy, 44, 285
Parallel single case study, 45, 79–80, 113–14, 131–2, 152–3, 285
    definition, 45, 285
    see also Replication; Single...

Partnership, collaboration, 98–119
Pattern, 95, 167, 211, 285
Pattern matching, 5–6, 15, 87–8, 94–6, 127–8, 133, 166–8, 171, 279, 285
    definition, 285
    see also Qualitative analysis; Score
Population, 44–7, 63–4, 76–9, 83–4, 183, 208–9
Population representativeness, 45–7
    see also Representativeness
Population selection, 46, 80–1, 286
Porter, Michael E., 37, 186, 203, 210
Practice
    definition, 52–3, 286
    domain, 221–2
    exploration of practice, 49–55, 56–8, 63–4, 92, 175–6, 217–28, 232
Practice-oriented research, 6–8, 9, 10–16, 23–4, 30–4, 52–9, 217–51, 272–5
    case selection, 230, 238–9, 250
    case study, 220–4, 227, 228–51
    comparative case study, 220–4, 227
    definition, 23, 30–1, 217, 286
    deterministic relation, 220–2, 237–8
    experiment, 220–2, 224, 226–7, 238, 270, 281–2
    exploration, 56–9, 217–232–51
    'flash case study', 231–3
    general research objective, 30–4, 52, 217–20, 222–6, 237–8
    how-to-do guide, 229–33
    intervention cycle, 53–5, 57–9, 218–28, 249
    knowledge need, 9, 30–4, 52–9, 217–51, 273–5, 286
    necessary condition, 220–2
    principles, 52–9, 84
    probabilistic relation, 220–2
    problem owner, 57–9, 218–28
    research objective, 9, 30–4, 52, 217–20, 222–6, 237–8, 241–4, 248–9, 251
    research strategiy, 220–2, 224–5, 226–8, 232, 238, 250
    sufficient condition, 219–22
    see also Descriptive...; Hypothesis-building...; Hypothesis-testing...; Theory-oriented research

Practitioner, 9, 30–4, 52–9, 92, 217–51, 273–5,
    286
  definition, 52, 217, 286
  exploration of practice, 49–55, 57–9, 92,
    217–28, 232
  knowledge need, 9, 30–4, 52–9, 217–51,
    273–5, 286
  theories-in-use, 50–1, 58, 75, 97–8
Pragmatic determinism, 69, 72–6, 82, 286
Preparation phase, case-study designs, 11–12, 17
Probabilistic necessary condition, 75
Probabilistic proposition, 66, 70–1, 72–6, 286
  definition, 66, 70, 286
Probabilistic relation, 7, 9–10, 32, 36–7, 66–7,
    72–6, 77, 82–4, 88, 112–13, 118, 156–72,
    177–83, 191, 194–5, 212, 220–2, 270, 273,
    286–7
  case study research, 77, 82–4, 88, 112–13,
    118, 156–72, 191, 194–5, 212, 220–2
  definition, 70–1, 156–7, 286–7
  how-to-do guide, 156–9, 191, 194–5
  hypothesis, 158, 163, 168–9, 171–2, 220–2, 273
  practice-oriented research, 220–2
  proposition, 156–72, 191, 194–5, 212
  research strategy, 77, 82–4, 88, 112–13, 118,
    157–8, 162, 170
  theory-building research, 177–83, 191,
    194–5, 212
  theory-testing research, 77, 82–4, 88, 112–13,
    118, 156–72
Probability sample, 47, 287
Probability sampling, 46, 83, 84, 157, 287
Problem owner, practice-oriented research,
    57–9, 218–28
Problem-solving
  intervention cycle, 53–5, 57–9, 218–28, 249
  management knowledge, 71–6
Process model, company standardization,
    242–51
Professional service providers, 200–13
Proposition, 6–8, 9–16, 31–52, 57, 63–89,
    90–137, 138–55, 159–72, 180–3, 197–213,
    230–3, 270–1
  business relevance, 71–6, 88

causal relation, 35–6, 65–6, 72–89, 176–83,
    185–91
conceptual model, 36–7, 84–9, 93–4, 101–2,
    123, 130–1, 140–2, 145, 160–2, 176–83,
    185–8, 279
  definition, 231–3, 287
  expert, 49, 64–5, 92, 133
  literature reviews, 48–9, 59, 130, 131–2, 135
  necessary condition, 9–10, 35–7, 66–7,
    68–9, 72–5, 77, 80–1, 90–137, 212, 270,
    273, 284
  one-shot study, 41–5, 47–8, 88
  research strategy, 76–89, 90–1, 102–3, 113–15,
    123, 131, 145–6, 152–3, 162, 170, 181–3
  sufficient condition, 9–10, 35–7, 66–7, 77–9,
    88–9, 90–137, 186, 189–90, 191–2, 205–13,
    270, 273, 289
  theory, 34–7, 76–89, 290
  theory-building research, 180–3, 192–213
  theory-testing research, 63–4, 76–89, 90–172,
    230–1
  types, 9–10, 65–89, 90–1, 177–83
  see also Concepts; Deterministic…;
    Hypothesis; Probabilistic…; Theory…
Protocol, 259–60

Qualitative analysis, 5–6, 15, 40–1, 87–8, 95,
    149–51, 287
  definition, 5, 40–1, 287
  quantitative analysis, 40–1
  see also Data analysis; Pattern matching;
    Visual analysis
Qualitative measurement, 3–4, 15, 40–1, 64,
    87–8, 149–51, 253, 262
  see also Interview
Quality criteria, case studies, 26–7
Quantitative analysis, 5–6, 15, 40–1, 87, 287
  definition, 5, 40–1, 287
  qualitative analysis, 40–1
  see also Data analysis
Quantitative measurement, 15, 40–1, 64, 253
  see also Questionnaire
Quasi survey, 46, 83–4, 157–8, 171
  see also Survey

Questionnaire, 5–6, 125–8, 132–3, 149–51, 154, 253, 257, 262
  see also Interrogation; Quantitative measurement

Radical/incremental innovation, 99–119, 120–36
Ragin, Charles C., 3, 75
Random sample, 83, 287
Random sampling, 83, 157, 287
Real life context, 4–5, 6, 30–2, 40–1, 72–6, 217, 287
  definition, 4–5, 6, 40–1, 287
Recording of evidence, 257–8, 261–2
Rejection,of a hypothesis, 42, 78–9, 87–8, 90–1, 95–8, 111–12, 114, 117–18, 123, 129–30, 133–6, 150–3, 168, 171–2, 230–1, 238
Reliability, 5–6, 24, 25–6, 116–17, 133, 164–5, 181, 210, 253, 262–4
  definition, 262
  validity, 5–6, 24, 25–6, 116–17, 133, 164–5, 181, 210, 262
  see also Measurement; Score
Replication, 6–8, 9–10, 39–45, 51–2, 64–5, 77–89, 96–7, 112, 113–15, 118–19, 130, 135–6, 142, 155, 169, 172, 183, 209, 269, 288
  definition, 39, 41–2, 288
  experiment, 42–4, 77–89
  serial tests, 43–5, 114–16
  survey, 43–4, 77–89
  see also Theory-testing…
Replication strategy, 88, 96–8, 112, 114, 118–19, 135–6, 288
Representativeness, 45–8, 83–4, 288
  definition, 45, 288
  see also Domain…; Population…
Research, 9, 11–16, 30–59, 288
  definition, 30, 288
  objectives, 24–5, 30–4, 52, 63–7, 77–89, 102, 113, 123, 131, 145, 152, 162, 170, 175–83, 217–20, 222–6, 237–8, 241–4, 248–9, 251, 288
  principles, 9, 11–16, 30–59, 84, 180–1

Research objective
  case study research, 24–5, 30–2, 52, 63–7, 77–89, 102, 113, 123, 131, 145, 152, 162, 170, 237–8, 241–4, 248–9, 251, 288
  general practice-oriented research, 30–4, 52, 217–20, 222–6, 237–8, 241–4, 248–9, 251
  specific theory-oriented research, 30–4, 52, 63–7, 77–89, 102, 113, 123, 131, 145, 152, 162, 170, 175–7
Research strategy, 6, 9–10, 12–14, 63–4, 76–89, 102–3, 113–15, 123, 131, 145–6, 152–3, 157–8, 162, 170, 181–3, 232, 238, 250, 288
  definition, 6, 288
  descriptive research, 226–8, 250
  deterministic relation, 77, 81–2, 88–9, 138–9, 145–6, 152–3, 238
  hypothesis-building research, 224–5
  hypothesis-testing research, 220–2, 238
  necessary condition, 77, 80–1, 90–1, 102–3, 113–15, 123, 131, 186
  practice-oriented research, 220–2, 224–5, 226–8, 232, 238, 250
  probabilistic relation, 77, 82–4, 88, 112–13, 118, 157–8, 162, 170
  proposition, 76–89, 90–1, 102–3, 113–15, 123, 131, 145–6, 152–3, 162, 170, 181–3
  sufficient condition, 77–9, 90–1, 102–3, 113–15, 123, 131, 186
  theory-building research, 181–3
  theory-testing research, 63–4, 76–89, 102–3, 113–15, 123, 131, 145–6, 152–3, 157–8, 162, 170
  see also Case…; Experiment; Survey
Results, 11–16, 17, 25–6, 34, 94–6, 111–13, 117–18, 129–30, 150–1, 154, 166–8, 171–2, 195–6, 206–7, 210–12, 232–3, 236–7, 239–40, 245–9, 251
  see also Outcome
Retailers' distribution costs, urban time access windows, 142–55, 160–72
Reviews, case studies, 19–29, 48–9

Robustness of a theory, 88, 183, 209, 288
  see also Generalizability; Replication; Theory

Sample, 43–8, 83–4, 157, 288, 289
  definition, 46, 288, 289
Sampling, 43–5, 83–4, 157
Sampling frame, 83, 289
Sarker, Suprateek, 97
Scientific realism, 40–1
Scorecard, 247–8
Score, 5–6, 14–15, 77–89, 90–1, 94–6, 127, 184, 188–9, 246–8, 258–64, 289
  definition, 87, 289
  see also Measurement; Reliability
Self-reporting bias, 126, 129–30
Serial replication strategy, 44, 289
Serial single case study, 45, 114–16, 289
  definition, 45, 289
  see also Multiple case study; Parallel single case study; Replication; Single…
Serial tests, replication, 43–5, 114–16
Services, business-services providers, 184, 197–213
Shell, 241–51
Single case study, 4–5, 37, 40–1, 44–5, 46, 63–4, 77–82, 91–137, 220–2, 289
  definitions, 4–5, 45, 289
  see also Mutiple …; Parallel…; Serial…
Sociocentric (SC) theories of redesign, 97–8
Sociotechnical (ST) theories of redesign, 97–8
Standardization
  best practice, 229, 240–51
  new products, 234–40
Starr, Harvey, 72
Statistical generalizability, 47–8
  definition, 47
  see also Generalizability
Statistical methods *see* Quantitative…
Stepwise procedures, 11, 17, 253–64
Strategic flexibility, 234–40
Strategy case studies, 19–29, 265–6
  journals, 20–9, 265–6
Study, 30, 289
Sufficient condition, 9–10, 35–7, 66–7, 77–9, 88–9, 90–137, 186, 189–90, 191–2, 205–13, 219–22, 270, 273, 289

case study research, 77–9, 88–9, 90–137, 186, 189–90, 191–2, 205–13, 219–22
  definition, 67–8, 91, 289
  how-to-do guide, 10, 90–8, 189–90, 191–2
  hypothesis, 104, 110–11, 116–19, 124–5, 129–30, 132–6, 219–22, 273
  practice-oriented research, 219–22
  research strategy, 77–9, 88–9, 90–1, 102–3, 113–15, 123, 131, 186
  theory-building research, 178–83, 186, 189–90, 191–2, 205–13
  theory-testing research, 77–9, 88–9, 90–137
Support for a proposition, 90, 289
Survey, 4–5, 7, 9–10, 13–14, 26, 40–1, 42–4, 46, 63–4, 76–89, 92, 157–8, 170, 220–2, 226–7, 228, 289–90
  definition, 5, 40–1, 289–90
  quasi survey, 46, 83–4, 157–8, 171
  replication, 43–4, 77–89
  sampling, 43–5, 83–4, 157
  theory-testing research, 76–89, 92, 157–8, 170
  see also Population; Probabilistic proposition; Quantitative analysis; Research strategies
Survey research, 5, 290
Szanton, Peter L., 196

Task integration, organizational configurations, 121–36
Teams, innovation projects, 191–6
Technocentric (TC) theories of redesign, 97–8
Technological capabilities, collaborations, 99–119
Telecommunications industry, 124–36, 199–213
Test, 90, 290
Theoretical domain, 36, 290
Theory, 6–8, 34–7, 46–51, 53, 56–9, 63–4, 92, 95–6, 99–102, 111–13, 117–18, 119–23, 129–31, 134–6, 138–9, 169, 175–83, 187–9, 290
  characteristics, 34–5, 46
  definition, 34, 37, 290
  expert, 49, 58–9, 64–5, 92, 133
  exploration of theory, 48–51, 53, 56–9, 63–4, 92, 175–83, 187–9, 217–18, 232
  generalizability, 47, 282

robustness, 44, 88, 183, 288
see also Concept; Domain; Object of study;
    Proposition
Theory development, 30–1, 38–41, 51–2, 87–8,
    97, 102, 111–13, 117–18, 119–23, 129–31,
    134–5, 142, 151–2, 154–5, 168–9, 172,
    175–7, 290, 291
    definition, 38–9, 290
Theory-building, 6–8, 10–16, 23–5, 26–7,
    38–41, 49–52, 63–4, 175–213, 290
    see also Exploration
Theory-building comparative case study, 182,
    290
Theory-building research, 6–8, 10–16, 23–5,
    26–7, 38–41, 49–52, 63–4, 175–213, 223–4,
    269, 271, 290
    costs, 181–2
    definition, 38, 39, 176, 290
    deterministic relation, 177–83, 190–1, 194,
        212
    how-to-do guide, 184–96
    known/unknown concept, 176–83, 184–213,
        223–4
    necessary condition, 178–83, 186, 190, 193,
        212
    outcome, 195–6, 206–7, 211–12
    principles, 180–1
    probabilistic relation, 177–83, 191, 194–5, 212
    proposition, 180–3, 192–213
    research objective, 175–83
    research strategy, 181–3
    sufficient condition, 178–83, 186, 189–90,
        191–2, 205–13
    theory-testing research, 181
    types, 176–7, 183
    see also Theory-oriented research; Theory-
        testing research
Theory-in-use, 50–1, 58, 72–3, 75, 97–8, 175–6
Theory-oriented research, 6–16, 23–4, 30–52,
    63–7, 175–83, 229–30, 269–71
    definition, 30–1, 38–9, 291
    exploration, 48–51, 63–4, 92, 175–83
    research objective, 30–4, 52, 63–7, 77–89,
        102, 113, 123, 131, 145, 152, 162, 170,
        175–7

principles, 34–52, 84, 180–1
    see also Practice-oriented…; Theory-
        building…; Theory-testing…
Theory-testing, 6–16, 23–4, 25, 26–7, 38–45,
    48–51, 63–89, 291
    definition, 38, 291
Theory-testing comparative case study, 43, 291
Theory-testing research, 6–16, 23–4, 25, 26–7,
    38–45, 63–89, 90–137, 138–55, 156–72,
    220–1, 269–70, 291
    complex conceptual model, 84–9
    definition, 38, 291
    deterministic relation, 77, 81–2, 88–9,
        138–55
    experiment, 76–89, 170
    how-to-do guide, 10, 90–8, 138–42
    hypothesis-testing research, 220–1, 230–1
    necessary condition, 77, 80–1, 90–137
    probabilistic relation, 77, 82–4, 88, 112–13,
        118, 156–72
    research strategy, 63–4, 76–89, 102–3,
        113–15, 123, 131, 145–6, 152–3, 157–8,
        162, 170
    sufficient condition, 77–9, 88–9, 90–137
    survey, 76–89, 92, 157–8, 170
    theory-building research, 181
    see also Initial theory-testing; Replication…;
        Theory-building…; Theory-oriented…
Time access windows, 142–55, 160–72
Trivial necessary condition, 96–7, 186

Unknown/known concept, theory-building
    research, 176–83, 184–213
Unknown/known variable, hypothesis-building
    research, 223–4, 227, 230
Urban time access windows
    distribution costs, 142–55, 160–72
    distribution strategies, 159–72
UWV, 200–13

Validity, 5–6, 24, 25–6, 47, 116–17, 133, 164–5,
    181, 210, 231, 253, 260–4, 282
    definition, 260
    reliability, 5–6, 24, 25–6, 116–17, 133, 164–5,
        181, 210, 262

Validity (*Cont'd*)
  types, 47
  see also Ecological...; External...;
    Measurement
Van de Ven, Andrew H., 31, 76
Variable, 6–8, 35–7, 45–8, 65–6, 72–3, 93–4,
    217–28
  conceptual model, 36–7, 84–9, 93–4,
    140–2, 279

definition, 35, 65–6
see also Concept
Visual inspection, 5–6, 15, 95, 166–8, 171,
    232–3, 291
  definition, 5, 291
  see also Pattern matching; Qualitative analysis
Voss, Chris, 25

Yin, Robert K., 3, 43, 44, 196